Careers in Criminal Justice

Second Edition

SAGE was founded in 1965 by Sara Miller McCune to support the dissemination of usable knowledge by publishing innovative and high-quality research and teaching content. Today, we publish over 900 journals, including those of more than 400 learned societies, more than 800 new books per year, and a growing range of library products including archives, data, case studies, reports, and video. SAGE remains majority-owned by our founder, and after Sara's lifetime will become owned by a charitable trust that secures our continued independence.

Los Angeles | London | New Delhi | Singapore | Washington DC | Melbourne

Careers in Criminal Justice

Second Edition

Coy H. Johnston

Arizona State University School of Criminology and Criminal Justice

Los Angeles | London | New Delhi
Singapore | Washington DC | Melbourne

FOR INFORMATION:

SAGE Publications, Inc.
2455 Teller Road
Thousand Oaks, California 91320
E-mail: order@sagepub.com

SAGE Publications Ltd.
1 Oliver's Yard
55 City Road
London, EC1Y 1SP
United Kingdom

SAGE Publications India Pvt. Ltd.
B 1/I 1 Mohan Cooperative Industrial Area
Mathura Road, New Delhi 110 044
India

SAGE Publications Asia-Pacific Pte. Ltd.
3 Church Street
#10-04 Samsung Hub
Singapore 049483

Acquisitions Editor: Jessica Miller
Content Development Editor: Laura Kirkhuff
Editorial Assistant: Rebecca Lee
Production Editor: Nevair Kabakian
Copy Editor: Diana Breti
Typesetter: Hurix Digital
Proofreader: Caryne Brown
Indexer: Julie Grayson
Cover Designer: Gail Buschman
Marketing Manager: Jillian Oelsen

Printed in the United States of America.

Library of Congress Cataloging-in-Publication Data

Names: Johnston, Coy H., author.

Title: Careers in criminal justice / Coy H. Johnston, Arizona State University School of Criminology and Criminal Justice.

Description: Second edition. | Thousand Oaks, Calif. : SAGE, [2019] | Includes bibliographical references and index.

Identifiers: LCCN 2017035291 | ISBN 9781506363950 (pbk. : alk. paper)

Subjects: LCSH: Criminal justice, Administration of—Vocational guidance. | Law enforcement—Vocational guidance—United States. | Police—Vocational guidance—United States. | Job hunting—United States.

Classification: LCC HV8143 .J642 2019 | DDC 364.73023—dc23 LC record available at https://lccn.loc.gov/2017035291

This book is printed on acid-free paper.

18 19 20 21 22 10 9 8 7 6 5 4 3 2 1

BRIEF CONTENTS

DETAILED CONTENTS

PREFACE TO THE SECOND EDITION

Career development is a lifelong process for students that involves their personalities, interests, values, abilities, circumstances, and backgrounds. It is constantly taking place regardless of a student's awareness of it. Career counseling can be beneficial, especially from someone who is trained in how to use the tools that are available. The counseling process helps students become more aware of themselves and how they fit into the work ambit, ultimately helping them make educational, career, and life choices. Combining development with counseling and applying it specifically to criminal justice is the crux of this book. The process of planning, pursuing, and preparing are three important components of students' career paths. Without devoting attention to all three, students may find themselves behind their peers in the job hunt.

Many students find it difficult to decide early on what they want to do for a career. They sometimes take irrelevant elective classes as fodder for needed credit hours. They may miss or dismiss unique opportunities. As in a game of chess, if students have no purposeful strategies, the moves they make may be of little benefit and possibly damaging. By using some of the same tools as career counselors, professors can combine development with counseling and play a huge role in helping students be realistic in their aspirations.

Although everything students ever want to know is available online, accessible from their laptops, tablets, and smart phones, they don't always take advantage of it. Every career imaginable is right at their fingertips. They rarely have the time or initiative to do more than the required homework. Being aware of this reality, professors try to sneak career and hiring information into their lectures. A book containing career and hiring information is one that professors can use in lectures and assignments, thus nudging students in the right direction.

After students learn about the criminal justice system and decide where they hope to fit in, they enter the world of applying, interviewing, facing disappointment, learning from their experiences, trying again and again, and, for some, settling for less than what they had hoped for. Students compete against other students for jobs, and universities compete against other universities for rankings. Providing students with tools for preparation gives them an edge and enhances their confidence. There is a great feeling of vicarious pleasure and satisfaction when professors get thank-you letters from prior students who landed their dream jobs.

In response to the needs of professors and students, I have partnered with SAGE to provide this textbook as a supplement to criminal justice courses, preferably in the introductory stages of a degree program. This book offers career counseling tools to help students plan their paths, core information about criminal justice careers, and advanced training for the hiring process. Students who employ this "career-focused" book will be prepared for the hiring process with an enhanced probability of landing their dream jobs.

Coy H. Johnston
Arizona State University
August, 2017

ACKNOWLEDGMENTS

I would like to thank Acquisitions Editor Jessica Miller and her staff members at SAGE Publishing for dedicating so much work to this book. Their timely assistance was given with patience, expertise, tact, and professionalism. It was a pleasure working with Jessica and her support staff as they took the collection of unrefined material and transformed it into a polished supplemental textbook.

I would like to acknowledge the expert guest speakers who participated in relevant chapters. Their written dialogue is just a small part of their overall contribution to the quality of the book. Face-to-face guests who have inspired students in my classes and have had a profound effect on the overall psyche of this book include Sergeant Mike Pooley and Lieutenant Noah Johnson of the Tempe Police Department; Detective Jerry Gissel, Lieutenant Rod Johnston, Commander Dave Ashe, and Chief Janice Strauss, all retirees of the Mesa Police Department; Special Agent Steve Palmer with the Federal Bureau of Investigation and Detective William Weigt with the Peoria Police Department.

Finally, I would like to thank the reviewers of the initial proposal for their advice and critiques:

George Ackerman

Charisse T. M. Coston, University of North Carolina at Charlotte

Michael A. Langer, National Louis University

Barry R. Langford, Columbia College

Emil Moldovan, Radford University

Quanda Watson-Stevenson, Athens State University

Courtney A. Waid-Lindberg, Northern State University

Thomas F. Adams, Del Mar College

Rosemary C. Arway, Federal Bureau of Investigation National Academy #234

James W. Beeks

Byung Jun Cho, Westfield State University

Ronald J. Curtis, Florida Gulf Coast University

Judith A. Harris, University of South Carolina Upstate

Julia Mack, Gannon University

Paul Nunis, Arkansas State University

James Kane Record, California University of Pennsylvania

Jerry L. Stinson, Southwest Virginia Community College

I would also like to thank the reviewers who helped shape the second edition:

Kelley Christopher, lecturer, University of West Georgia

Kimberly A. Kampe, adjunct, University of Central Florida

Paul M. Lucko, Murray State University

Patrick Webb, PhD, assistant professor of criminal justice and sociology, Savannah State University

Dr. Elizabeth K. Ayers, University of West Georgia

Susan R. Takata, University of Wisconsin, Parkside

ABOUT THE AUTHOR

Coy H. Johnston is a professor in the School of Criminology and Criminal Justice at Arizona State University. He earned his bachelor's degree in business management at the University of Phoenix and his master's degree in community counseling from Northern Arizona University. He has been a nationally certified counselor since 2004. For more than 27 years, Johnston worked in law enforcement, specializing in sexual crimes and domestic violence. During his career, he co-organized the Mesa Police Benefit Fund, which offered financial assistance to needy employees; the Mesa Police Department RCVR program, which provided additional funds for victims of crime; the statewide domestic violence awareness committee, involving more than 1,200 domestic violence professionals; and the annual statewide law enforcement domestic violence roundup. Noteworthy awards during the last decade of his career included the Distinguished Service Award of Victims of Crime from Attorney General Terry Goddard and a certificate of recognition from Arizona Governor Janet Napolitano for the law enforcement domestic violence roundup. Johnston served on the governor's grant approval committee for STOP and Recovery grants from 2007 to 2013. Since retiring from law enforcement in 2007, he has taught psychology and criminal justice classes at University of Phoenix (AXIA), ITT Technical Institute, Chandler-Gilbert Community College, Everest College, CARLOTA Police Academy, and Arizona State University. This book is his fourth official publication.

SECTION 1

PLANNING

KNOW YOURSELF

INTRODUCTION

Two questions that regularly stump candidates in hiring interviews are "What are your strengths?" and "What are your weaknesses?" An interviewee who has been well coached may offer some scripted examples of strengths, such as being a great communicator or having a fun personality or being a quick thinker. A well-coached interviewee will also know better than to give a long list of weaknesses. As discussed in more detail in the final chapter, there is nothing wrong with being coached for an interview, and it is actually highly recommended.

One important purpose of the hiring interview is to give an employer an opportunity to assess certain personality and character traits of an individual that can't be sufficiently discovered through a written test or from the application paperwork. The ability to communicate well and to think quickly and to be a fun person may be exactly what an agency is looking for. It is refreshing for interviewers when candidates meet their criteria and are self-aware and genuinely know who they are. Other traits commonly sought by most agencies are assertiveness, ability to work well with others, willingness to work hard, capacity for independent thought, ability to follow a chain of command, and a high level of integrity, which is often determined through background checks and polygraph tests.

When answering interview questions, it is always a good idea to be truthful. However, truth is somewhat subjective in the area of self-awareness. It is my experience that some students aren't fully aware of their strengths and weaknesses. An uncoached student with desirable qualities might not adequately describe his or her strengths in an interview and might subsequently be passed over in favor of others who are better prepared. Sadly, some well-qualified students don't feel ready and therefore don't even apply. There are also those students who aren't ready (or are not a good fit for the jobs they seek), but they aren't aware of it.

The overall usefulness of this book depends largely on how well you know yourself. This first chapter is dedicated to helping students become more in touch with their individual personalities, their temperaments, their strengths and weaknesses, their biases and beliefs, and what types of careers might be a good fit. Just as a house needs a good foundation, learning about oneself is the right place to start if the best results are to be achieved. It is fundamentally important, and when self-assessment exercises are used in college courses, students report them as among their favorite activities.

WHAT YOU DON'T KNOW CAN HURT YOU

Self-awareness is the gateway to self-improvement. Learning should be a lifelong interest, but the biggest stumbling block for some students is the belief that they already have a handle on the way things are. This way of thinking is normal, especially in early adulthood. It develops naturally from everything a person has experienced throughout his or her life using the five senses, coupled with reassurance and confirmations from peers. This type of person is stagnant. Stagnant people have slowed their growth and sometimes never crawl out of the holes they dig for themselves. Stagnant people feel comfortable around others who think as they do. It is a natural tendency for people to consider someone who thinks as they do to be normal or even intelligent. Instead of desiring and trying to understand everyone and appreciate the differences, stagnant individuals tend to divide people into "us versus them." This poem by John Godfrey Saxe (1873) helps demonstrate how people get stuck in such a rut:

I.

It was six men of Indostan

To learning much inclined,

Who went to see the Elephant

(Though all of them were blind),

That each by observation

Might satisfy his mind.

II.

The *First* approach'd the Elephant,

And happening to fall

Against his broad and sturdy side,

At once began to bawl:

"God bless me!—but the Elephant

Is very like a wall!"

III.

The *Second*, feeling of the tusk,

Cried, "Ho!—what have we here

So very round and smooth and sharp?

To me 't is mighty clear

This wonder of an Elephant

Is very like a spear!"

IV.

The *Third* approached the animal,

And happening to take

The squirming trunk within his hands,

Thus boldly up and spake:

"I see," quoth he, "the Elephant

Is very like a snake!"

V.

The *Fourth* reached out his eager hand,

And felt about the knee.

"What most this wondrous beast is like

Is mighty plain," quoth he;

"'T is clear enough the Elephant

Is very like a tree!"

VI.

The *Fifth*, who chanced to touch the ear,

Said: "E'en the blindest man

Can tell what this resembles most;

Deny the fact who can,

This marvel of an Elephant

Is very like a fan!"

VII.

The *Sixth* no sooner had begun

About the beast to grope,

Than, seizing on the swinging tail

That fell within his scope,

"I see," quoth he, "the Elephant

Is very like a rope!"

VIII.

And so these men of Indostan

Disputed loud and long,

Each in his own opinion

Exceeding stiff and strong,

Though each was partly in the right,

And all were in the wrong!

MORAL.

So, oft in theologic wars,

The disputants, I ween,

Rail on in utter ignorance

Of what each other mean,

And prate about an Elephant

Not one of them has seen!

This poem has an important message for all of us. There is so much we do not know and will never have the opportunity to know. It is the realization of our vulnerabilities and inefficiencies that prepares us for learning, changing, and improving. Narcissistic people we may come across in our lives would benefit greatly from self-awareness, but they will never realize that they don't already have it.

What You Don't Know

To learn more about ourselves, we should first put our own existence into the proper perspective. Current estimates suggest that there are more than 165 billion galaxies in the universe, each with hundreds of billions of stars (National Aeronautics and Space Administration, n.d.). The universe is estimated to be more than 12 billion years old (National Aeronautics and Space Administration, 2012). Compare that with the average lifespan of humans, which is estimated to be 78 years (U.S. Census Bureau, 2012).

Let's just consider what we can learn about our own planet. There are seven continents, containing 195 countries, on which approximately 7 billion people reside, speaking more than 6,000 different languages (O'Neil, 2013). Our planet has an estimated 146 million books (Taychir, 2010). If someone were to read one book per day between the ages of 6 and 86 years, he or she could read only 29,200 of those books in a lifetime. In reality, the average American reads only about 15 books a year.

There are hundreds of degrees available, but according to the U.S. Census Bureau (Stoops, 2004), only 29% of young adults in America receive a bachelor's degree or higher.

Seldom does anyone devote the time and money to obtain more than one bachelor's or master's degree. Like the blind men who each felt only one part of the elephant, there is so much we don't know. Realizing and accepting this truth is the key to having the learning attitude we need. "Do you wish to rise? Begin by descending. You plan a tower that will pierce the clouds? Lay first the foundation of humility" (Saint Augustine, CE 354–430).

GUEST SPEAKER
STEVE PALMER, FBI SPECIAL AGENT

I began my career as an FBI special agent in 1998. After graduating from the FBI Academy in Quantico, Virginia, I was assigned to the Laredo, Texas resident agency out of the San Antonio, Texas, field office. Because the Laredo agency is a fairly small office, I was able to investigate a broad range of violations. My primary responsibility was to investigate public corruption. I found this work to be very rewarding. I also investigated kidnappings, extortion, bank robberies, fraud, and many others. In 2004, I transferred to the Phoenix, Arizona, field office. In Phoenix, I still am involved in all types of investigations, but my primary area of responsibility is counterterrorism. In 2011, I was given the opportunity to move to Washington, D.C., to work with the FBI's Counterterrorism Division. I was privileged to work jointly with all of the U.S. agencies that play a part in the war on terror, both in the United States and overseas. While there, I was involved in some of the biggest terrorism investigations in the United States and abroad. It was inspiring to see all of the work that goes on behind the scenes and the dedication of the men and women from all of the U.S. intelligence agencies. I have had many diverse and exciting experiences while working for the FBI. As an FBI agent, I have worked on cases all over the United States, and on several occasions, I have traveled overseas in support of the FBI's mission. I have had the opportunity to work with people from many different U.S. agencies and all branches of the military, as well as officials from foreign governments.

My advice to those interested in a career in the FBI:

- Get a college degree in a field in which you wouldn't mind working; sometimes getting hired by the FBI takes a while, and you might need to work in your field of study for a while.
- Get experiences working and, through other activities, interacting with strangers. Strong people skills will serve you very well in the FBI.

The foregoing is based on my own personal experiences and does not represent the official view of the FBI.

SELF-ASSESSMENTS

Working in the criminal justice field can be a very rewarding and even exciting career. Many students entering criminal justice degree programs have particular fields in mind because they are either jobs they have always wanted or jobs that sound enjoyable. A common question for a professor to ask a group of students is "What do you want to do with your degree?" Then there are the follow-up questions that solicit the raising of hands: "Who is interested in being a police officer?" "Who is interested in being an attorney?" "How many want to work in the forensic field?" "How many want to work in corrections?" Other typical interests usually include the Federal Bureau of Investigation, the Drug Enforcement Administration, the U.S. Marshals Service, victim services, child interviews, and criminal profiling. There are also students who are not sure where they want to work or are not sure what they can qualify for.

As students progress through their bachelor's degrees in criminal justice, they learn more about the types of jobs available as well as the positive and negative aspects of each field. It is common for a professor to hear comments such as, "I don't think I could ever defend a murderer in court" or "I could never interview child molesters because I would want to strangle them." Students start to become aware of personal issues that might affect their job performance or their happiness in certain careers. Similarly, professors have the opportunity to recognize students' strengths and weaknesses and can either confirm that students are a good fit for the careers they wish to pursue or direct students to better choices. This is easier to do if the students are somewhat aware of their own strengths, preferences, and natural tendencies. The ideal situation is for students to learn about themselves at the earliest point possible.

There are several tools available to help us recognize our temperaments, personalities, likes and dislikes, strengths and weaknesses, and even what types of people we would be happiest with and what careers we would be best fit for. These tools (and some useful books) will be discussed throughout the rest of this chapter. It is highly recommended that you learn all you can about yourself (and what makes you happy) before progressing far into your degree program. Having true insight early on will help you search out the best volunteer positions or internships that will get your foot not just in the door but in the right door.

What Color Is Your Parachute?

Richard Bolles published a book in 1970 titled *What Color Is Your Parachute?* It has been a very successful job hunter's book, with a new edition appearing each year, and it continues to be revised and reissued. The 2018 edition can be found on Amazon for as little as $13. More than 10 million copies have been sold, including one copy of the 30th edition that I purchased and read. The ideas and concepts in the book are very helpful and easy to retain.

Chapter 4 is titled "What Do You Have to Offer the World?" Bolles (2000) states, "You must figure out which of your skills you most delight to use." He gives these three steps to job-hunting success:

1. What: You must decide exactly what you have to offer to the world
2. Where: You must decide where you want to use your skills
3. How: You must go after the organizations that interest you the most, whether or not they are known to have vacancies

These three steps are in line with the focus of this book in which we plan, pursue, and prepare. The first step, planning, is essential, but that is not to say that everyone goes through an identical, meticulous process. It is highly recommended, however, that students figure out their own preferences and skills, and ultimately their ideal career paths, at the earliest point possible. According to Bolles, everyone has skills, but "there is such a thing as being deeply unaware of our skills." I have witnessed students' unawareness when they have been asked to write self-reflection essays to articulate the skills they use to accomplish group work. The assignment is didactic, intended to trigger students' awareness of the skills they possess and how they use them to influence, encourage, and motivate others. The essays usually end up being more narrative, describing the work they've done or what they normally do. The essays rarely include actual skills. They are usually more like very short accounts of what results have been accomplished instead of how they were accomplished. What Bolles wrote about, people's being deeply unaware of their skills, is surprisingly ubiquitous. Candidates who are not ready for questions about their strengths and weaknesses in hiring interviews often find themselves surprised at how hard it is to articulate one's own skills. We will visit this issue again in Section 3, "Preparing."

Keirsey Temperament Sorter

In 1984, David Keirsey and Marilyn Bates published *Please Understand Me*. The book focuses on the concept that everyone is fundamentally different and that differences are neither good nor bad. They asserted that self-assessment is "foreign" to most people, so using some kind of examination tool is very helpful. Keirsey and Bates created the Keirsey Temperament Sorter, which can be accessed at http://www.keirsey.com/sorter/register.aspx. It consists of 70 questions, which can also be found on page 5 of their book. The questions each offer two choices, for example,

20. On the job do you want your activities
___(a) scheduled ___(b) unscheduled

The value of this tool hinges on the test taker's being as honest as possible. The answers are recorded on a scoring form that ultimately identifies where the test taker fits among 16 different personality types. The book follows up with detailed information about each personality type.

Keirsey wrote a follow-up book in 1998 titled *Please Understand Me II*. This book is 140 pages longer than the 1984 book. The 70 Keirsey Temperament Sorter II questions and score sheet are available in the book on page 4. The questions are similar to those in the original book, but the follow-up information is much more comprehensive.

A website was created allowing people to answer the Keirsey Temperament Sorter II questions online, free of charge, and to receive a scored report (Keirsey.com, n.d.). The report has minimal information to help students better understand their own temperaments and styles. For a more detailed report on the results, one would have to pay a small fee. The free report includes your basic personality type (Artisan, Guardian, Idealist, or Rationalist) and four subtypes. As an example of the details, if your results show that you are a Guardian, you will find out that the four types of Guardians are supervisors, protectors, inspectors, and providers. A few things the free report briefly explains about Guardians are that they pride themselves on being dependable, helpful, and hard working. They make loyal mates and reasonable parents, and they are stabilizing leaders. A Guardian is also a concerned citizen who trusts authority, joins groups, seeks security, and dreams of meting out justice.

To get detailed information on these four subtypes, you would need to pay a fee for the type of report you want. You can order the 18-page "Classic Temperament" report ($14.95), the 18-page "Career Temperament" report ($19.95), the 15-page "Learning Style Temperament" report ($14.95), or the 3-page "Temperament Discovery" report ($7.95) at www.keirsey.com. The Keirsey Temperament Sorter II can also be accessed at that website. It takes only about 20 to 25 minutes to answer the questions, and the results come back immediately and can be printed out.

It is important to remember that you can buy the book, which contains the Keirsey Temperament Sorter II questions and score sheet, several pages of detailed information about each type of personality, careers you would be best fit for, and what type of person you are a good match for. The book can be found on Amazon for as little as $5.

True Colors

Roger Birkman published his book *True Colors* in 1995. The book can be purchased used on Amazon for as little as $4. Birkman was fascinated with the topic of perception and posited that our perceptions, whether right or wrong, influence everything we do. He felt that by gaining the proper perspective on one's own perceptions, other things would start to fall into place. According to Birkman, there are no criteria anywhere that define what is normal, and so "nobody is normal, and everyone is." Birkman also suggested that "there is great freedom in knowing one's own strengths and weaknesses, for as soon as these are identified, it becomes a much simpler matter to focus on the things you do well and look for help in your weaker areas."

In *True Colors*, Birkman explains that there is no limit on the number of "normal" or "right" behaviors, but the unlimited number of normal and right behaviors can be categorized, to some extent. Birkman categorizes people in four quadrants, using the colors red, yellow, green, and blue. He explains in the book what these colors represent. He also notes that the best way to learn which of the four quadrants is the most indicative of one's personality is to take a personalized, individual assessment. Birkman also gives two other ways to help someone determine his or her self-perception. He includes in the book (pp. 42–43) 16 true-or-false questions as well as instructions on how to score the answers. The other way to determine your perceptions is to read the explanations and examples throughout the book. On page 44, there is a chart that gives just a few examples of what falls under the different quadrants. If you fall under the red quadrant, you are friendly, decisive, energetic, frank, and logical. If you favor the yellow quadrant, you are orderly, concentrative, cautious, and insistent. Green people are competitive, assertive, flexible, and enthusiastic about new things. Blues are insightful, selective sociable, thoughtful, reflective, and optimistic.

Chances are that you could look at these examples and guess which color quadrant you would fall in before you even take the 16-question test. You might also find that you have some characteristics from more than one quadrant. Birkman dedicated many pages to explaining how to interpret the results. In the book, there are details about different operating styles, what motivates you, understanding your needs, how to relate to people of other colors, and several other categories of helpful information.

In *True Colors*, Birkman lists 10 classifications of interest with possible occupations that are a good fit for each category. Here are some examples:

Artistic: photographer, architect, artist, florist, designer, painter, or decorator

Clerical: secretary, typist, office worker, or financial manager

Literary: writer, editor, literary scholar, reporter, or librarian

Mechanical: engineer, machine designer, auto mechanic, carpenter, pilot, or plumber

Musical: professional singer, musician, or songwriter

Numerical: cashier, accountant, mathematician, or administrative office worker

Outdoor: carpenter, farmer, animal trainer, sportsman, forest ranger, or field engineer

Persuasive: salesperson, teacher, counselor, public relations director, politician, or auctioneer

Scientific: scientist, lab worker, detective, meteorologist, doctor, or dentist

Social services: teacher, social worker, counselor, personnel or employment manager

Birkman states in his book (pp. 58–59) that strong interests have the same status as a need and that our interests influence us more than we realize.

What Type Am I?

In 1998, Renee Baron published a book titled *What Type Am I?* This book can be purchased on Amazon new for less than $7. Baron also wrote a follow-up book titled *The Four Temperaments,* which we will explore later. In *What Type Am I?* Baron tells us that she began to learn about personality temperaments when she came upon the book *Please Understand Me* by Keirsey and Bates. She explains that learning her own temperament gave her a strong sense of relief to finally identify her real self. It was this great feeling of self-worth that inspired her to teach it to others for the next 18 years. In this book, Baron shares the Myers-Briggs system the way it was first taught to her. She starts her book with an overview of the Myers-Briggs system, which is one of the most popular and comprehensive personality assessments to date. The Myers-Briggs scheme measures both preferences and temperaments. The first part of the book deals with preferences. The four pairs of preferences are listed as opposites:

Extraversion (E) and Introversion (I)

Sensing (S) and Intuiting (N)

Thinking (T) and Feeling (F)

Judging (J) and Perceiving (P)

Baron wrote full chapters on each of these opposite pairs. She starts each of the chapters with a 20-question inventory to help the reader distinguish which preference is dominant. The second part of the book delves into temperament, which is "a pattern of characteristic behaviors that reflect a person's natural disposition" (Baron, 1998). Myers-Briggs lists the four temperaments' themes as follows:

SJ–Sensing Judging: duty seekers

SP–Sensing Perceiving: action seekers

NT–Intuiting Thinking: knowledge seekers

NF–Intuiting Feeling: ideal seekers

Ultimately, the Myers-Briggs system classifies a person into one of 16 categories:

ESTP	ESFP	ISTJ	ISFJ
ENTP	ENFP	INTJ	INFJ
ESTJ	ENTJ	ISTP	INTP
ESFJ	ENFJ	ISFP	INFP

Baron explains the meaning of these types in great detail. She says in the last paragraph of the book that this valuable information changed her life. She says that it started her on the path to acceptance and "that it was all right to be me, an ENFP" (Baron, 1998).

The Four Temperaments

Baron's 2004 follow-up was titled *The Four Temperaments*. The book can be purchased on Amazon (used) for less than $5. This book contains a personality inventory that starts on page 9 and consists of 80 questions. These 80 questions are divided into four different groups of 20 questions each. The four groups are Security Seeker, Experience Seeker, Knowledge Seeker, and Ideal Seeker. You answer each question with one of these three choices:

0—Not like me

1—Somewhat like me

2—Exactly like me

An example item is "I dislike wasting time talking about policies and procedures. I want to take immediate action." At the end of the inventory, you total your points and mark on a chart where you fall in each of the four categories. The remainder of the book gives an in-depth description of the four temperaments.

Security Seekers make up approximately 40% of the U.S. population (Baron, 2004). Baron tells us that Security Seekers are responsible, dependable, and solid citizens. They feel obligated to do their part and work hard. They respect customs, traditions, and social standards. Security Seekers place a high value on family and are the most marriage minded of all the temperaments. This type of person is also organized and thrives on routine and structure. Security Seekers like to communicate in a clear way, with things stated specifically, without having to draw assumptions. As teens, they are generally cooperative and respect authority. As parents, they provide a secure and consistent home environment. Security Seekers are well suited for careers in health care, finance, clerical work, sales, education, social service, counseling, legal or civil service, and a variety of creative fields, such as painting and photography.

Experience Seekers make up approximately 40% of the U.S. population (Baron, 2004). According to Baron, Experience Seekers have the need to act spontaneously for fun and also for problem solving. They value independence and freedom. They don't like to be burdened by obligations. Experience Seekers thrive on crisis situations. They feel comfortable acting spontaneously in the moment. As teens, Experience Seekers learn best in a hands-on setting, such as building, playing instruments, and playing sports. As parents, Experience Seekers like to expose their children to adventures and encourage them to be physically active. Experience Seekers are well suited for careers in sports, entertainment, creative fields, sales, service, travel, health care, education, social service, and miscellaneous related fields, including the law and private investigation.

Knowledge Seekers make up approximately 10% of the U.S. population (Baron, 2004). Baron tells us that Knowledge Seekers need competency and seek understanding of things such as the world and universal truths. Knowledge Seekers see patterns and connections and the relationship between things. They thrive on developing theories and focus on long-range goals. As teens, Knowledge Seekers are challenged by learning and are bright and clever. They can become bored if not challenged mentally. They are curious and inquisitive and constantly investigating and experimenting. As parents, Knowledge Seekers expect their children to challenge themselves intellectually. They challenge their children to accept responsibility, but they can be so busy that they neglect the normal tasks of family life. Knowledge Seekers are well suited for careers in education, medicine, science, engineering, business, finance, creative fields, and miscellaneous professions including the law, organizational consulting, and computer programming.

Ideal Seekers make up approximately 10% of the U.S. population (Baron, 2004). Baron writes that Ideal Seekers need to express themselves authentically and genuinely. They are passionate about things they believe in and spend a lot of time fostering relationships. They are insightful, perceptive, and sensitive. As teens, Ideal Seekers can have rich imaginations and are usually cooperative. They do their best when competing against themselves because competing against others causes disharmony. They try to be like those they admire. As parents, Ideal Seekers are concerned about their children's emotional development. They encourage their children's individuality and allow the children their free expression. Ideal Seekers are well suited for careers in helping professions, education, creative fields, health care, business, sales, and professional positions such as fundraiser, conference planner, program coordinator, and public relations specialist.

Baron includes some closing thoughts at the end of her book in which she says, "Although temperaments do not explain everything about people, they certainly give us a great deal of practical insight into human behavior, which can have a life-transforming effect on our relationships with ourselves and others" (Baron, 2004). I agree wholeheartedly with this message. We can better understand and relate to others after we sufficiently understand ourselves.

What Color Is Your Personality?

Carol Ritberger published *What Color Is Your Personality?* in 1999. This petite and colorful book can be purchased on Amazon new for less than $9. Ritberger's book includes a personality assessment that helps you determine whether you are a red, orange, yellow, or green personality type. She explains that it is more crucial to understand ourselves than it is to understand others. By paying attention to our own habits, why we do what we do, and how we respond to challenges, we can see what characteristics are stumbling blocks and need to be changed.

Ritberger categorizes the colors briefly for the reader prior to the actual personality assessment. She tells us that red is a personality style that needs to be in control. This need causes stress, which could be released through physical activity.

Individuals with the orange personality always need to be doing things for others, so there is hardly any time for themselves. People with this personality type could pamper themselves more; perhaps they could learn yoga. Yellow types find themselves frustrated by indecision because they can see both sides very well. Such individuals could help themselves by creating stimulating mind diversions such as reading a book or even playing video games. Greens can get angry when they feel disorganized or out of control; they could read books on how to better manage time and how to get better organized.

The personality assessment Ritberger uses is found on pages 60 to 65 and consists of 60 statements. Each statement has a letter next to it: A, B, C, or D. When taking this assessment, you are asked to circle any of the 60 statements that represent your most frequent and habitual patterns. An example of one of the statements is "I have a lot of thoughts in my head simultaneously, and I am often accused of not listening or of being preoccupied." At the end of the assessment, the total circled answers are added up separately for the A's, B's, C's, and D's. The last step is to combine A's and C's to get a red score, B's and C's to get a yellow score, A's and D's to get an orange score, and B's and D's to get a green score. One of the strong points of Ritberger's assessment tool is her coverage of the weak side of each personality type and potential health issues. She states at the end of her book that the "state of our mind directly affects the chemistry of the body in such a way that we are either becoming ill or overcoming illness every moment of our lives" (Ritberger, 1999). She further explains that our health is directly related to our success and happiness, which is in direct relation to understanding ourselves and changing unhealthy habits and thoughts.

Jung Typology Test

Another free online personality test is the HumanMetrics (2013) Jung Typology Test accessible at http://www.humanmetrics.com/cgi-win/jtypes2.asp. The test is based on Carl Jung's and Isabel Briggs-Myers's typological approach to personality. To take this assessment, you answer 72 yes-or-no questions and then submit the test for grading. An example questions is

2. You like to be engaged in an active and fast-paced job.

The results of your answers come back immediately. I answered the questions as honestly as possible, and according to the results, I am an INTJ, preferring Introversion (33%), Intuition (12%), Thinking (1%), and Judging (44%). The following analysis was provided:

- You have *moderate* preference of Introversion over Extraversion (33%)
- You have *slight* preference of Intuition over Sensing (12%)
- You have *marginal or no* preference of Thinking over Feeling (1%)
- You have *moderate* preference of Judging over Perceiving (44%)

On the same screen with your results, you can choose other free results. By clicking on the career choices for your type, you will be directed to another screen with helpful career information. The information for INTJs is as follows:

> Generally, INTJs have successful careers in areas requiring intensive intellectual efforts, presenting intellectual challenge, and creative approach.
>
> Due to the characteristics mentioned above, successful INTJs are found in technological companies, particularly in research and development, and also found among corporate lawyers, high- and mid-rank managers in technology companies and financial institutions.

The various careers suggested for INTJs fall into areas of computer programming, natural science, teaching, engineering, management, entrepreneurship, the law, and libraries. The results even list the names of famous personalities who share the same personality type. These individuals are INTJs:

- Stephen Hawking, a theoretical physicist, cosmologist, and author
- Andrew Grove, a businessman, engineer, and author
- Marie Curie, a physicist and chemist famous for her pioneering research on radioactivity
- Guy Kawasaki, a venture capitalist, best-selling author, and Apple fellow
- Igor Sikorsky, a pioneer of aviation
- Hillary Clinton, the 67th U.S. secretary of state
- Arnold Schwarzenegger, governor of California

Another option from the results screen is to access a profile of your personality type. The profile of the INTJ is a comprehensive report of 1,400 words. This is one of the paragraphs from the INTJ profile:

> INTJs are perfectionists, with a seemingly endless capacity for improving upon anything that takes their interest. What prevents them from becoming chronically bogged down in this pursuit of perfection is the pragmatism so characteristic of the type: INTJs apply (often ruthlessly) the criterion "Does it work?" to everything from their own research efforts to the prevailing social norms. This, in turn, produces an unusual independence of mind, freeing the INTJ from the constraints of authority, convention, or sentiment for its own sake.

Minnesota State Careerwise Education

Another website with a career assessment tool and free results is the Career Cluster Interest Survey at https://www.careerwise.mnscu.edu/careers/clusterSurvey (Minnesota State Careerwise Education, 2017). This survey has you choose and rate activities you enjoy. It also explores your personal qualities and any school subjects you like. After completing the survey, you can see which careers might be a good fit for you. The careers are offered in groupings, called clusters, and you are able to enter each cluster and explore individual careers within them. I wasn't surprised that my top three recommended career clusters were hospitality and tourism, education and training, and government and public service work. However, I think I would have been surprised had I taken this survey when I was 18 years old. At that time, I had no motivation to become a police officer or a professor, but I learned eventually that I was a good fit for both.

Entering the education and training link offered me four more groupings:

1. Careers in this cluster
2. Industries in this cluster
3. Pathways in this cluster
4. Majors in this cluster

By entering the careers cluster, I found 76 career suggestions. I was able to click on any of the careers, which would take me to a new page containing information about the career, including an overview, wages and outlook, education and credentials, skills and knowledge, tools and technology, and jobs.

Monster

At https://www.monster.com/career-advice/article/best-free-career-assessment-tools you will find nine assessment tools (Monster Worldwide, 2017). Just as with some of the other tools listed in this chapter, you can usually get a brief report for free, but some assessments require that you pay a fee for more comprehensive feedback. The following assessment tools are available on this website:

- Myers-Briggs Type Indicator
- Keirsey Temperament Sorter
- MyPlan.com
- Big Five Personality Assessment
- 16personalities
- iSeek "Clusters"
- MyNextMove
- MAPP Test
- Holland Code Career Test

The Myers-Briggs Type Indicator is one of the best-known assessments and takes longer than most other career assessment tools. Its main purpose is to make Jung's psychological "type" theory understandable and useful in people's lives. You have to pay to receive the results of the Myers-Briggs survey, but there is an option to click a link to the Jung Typology Assessment, which is shorter and offers a free report.

The Keirsey Temperament Sorter (discussed earlier) is the most frequently used personality instrument worldwide. The questions are offered in several languages, but the results are offered only in English. An advantage to using this tool is the short amount of time it takes and the free report that gives quite a bit of helpful information.

MyPlan.com helps students identify their motivations and what's really important to them in their career. The results rank different aspects of work that can encourage students to look at jobs or industries they may not have considered before. Students can walk away from this test with a list of 739 jobs, ordered by how well the job fits the student's profile. The test is 20 questions that should only take about 10 to 15 minutes.

The Big Five Personality Assessment measures five personality traits: openness, conscientiousness, extraversion, agreeableness, and neuroticism. The assessment will identify a dominant trait out of the five and can help students identify learning styles as well as work preferences. This assessment tool is the best accepted and most commonly used model of personality in academic psychology. It consists of 50 items that students must rate on a five-point scale (1 = disagree, 3 = neutral, and 5 = agree). It takes most students 5 to 10 minutes to complete.

The 16 Personalities Assessment starts with Myers-Briggs classifications and adds standards from Jung's theory and the Big Five. Students learn whether they are an introvert or extrovert and are labeled with one of 16 personality types, such as "Mediator," "Commander" or "Defender." This test is short and should take students only about 10 to 15 minutes. I took the survey and was quite impressed with the free information it offered after answering the questions. The results were separated into the following categories:

1. Introduction
2. Strengths & Weaknesses
3. Romantic Relationships
4. Friendships
5. Parenthood
6. Career Paths
7. Workplace Habits
8. Conclusion
9. Premium Profile

The premium profile is an easy-to-read downloadable e-book containing 158 pages of insights and advice created specifically for each individual result. Students taking this survey will find plenty of helpful information without needing to pay for more.

iSeek "Clusters" is a link to the Careerwise assessment mentioned earlier. It lets students rate activities they like, their personal qualities, and school subjects they enjoy. After answering the questions, students can see which career clusters are matches for their interests. This survey usually takes students 5 to 10 minutes to complete.

MyNextMove uses O*Net information, which is sponsored by the U.S. Department of Labor, to help determine students' interests as they relate to work. This test asks students to rate how much they would enjoy performing specific work tasks such as "building kitchen cabinets," "laying brick," or "buying and selling stocks and bonds." This is a 60-question survey, so it may take more time than some of the other tools.

More than 8 million people around the world have taken the MAPP Test. The hook is the claim that it helps students find their way in life and tells them what they love to do and what they don't love to do. It also draws from the O*Net job list to match jobs to students' profiles. The problem is that students have to pay for their "starter package," in which they will see their top 20 general career matches. The costlier "executive package" provides a 30-page assessment and ranked recommendations to 900 careers. But students can still try it for free and be matched with five potential careers.

The Holland Code Career Test examines students' suitability for various careers based on six occupational themes: Investigative, Realistic, Artistic, Enterprising, Social, and Conventional. The test reveals students' top interest area and what it means for their career interests. This test takes about 20 minutes to answer the 87 questions.

Students invest 4 years of their life to earn a college degree in order to land a job that may potentially fill 20 more years of their life. Giving an hour or two early on to enhance self-awareness is not too much of a sacrifice. It could help steer students in the right direction as they choose their classes and seek volunteer opportunities. The books and assessments presented in this chapter are free or very low cost. A student who assertively does whatever it takes to plan, prepare for, and pursue a career is exactly what employers are looking for.

SUMMARY

Two questions that stump applicants in an interview are "What are your strengths?" and "What are your weaknesses?" Sometimes a person has great strengths and skills but has trouble articulating them in an interview. Many students aren't adequately aware of their strengths and weaknesses. Just as a house needs a good foundation, learning about oneself is the right place to start if the best results are to be achieved. Some people lack self-awareness and are stuck in a rut. They are not likely to change and improve their lives, simply because they feel as if they already know enough. In reality, there is so much we do not know and will never have the opportunity to know. It is the realization of our vulnerabilities and inefficiencies that prepares us for learning, changing, and improving.

Professors recognize students' strengths and weaknesses and can either confirm to students that they are a good fit for the careers they are pursuing or help direct them to better choices. It is best if students are aware of their own strengths, preferences, and natural tendencies. The ideal situation is for students to learn more about themselves at the earliest point possible.

There are several books and self-assessment tools available to assist students in reaching a deeper understanding of their strengths and weaknesses and what types of jobs they might be best suited for. Some online assessment tools are free and offer concise reports of the results. There are books available to clarify the results with much more comprehensive information. Once you gain a deeper understanding of your own strengths and weaknesses, you will have the insight early on that will help you search for the best volunteer positions or internships that will get your foot not just in the door but in the right door.

DISCUSSION QUESTIONS

1. What is the difference between group skills we possess and use and the actual work we do in group projects?
2. Do you agree with the statement "Self-awareness is the gateway to self-improvement"? Why or why not?
3. What is the moral of the poem about the six blind men from Indostan?
4. Do you agree with Bolles's statement that "everyone has skills, but there is such a thing as being deeply unaware of our skills"? Why or why not?
5. What does Birkman mean when he says "Nobody is normal, and everyone is?"
6. Do you agree with Ritberger when she explains that "it is more crucial to understand ourselves than it is to understand others?" Why or why not?
7. If you tried any of the free online tests, do you agree with the results you got? Were there any surprises?

REFERENCES

Baron, R. (1998). *What type am I? Discover who you really are.* London, UK: Penguin Group.

Baron, R. (2004). *The four temperaments: A fun and practical guide to understanding yourself and the people in your life.* New York, NY: St. Martin's.

Birkman, R. W. (1995). *True colors: Get to know yourself and others better with the highly acclaimed Birkman method.* Nashville, TN: Thomas Nelson.

Bolles, R. (2000). *What color is your parachute? A practical manual for job-hunters and career changers* (30th ed.). Berkeley, CA: Ten Speed Press.

HumanMetrics. (2013). *Jung typology test.* Retrieved from http://www.humanmetrics.com/cgi-win/JTypes2.asp

Keirsey, D. (1998). *Please understand me II: Temperament, character, intelligence* [Kindle version]. Del Mar, CA: Prometheus Nemesis.

Keirsey, D., & Bates, M. M. (1984). *Please understand me: Character & temperament types* (5th ed.). Del Mar, CA: Prometheus Nemesis.

Keirsey.com. (n.d.). *Welcome to the Keirsey Temperament Sorter II (KTS-II)!* Retrieved from http://keirsey.com/sorter/register.aspx

Minnesota State Careerwise Education. (2017). *Career cluster interest survey.* Retrieved from https://www.careerwise.mnscu.edu/careers/clusterAssessment

Monster Worldwide. (2017). *Ten awesome free career self-assessment tools on the internet.* Retrieved from https://www.monster.com/career-advice/article/best-free-career-assessment-tools

National Aeronautics and Space Administration. (n.d.). *Counting galaxies with the Hubble space telescope.* Retrieved from http://spacemath.gsfc.nasa.gov/weekly/6Page14.pdf

National Aeronautics and Space Administration. (2012). *How old is the universe?* Retrieved from http://map.gsfc.nasa.gov/universe/uni_age.html

O'Neil, D. (2013). Introduction. In *Language and culture: An introduction to human communication.* Retrieved from http://anthro.palomar.edu/language/language_1.htm

Ritberger, C. (1999). *What color is your personality? Red, orange, yellow, green.* Carlsbad, CA: Hay House.

Saxe, J. (1873). *The poems of John Godfrey Saxe.* Washington, DC: Library of Congress.

Stoops, N. (2004). Educational attainment in the United States: 2003. *Current Population Reports*, P20-550. Washington, DC: US Census Bureau.

Taychir, L. (2010). Books of the world, stand up and be counted! All 129,864,880 of you. *Google Books Search*. Retrieved from http://booksearch.blogspot.com/2010/08/books-of-world-stand-up-and-be-counted.html

U.S. Census Bureau. (2012). *Births, deaths, marriages, & divorces: Life expectancy*. Retrieved from http://www.census.gov/compendia/statab/cats/births_deaths_marriages_divorces/life_expectancy.html

SETTING REALISTIC GOALS

INTRODUCTION

Career development is a process that takes time, patience, hard work, and, for those without a full-ride scholarship, money. Like climbing a ladder, the process involves a beginning step. Trying to skip the first step and going straight to the second is very arduous and, for most, not possible. Trying to start on the third step is almost impossible, leaving those attempting it with feelings of disappointment and failure. To take this analogy even further, we can factor in those who get a boost and can actually reach the second or third rung immediately. Boosters include family members or friends who are already in position and willing to give a boost. Our analogy also includes supporters who help steady people and therefore enable them to climb each step more quickly and with less difficulty. This chapter is important for those who can't depend on boosters and supporters to land that dream job.

The two factors that affect your happiness the most are your relationships and your job. These areas also have a profound effect on each other. It is common for a person who is not happy at work to bring the discord home and make others miserable as well. The same happens when a person is experiencing difficulty at home and then tries to muster up some positive energy at work. Without our jobs and our relationships being in harmony, we can't be our happiest, and our trials are more difficult to overcome.

The self-assessment tests in Chapter 1 can show you a multitude of information if you actively seek it. If you are searching for understanding in relationships, those types of tests can clarify what kind of person might be a good fit for you and why. If you are looking for happiness in a career, self-assessments can accomplish the same thing. If you seek a career that is not a good fit, you may find yourself unhappy at work and at home. If you are afraid of needles, you might need to reevaluate your dream of being a doctor. If you get sick to your stomach before giving a presentation in front of your college class, being a prosecutor might not be something you would be happy doing.

Desire to do a particular job doesn't necessarily translate into being good at it, and disinterest doesn't mean that you're deficient in the skills needed to do the job. However, people tend to like doing what they are good at, and people excel at things they like to do. Therefore, being or becoming good at what you choose to do for your job correlates with being happy in your career. Some people become knowledgeable and somewhat skillful in certain areas through exposure, and they subsequently transition into careers without much trouble. This type of experience is common when someone follows in the footsteps of a parent or older sibling. Someone raised by a parent who is an attorney would develop insight into that type of thinking, just as the daughter of a police officer is likely to be somewhat familiar with the police personality. How does a person who has not had these learning opportunities choose a career? How do you know what you can be good at if you haven't tried it?

SET REALISTIC GOALS

A popular quotation from Laurence J. Peter (1919–1988) goes like this: "If you don't know where you are going, you'll probably end up somewhere else." In 2007, David P. Campbell published a book titled *If You Don't Know Where You're Going, You'll Probably End Up Somewhere Else: Finding a Career and Getting a Life*. According to Campbell, we all want choices, but to create choices, we must have goals. To reach your goals and expand your choices, you need assets, and the more the better. These assets can include a good education, good health, broadening experiences, talents, and help from family and friends. In fact, Campbell asserts, the assets with the greatest impact on your future are the following, in this order:

1. Talents and skills
2. Intellectual intelligence
3. Emotional intelligence
4. Education
5. Friends
6. Family
7. Experiences
8. Appearance
9. Health

The more assets you have going for you, the more choices you will have. What talents and skills do you already have? As we discussed at the beginning of this book, one of the questions many applicants are most unprepared for is "What are your strengths?" Often applicants have the relevant skills needed for a job but can't articulate them. Likewise, some applicants are dreadfully lacking the necessary skills for a job but unfortunately do not realize it. Consider some of the popular talent shows, such as *American Idol*, *America's Got Talent*, and *So You Think You Can Dance*, as extreme examples of candidates not right for the job. Before the judges select the final competitors, they view hundreds to thousands of contestants, many of whom are embarrassingly humorous. Believe it or not, professionals in the criminal justice system witness similar humorous tryouts. If some of those interviews were videotaped, they would make for an entertaining television show.

To set realistic goals, you should evaluate the talents and skills you already have as well as those you need for the career you are interested in. You then need to be realistic with your goals. One advantage of getting a degree is improving your knowledge and skills for a career. Improving your abilities often means stepping outside your comfort zone. Consider public speaking, which is a valuable skill for many professions. How does a person who is frightened of public speaking become skilled at it? Those who are afraid to speak in public generally avoid it. Some people have personality or cognitive limitations that hinder their ability to become great public speakers no matter how much they practice.

Sometimes improving ourselves involves altering our way of thinking first. There is a prayer by American theologian Reinhold Niebuhr (1892–1971) that has been adopted by Alcoholics Anonymous and other 12-step programs. It has become known as the Serenity Prayer. The part of the prayer most widely used goes like this:

> God, grant me the serenity to accept the things I can't change, the courage to change the things I can, and the wisdom to know the difference.

Once you know the difference between what you can and can't change, you can concentrate more time and effort in the areas that will be of the most benefit. Most of our skills are improvable with practice. Some traits are not easily changeable, such as our demeanor and personality. Some skills are more important than others in different careers.

There are special talents and skills specific to particular jobs in the criminal justice field. Some say you practically need to "walk on water" to become a police officer. Some lawyers would tell you that it is equally challenging to be accepted to a "top 40" law school. Employees in correctional facilities would likewise agree that special skills are needed to succeed, including the "gift of gab"; the wrong candidate would get swallowed up by the argot working as a corrections officer. Throughout the remainder of this chapter, we will explore certain skills needed to work in some of the more predominant positions of the criminal justice system: law enforcement, the courts, and corrections.

ISSUES IN POLICE WORK

Law enforcement is a field highly sought after, yet one in which it can be difficult to land a job. This field encompasses the federal, state, county, and city levels, as well as other miscellaneous agencies, such as campus police and gaming officers. As we explore the skills necessary for law enforcement, we will refer to it broadly as "police work." By understanding some of the more advanced matters in police work, you can better appreciate what skills are needed and determine whether it is a career you could actually excel in and enjoy. The more one knows about what a police officer is and does, the better one can understand what type of person an agency is looking for. This knowledge can help you decide whether you are a good fit for police work and can help you prepare for the hiring interview. It is important to note that it is not possible to fully comprehend the jobs and thought processes of police officers by reading a textbook. A graduate of an 18-week police academy, with another 18 weeks of field training and more than 5 years on the street, would tell you that every call is different, and doing the job requires a variety of approaches every day. Additionally, most officers with 3 to 5 years of experience would say that they are confident they can handle anything that comes along. Police agencies are looking for that type of person.

Agencies invest a lot of time in the hiring process and a substantial amount of money in the training of their recruits. They want a person who, after sufficient training, can handle the variety of incidents that occur. What types of things do police officers have to handle? Do you have an adequate understanding of what is expected of you as a police officer?

Some of the best introductory textbooks on policing are comprehensive and cover the topic in a way that is easy to understand (e.g., Scaramella, Cox, & McCamey, 2010). I recommend studying an all-inclusive textbook for a basic understanding of policing. However, getting hired as a law enforcement officer and performing the job with competence requires a deeper insight. Knowledge of topics such as evidence-based policing and intelligence-led policing is not exactly what recruiters are looking for in new hires. Although a degree and a strong knowledge base are great assets, recruiters will be looking for someone who can do the job at the entry level, with the potential to be great. Factors such as the proper thought process, personality, communication skills, and temperament are of higher importance to recruiters.

If you have not yet had a chance to study from an introductory policing textbook, you should ask yourself what you already know about police work. Ask yourself where you got that knowledge. The average citizen has not taken the opportunity to experience a police ride-along or to take criminal justice classes in college. Their knowledge of police work has been gleaned through media reports, stories from family and friends, and brief encounters during traffic incidents or filing police reports. To get the most out of this chapter, it is recommended that you consider the poem in Chapter 1 about the blind men and the elephant. Be open minded to the reality that there is more to learn and, thanks to selective and fragmented media coverage, plenty to unlearn.

An example of how police work is distorted by the media is the illusion that police often use force against citizens. In reality, there is relatively little use of force by police officers in the United States. In fact, according to a database of the International Association of Chiefs of Police (2001), law enforcement officers in 1995 used some level of force only 4.19 times every 10,000 calls for service. The data in 1999 showed that force was used only 3.61 times for every 10,000 calls for service.

The following information is intended to help you better understand the police "reality," which can help you start developing the necessary way of thinking to stand out in the hiring interview or, as a possible consequence, sway you to consider a different career. Some of the skills and expectations relative to police work might shock you as we visit some important and controversial issues in the field of policing.

The Use of Deception

An important paradox in policing that might be too conflicting for some to appreciate and accept is that an exceptional law enforcement officer is one who can use deception in the appropriate settings and yet be conclusively honest enough to pass a polygraph test. As mentioned earlier, it is difficult for interviewees to articulate their strengths in hiring interviews if they are not prepared. You can imagine the irony in an interview were you to answer the strength question by saying that you are a really good liar. It is not recommended that you answer the question that way, but recruiters are essentially looking for honest people who can be actors with the ability to deceive. A person who has never done anything wrong might be a great bank teller or maybe even a priest but might lack the unusual characteristics needed to be a law enforcement officer. However, anybody in law enforcement will tell you that dishonesty will get you fired faster than almost anything else you do wrong.

This contradiction can put police work in a bad light if not clearly understood. Mothers usually teach their children that they can trust certain professionals, such as teachers, doctors, and police officers, but you will rarely see a mother, after her child tells a lie, say to her child, "You would make a great police officer!" When trickery is used by law enforcement to develop criminal cases, defense attorneys often enjoy letting the jury know about it in a way that shocks them. Some citizens believe that police officers should never lie. Some citizens also feel that the police should disarm a knife-wielding suspect by using martial arts techniques or should shoot the gun out of the hands of a would-be cop killer. If you are one of these citizens, police work might not be the right job for you. However, if you can develop a "reality" mindset like that of a police officer, you will not be far out of your wheelhouse during the hiring interview.

When is it okay for a police officer to lie? One of the few allowable circumstances is when it is done for the purpose of obtaining the truth. Police officers are fact finders. Regardless of the purpose at hand, such as to prevent crime or to protect and serve citizens, police officers must report the facts of an incident as accurately as possible. This includes honestly reporting any trickery or lies that were used to accomplish the task. If an officer obtains a confession from a suspect by falsely telling him that there were witnesses who saw him commit the crime, the officer must be honest and accurate in the report and in court testimony about the lie told to the suspect. When police are faced with a child molestation case in which there is little or no physical evidence, a confession from the suspect is likely the only way justice will be served. It is common for the police to ask a victim to make a phone call (monitored and recorded) and deceive the perpetrator in an effort to solicit incriminating comments. This type of trickery by the police can shock people who are naive to police strategies. In such a situation, an officer may need to educate the jury on police tactics to help them understand that deception is allowable and necessary. Some jury members may still be appalled. Police officers also work a variety of undercover operations in which deception is the norm. You need to decide how you feel about the methods police use to achieve their goals. Can you lie to a suspect in an investigation to gain a confession?

Regardless of the need to use deception in police work, there are ethical issues and "gray areas" that officers learn to work with (and work around) through experience. However, when it comes to a suspect's rights, reporting writing, testifying in court, or answering questions during internal investigations, an officer must always be as honest as possible. Like so many other aspects of a police officer's job, the allowable situations for lying and deceiving are not specifically spelled out in policy. If you get hired as a police officer, you will need to learn how to survive with vague guidelines. Most officers don't stress over the ambiguity and just survive on faith that they will be treated fairly if their behavior is ever questioned. They continue to learn from veteran officers, court decisions, and trial and error.

The Role of Acting in Police Work

Being a good deceiver correlates with being a good actor. The necessity to act isn't limited to police work only, but it is a big part of a police officer's job. Some refer to it as the ability to "wear different hats." It is important that an interviewer knows that you have the ability to be an actor. If you can't show some level of fluctuation in your persona during your hiring interview, the recruiter might not feel that you can show it on the street. The interview is your one shot to demonstrate that you can. An officer needs to be able to leave a death scene where she just spoke softly and soothingly to the victim's family and arrive at a scene of melee and discord, yelling commands to unruly citizens in an authoritative fashion. This same officer may then need to interview a woman who was kidnapped by a stranger and brutally raped and then, 2 hours later, interview the perpetrator of the attack. Each of these scenarios requires a different demeanor on the officer's part. To do the job of a police officer well, one needs to be able to change hats from one call to the next. An officer might go home and have a good cry after handling a drowned baby incident earlier in the day, but during the shift, officers are expected to remain professional and wear whatever hat is necessary.

The Use of Discretion

Some of the toughest scenario-based questions that are asked in a hiring interview involve some kind of discretionary decision. Often these questions involve the use of force, integrity issues, and teamwork. To be prepared for these types of questions, one needs to be aware of the scope of an officer's discretionary powers. Police officers must constantly make decisions in situations in which there are several options. Even though there are many ways to accomplish things, the personnel who developed the interview questions have already decided what they feel would be the best answers. If a police officer makes a traffic stop, she can decide when and where to actually turn on the overhead lights to signal the driver to pull over. The officer can then decide whether to approach the car from the driver's side or the passenger's side. The officer may choose to have the driver step out of the car. There may be passengers to deal with. The officer might see or smell something in the car that brings in new options to choose from.

Depending on the circumstances, the driver may get a warning, be ticketed, or be arrested. If the driver is arrested and transported to jail, the officer would have to decide what to do about the suspect's vehicle. She may choose to have the car towed, call someone to come get it, or lock it and leave it at the scene. The officer may choose to read the Miranda warnings to the suspect and can decide when and where to do so. If the officer decides to conduct an interview, another group of choices is introduced. In many cases, officers can choose between booking a suspect into jail or issuing a ticket and releasing the suspect with a future court date.

A difficult area for anyone to fully comprehend, including currently active police officers, is exactly what types of crimes are okay to give a citizen a "free pass" on. There is rarely a clear rule or policy that explains it. Protocols for these types of decisions are normally unwritten and passed down from veteran officers and supervisors through the years. A problem with this type of structure is that not all officers and supervisors agree on what should be tolerated and what should be strictly enforced. Police personnel bring their own opinions and values to the job. What is okay to overlook, and what is not, can become somewhat clouded throughout a career of working with different officers and supervisors. This ambiguous discretionary power can result in situations of unfairness to citizens, such as racial bias, gender bias, age bias, and other similar instances of inequity. It also opens up possibilities for corruption; officers may succumb when solicited with favors in exchange for a release without an arrest.

It is important to understand that most police departments avoid giving explicit permission (written in policy) for their officers to give breaks to citizens on anything. When an officer pours alcohol on the ground and tells underage drinkers to go home, with no record made of the incident, the officer puts his job on the line by not following the policy of the department. Most agencies in this scenario would require a police report, charges to be filed if appropriate, and the alcohol to be placed into evidence until trial or proper destruction. A police officer today might choose to be lenient simply because in the past, a different police officer was lenient with him or her. If an officer opts not to arrest a driver who is under the influence of alcohol and lets the driver call for a ride home, the officer is actually taking the risk of being disciplined. Again, there is no specific permission given in department policies to allow officers to make that type of decision, but discretion is used all the time. Officers face the dilemma, every shift, of trying to balance what they feel they should do and what policy tells them to do.

Just as with the example of underage drinking, when an officer chooses a certain course of action, it could be for numerous reasons. If the jail is overcrowded and the dispatcher is holding several high-priority calls, an officer may choose to cut some slack to a driver on marijuana possession. That same officer, during a slow shift on the following day, might arrest four to five people for driving under the influence and give absolutely no breaks. In the busy night scenario with the overcrowded jail, there may be other officers who do not cut any slack for any reason. They might not want to risk answering to a supervisor who doesn't agree with their decisions. The lenient officers might end up handling most of the workload and may even find themselves without sufficient backup because other officers are tied down with arrests. There may even be serious calls, such as robberies or aggravated assault cases, waiting on hold for long periods of time because officers are unavailable. Police officers often must choose between the letter of the law and the spirit of the law, but rarely is there express, written permission allowing officers to make any of the discretionary decisions they make.

One of the main reasons a police department has standards and policies is to protect it from lawsuits. If an officer follows his training and adheres to these policies, the department will likely back him up on lawsuits or citizen complaints. If the officer violates a policy, the department might not stand behind him in a civil lawsuit and could choose to discipline him, which can include termination. Even with this lose-lose quandary officers are faced with, they continue to make discretionary decisions on whom to arrest and whom to let go.

All officers bring to the job their own principles based on their life experiences. They have different agendas and particular violations they like to look for and enforce. They have different strengths and weaknesses. They have different personalities and approaches. They have different biases, too. If you enter the police world, you, too, will add to the diversity and bring your own heart and soul to the work. Can you survive in this type of work environment, with vast degrees of freedom and empowerment, yet with such ambiguity and, in some ways, insecurity?

One more peculiar fact about discretion in the police world is that the higher ranking a person has in a department, the less discretion that person can exercise. As a police officer climbs the supervisory ladder in a department (from operations to middle management to upper management), her hands are tied more and more the higher she gets. The chief of police, for example, must follow the standards, policies, and procedures to a tee, with little or no deviation. This bit of information is very important because you will want to answer questions in the hiring interview as though you are talking directly to the chief. In other words, for questions in which discretion is asked for, it is best to lean in the direction of what the chief would want to hear, not toward what you think most officers actually do in reality. We will be discussing this further in Chapter 11.

The Use of Force

Police officers periodically get shot and sometimes must shoot people. Do you have the fortitude to use lethal force against another human being? Do you know when it is appropriate to do so? Use of force is closely linked to the topic of discretion. There are often scenario questions in the hiring interview that involve a use-of-force decision. Besides the questions about strengths and weaknesses, this is another area for which many candidates are unprepared. Therefore, by scoring high on these questions, one can stand out and move ahead of other applicants.

There is more on this topic in Chapter 11 to help you prepare for interview questions, but here is a brief lesson on the use of force. Not many colleges offer full-semester courses on this topic, and many police recruits learn it for the first time in the academy. Again, you need to know what a police officer does in order to know whether this job is the right fit for you. If it is something you feel you can do, go for it!

There are different models for the use of force. We will briefly discuss two of them here. The first is the continuum model, and the second is the Federal Law Enforcement Training Center (FLETC) model. The continuum model tries to match appropriate actions by an officer to an offender's behavior. The continuum of force generally contains five to seven levels, which include officer's presence, verbal commands, soft hand techniques, hard hand techniques, less than lethal force, and lethal force. Less than lethal weapons can sometimes be broken into two different levels, with pepper spray being on a slightly lower level than Tasers, beanbags, and pepper balls. The amount of force an officer uses depends on what level of resistance or threat an offender poses. Officers are permitted to be "one up" on offenders, but this doesn't mean that an officer is restricted to a certain order, going from level 1 to level 2 to level 3 and so on. An officer can ratchet up several levels all at once, if necessary. When an offender is only passively resisting, an officer will normally use certain transport techniques or even step up to pepper spray.

The continuum model has been used for years, but it does have some downfalls in modern law enforcement. The U.S. Supreme Court in *Graham v. Conner* (1989) held that force used by police officers is judged by "objective reasonableness," a standard established by the Fourth Amendment, and incorporates the view of the totality of circumstances. In *Graham*, the court decided "the test of reasonableness under the Fourth Amendment is not capable of precise definition or mechanical application." However, that is what the use-of-force continuum attempts to do. Many continuum models do not address the concept of the totality of circumstances. Most continuum models are structured in such a way that a specific subject action equates to a specific officer response, regardless of the totality of circumstances known to the officer at the moment force was used. Experienced law enforcement officers know that each use-of-force incident is unique and therefore has a different totality of circumstances. Because many local and state law enforcement agencies use the continuum model, it is important to be familiar with it and be able to articulate your knowledge of the agency's use-of-force policy if asked about it in the hiring interview.

The FLETC model is a bit more general and basically follows the guidelines implied (and spelled out) in the Fourth Amendment. All the use-of-force training at FLETC is founded upon the Supreme Court's decisions in *Graham* and in *Tennessee v. Garner* (1985). FLETC focuses on the favorable law enforcement language used by the Supreme Court to teach students what the law tells them they can do, rather than what they can't. FLETC instructors attempt to resolve the various myths regarding the use of force, such as "an officer can never shoot someone in the back," "an officer can never shoot an unarmed person," and "an officer must exhaust all lesser means before using deadly force," "an officer must give a verbal warning before using deadly force," "an officer cannot use deadly force on a suspect wielding an edged weapon until the officer is within 21 feet," and "an officer must be in fear for his or her life before using deadly force." In dispelling these types of myths, students are less likely to err or hesitate during a use-of-force incident (Bostain, 2006).

One stumbling block some applicants run into is the fear of sounding too anxious or too aggressive. Although this is a legitimate concern, sounding too naive or hesitant is usually worse.

A good portion of applicants derive many of their opinions about police work from the media, which results in a feeling that police overuse their power. As stated earlier, very little force is actually used in comparison with the overall frequency of citizen contacts, and consequently, there is, in fact, very little brutality in law enforcement. Although even once is too often for police brutality, the misconceptions regarding the overuse of force can hinder a person from being realistic. The more you can think like a police officer rather than a citizen who has been misled about police work through watching the nightly news, the better you will be at answering use-of-force questions. Could you take someone's life if you had to, cope with the emotional aftermath, and handle all the negative press that goes along with it?

The Polygraph Test

Are you honest enough to be a police officer? Have you committed any crimes that may disqualify you? To be hired by a law enforcement agency, you are expected to be the best of the best. Most large agencies require an applicant to pass a polygraph test. After a thorough background check and polygraph test, a department can feel assured that it has done its best to hire a safe and honest employee. You should check the crime and drug history guidelines of the agency you want to work for. You can examine the basic requirements and disqualifiers for the position of police officer in Chapter 3.

Not all agencies include polygraph examinations in their hiring process, but almost all agencies do thorough background investigations. Large agencies almost always require polygraph testing for new hires, but that doesn't mean their agency is free of corruption. Because this is always a concern, there is often at least one scenario question in the interview that assesses an applicant's thinking process in the area of ethics. Some sample questions and answers appear in Chapter 11.

Interviewing and Interrogating

Interviewing and interrogating are important tasks in police work; hence, a recruiter needs to believe that an applicant has these abilities. We discussed earlier that police are allowed to deceive people in appropriate situations. Police officers also get deceived. In fact, some criminals are outstanding deceivers with years of practice. Officers are fact finders, and they need to be able to evaluate statements from citizens for accuracy and truthfulness. An officer who isn't naturally suspicious of ulterior motives may be easily tricked. Therefore, an applicant who appears too naive and trusting of others might not impress an interviewer. Interviewers for the hiring of law enforcement positions are generally experienced officers who are very good at what they do. Regardless of specific questions you are asked, the interviewer will continuously be observing and assessing you for numerous traits during the entire duration. Make sure the interviewer knows that you are not one of the naive ones. If you do not come across as clever, assertive, quick witted, and intelligent, you might not convince the interviewer that you have what it takes.

Internal Investigations

In police work, you are in the public eye and held to a higher standard. You are considered a police officer 24 hours a day, which means you are held to a higher standard at all times and in all places. Anything you do on your "off duty" time is subject to scrutiny from the department and the public. Citizen complaints about unpleasant confrontations with police officers spark investigations from internal affairs. The reality of police work is that the harder-working street officers (answering calls for service, writing tickets, and making arrests) will receive a greater number of citizen complaints because of the quantity and category of people they deal with. If a citizen complaint is serious enough, an officer may be suspended from work until the accusation is resolved. Often complaints are unfounded and officers are cleared for duty, but the damage caused by the stress (and sometimes media coverage) lingers in the officer's memory, and the investigative report lingers in the officer's personnel file. If an officer is determined to be guilty of wrongdoing, the punishment is usually more severe than what we see in other professions, and rightly so. This type of stress and other internal political issues can affect an officer's attitude, outlook on life, and overall happiness.

Police officers spend their careers surrounded by victimization, violence, and crime, which includes murders and other cases involving dead bodies, sexual assaults, kidnappings, child molestation, drugs, robberies, and many other experiences of sadness, chaos, and evil. A police officer is vulnerable to injury and death in the line of duty. Because you patrol in a marked car, criminals will know you are a police officer before you know they are criminals. Most deaths among police officers take place during arrests and transport, but some officers are murdered just because they are police officers. Faced with all of this, coupled with other miscellaneous external hurdles, police officers have above-average divorce and suicide rates. As hard as it is to get hired by a law enforcement agency, it is not surprising that many officers leave during their academy training or during the first 5 years of service, once the "reality" sets in. Are you the type of person who can remain positive, maintain harmony in your home, and work 40 to 60 hours a week, dealing with some of the most vile people and most depressing experiences? Police work isn't for everyone, but most officers will tell you that it is a very rewarding career with more positives than negatives.

ISSUES IN THE JUDICIAL SYSTEM

A legal career may be a better option for those who might not appreciate some of the negative aspects of police work. You can be a police officer in most agencies with just a high school diploma or General Educational Development (GED) certificate. To be a lawyer, however, you will need a 4-year bachelor's degree, followed by 3 years of law school, and then you must pass a complex bar exam that qualifies you in the state where you wish to practice. Here we will examine some specific skills and difficulties relevant to working in this field.

The Power of Persuasion

Are you a good manipulator? Do you know how to get what you want from people? How influential are you? If you litigate in the courtroom as a prosecutor or defense attorney, you will constantly be using your skills of persuasion with witnesses, the jury, and the judge. Aside from the actual skills required, one of the most important factors in influencing others is attractiveness. How do you fare? Actually, there is much more to attractiveness than a chiseled figure and picturesque facial features. You can't do much about your height, gender, or race, but your ability to persuade can be enhanced. This is done through good hygiene, good grooming, staying in good physical shape, maintaining a professional wardrobe, and exuding confidence.

You also need to be cognizant that the colors you wear will have an effect on how others perceive you. For example, dark colors (black, dark gray, and dark blue) are considered power colors and can boost your influence. The color of a necktie is important, too. A red tie can be too emotionally strong, but a blue tie represents peace and tranquillity and is considered the opposite of red. Green is calming and refreshing, and yellow is considered cheerful and an attention getter.

Another important area of influence is using the proper language. An effective litigator knows when to use an active or a passive voice. An example of a passive way to phrase a very familiar question is "Why was the road crossed by the chicken?" Knowing when to use which type of language is a skill that can be developed with practice. These little tricks of persuasion (attractiveness, wearing the right colors, and using the right language) are all important in your hiring interview, too. If you are seeking a career in law, you have several years of schooling ahead during which you can practice and prepare.

Attitude

To work in a courtroom environment, you must be assertive. When it comes to litigation, you need to be a pit bull. Chihuahuas need not apply! No client wants a pushover to represent him or a lawyer who sits back and waits for things to happen.

Clients want lawyers who are hungry and not afraid of a confrontation or an all-out fight. Just like Dorothy's friends along the yellow brick road, to be a good lawyer, you need a brain, you need heart, and you need courage.

In hiring interviews for police officers, applicants want to show off their respect for the chain of command with a soupçon of humility. In a hiring interview for a position in the judicial system or at a private law firm, you will want to demonstrate your confidence, assertiveness, control, and poise. Likability is important for all jobs, but that alone will not land you a job in the law field. It is highly competitive, and the firm needs to know that you can do the job. The key is to find that balance between confidence and zealousness. Make them like you because you are a good fit for what they need.

Communication Skills

Lawyers are master communicators, written and verbal. They must be comfortable teaching clients the details and complications of the law in a way they can understand. They are held to the highest standards in society for professionalism. Their ethical standards are highly criticized and monitored. Failure to effectively represent clients may subject attorneys to malpractice claims and loss of license. Attorneys' jobs can be stressful, as their clients are typically in some of the most desperate and worst circumstances of their lives.

Working anywhere in criminal justice involves some paperwork. In the law field, it isn't just the amount of paperwork that is astounding but also the precision and accuracy that are required. Lawyers draft contracts, briefs, pleadings, motions, and numerous persuasive letters every year. Lawyers and judges (who are usually lawyers) have the highest degree of liability and responsibility when it comes to the written word. The vocabulary one needs to master is substantial. You will be using words and phrases such as *adjudication*, *amicus curiae*, *arrearages*, *capias mittimus*, *probate*, and *peremptory challenge*. You will be expected to master legal jargon once you graduate from law school. You will also be expected to be professional in your writing style. If you are a good writer, you have already cleared an important hurdle required to survive in this field.

Salary Issues

The majority of law students survive on student loans. Some graduate from law school with debts of more than $100,000. Are you the type of person who can handle the added pressure of a huge debt early on in your career? If you are currently married and plan to start a family while in school, are you prepared to live on a student loan of approximately $24,000 per year?

Most law schools won't allow students to work while going to school, at least during the first year. Most students wouldn't find time to work anyway, with the additional homework necessary to keep up with their courses. Is your spouse okay with tending to the children while you are in class and then continuing to tend to them while you spend time in the library?

It bears repeating that the law is a highly competitive field. After your schooling is complete and you have passed the bar exam, you are really only on the first rung of the ladder. Without boosters and supporters, you can expect to start at a relatively low-paying job, working 60 or more hours a week. Some of the best and most experienced attorneys work even longer hours. Just as in police work, you can make a living working for the government, but it is doubtful you will own a swimming pool, a boat, an RV, and a time-share until you move up in rank or live in a two-income home. Ironically, a police recruit who possesses only a high school diploma may start at a higher pay rate than a new lawyer with 7 extra years of schooling. Nevertheless, the potential for a lucrative law career motivates countless students to seek bachelor's degrees that will benefit them in their applications to law schools.

Law degrees offer countless opportunities outside the criminal justice system. One can land jobs for a variety of private businesses in numerous areas of law. A lawyer can work in the criminal justice system as a prosecutor, defense attorney, or judge and, at the same time, work for private clients. However, without some flourishing networking, or boosters and supporters, these opportunities seldom drop into your lap. To succeed in law, you often need to create your own breaks. Are you this type of person?

Power and Responsibility

Prosecutors have tremendous power in the criminal justice system, especially over the police departments in their jurisdictions. Judges have a great deal of power, responsibility, and control over trials and some discretionary leeway in sentencing. Police officers hold a great deal of discretionary power in the initial stages of an investigation and some leeway in which suspects they arrest. However, prosecutors ultimately decide who will be charged with a crime and who won't.

Prosecutors benefit by communicating clearly with police departments about what they need done in order to prosecute certain crimes. If prosecutors see a trend or a change in what defense attorneys do, or in how juries react to particular crimes or evidence, the prosecutors have the responsibility to respond to it appropriately. They may start turning down cases that were once prosecuted routinely, or they may start requiring a different type of procedure from a police department before they consider prosecuting certain crimes. An example of this is adultery. In 1982, adultery was a misdemeanor in Arizona, requiring the spouse or victim to desire prosecution. However, prosecutors quit taking those cases to court well before 1980, regardless of what the spouse or victim desired. It took a while before Arizona police departments refrained from making arrests for adultery. Once they realized that prosecutors were turning down these cases, police no longer investigated the crime of adultery. Because the crime of adultery remained in the Arizona Revised Statutes, police officers had to explain the conundrum to would-be prosecuting spouses.

Ethics in Court

Prosecutors and public defenders work for the government. Public defenders are a necessary part of the judicial system. They are generally more experienced in criminal court than private attorneys. Public defenders get to know prosecutors and judges very well because of the number of hours spent with them in court. Public defenders (and prosecutors) are subjected to more scrutiny than private attorneys. This is not to say that private attorneys are louche. Private attorneys work for a different boss. If a private attorney steps over the line ethically during a trial, his or her boss might never know about it or might not discipline the attorney if it is reported. This is also true with police officers. Unless a prosecutor takes the time to report a police officer who may have acted questionably to his or her sergeant, a dishonest officer may be able to continue unethical practices undetected.

Secrecy is an important element in court proceedings. All the participants in the courtroom (judge, jury, prosecutor, defense attorney, police officers, and witnesses) are bound by confidentiality about certain information at different stages in the court process. This can make the process very difficult at times. At home, a prosecutor might be unable to discuss a case with the family. A prosecutor may know that a child molester has four prior convictions for child molestation, but she must keep that fact secret from the jury during the trial of a new case. Breaking the court's rules of secrecy can result in a mistrial and disciplinary action. Can you defend a child molester? Can you prosecute a murderer or a rapist and follow the rules to the letter, even if you know the defendant might strike again if he wins the trial?

The Battle of Wits

Attorneys want to win their cases. As they gain experience, they develop their preferred styles and strategies, but just like police officers who face new experiences every day, attorneys face new cases, new witnesses, and new juries. Attorneys, therefore, must be flexible and willing to react and adjust quickly and cleverly when necessary. Although a trial is very serious for all involved, it is easier to understand some of the clever strategies that take place in the courtroom (and behind the scenes) if you compare it to a game. We will use the game of poker, since it is rich with chicanery and is universally familiar. The game starts when the prosecuting attorney is dealt a case. He or she will review the case to decide what can be used and what is of little benefit. Instead of cards, the prosecutor has witnesses and physical evidence to work with. Like cards, the witnesses and pieces of evidence are of different strengths, such as an unlikable victim or a well-respected politician as a witness. The prosecutor can then request further follow-up from the police department in the hope of strengthening the case even more, or the prosecutor can fold and decide that the case isn't worth playing out. Follow-up can include a variety of tasks, such as additional interviews, lab work, or searches. Although the trial is similar to a poker game, one difference is that when the prosecutor is ready to play his hand, the defense attorney gets to see it. The defense attorney then develops a strategy to defeat the prosecutor's hand. Part of the strategy a defense attorney uses is to find (or create) weaknesses in the prosecutor's case. This is done mainly through interviews with witnesses, including police officers. A seasoned defense attorney approaches interviews with the strategy of creating weaknesses in the case. This is done cleverly and often results in inexperienced police officers' giving ammunition to the defense attorney without even realizing it. Defense attorneys delight in any conflicting statements made by officers and any sloppy police work.

Defense attorneys must be actors just as good as police officers on the street. If there are no mistakes in the interview or no sloppy police work, a defense attorney may talk the defendant into accepting a plea bargain. The defense attorney works hard to minimize the sentence on a plea bargain by pointing out the weakness of the prosecutor's case and providing a short summary of what is predicted to happen if the case goes to trial. Each attorney uses carefully selected words in selling his or her case to the other, hoping to get the opposing side to cower and give ground. This is one of the opportunities you would encounter as an attorney to exercise your skills in persuasion. You will also use your cleverness and influential panache when interviewing witnesses and performing in front of the jury. A prosecutor might feel very confident in a case and insist that the defendant plead to the charge without any guarantee of a lighter sentence. The defense attorney might riposte by reminding the prosecutor that a particular witness has already changed his story a couple of times and, therefore, might cause the jury to come back with a "not guilty" verdict. Just as in a poker game, what will happen if the hand is played out is unknown, but the players hope the other will fold.

The jury trial is where attorneys need their poker faces most. They are playing against each other, but it is the jury they must convince. The prosecutor must convince the jury that the accused is guilty beyond a reasonable doubt. The defense attorney will try to convince the jury that the prosecution has not proved its case. This is sometimes done by the clever use of influential dialogue and creative subtleties. It might appear to a jury that the opposing attorneys are not fond of each other, but in reality, most attorneys who oppose each other have mutual respect and can often be seen having friendly conversation when the jury is out of view. Can you work in such an adversarial environment? Litigation might not be for you, but there are plenty of other career options once you have your law degree.

ISSUES IN CORRECTIONS

Corrections is a field in which polygraph tests are not routinely conducted as part of the hiring process. This is important to many students. Too many students make mistakes early in life that disqualify them from some government jobs because of criminal histories or drug use. Such persons who are seeking careers with the thrill and excitement of law enforcement might find jobs in corrections or private security relatively satisfying. Although there is less variety in corrections than in police work and the pay is lower, it is easier to be hired in corrections, and the academy training is shorter as well. Not all applicants for corrections consider it a step on the ladder toward a different goal, such as police work or federal law enforcement. There are correctional officers who complete their whole careers in jails and prisons and are quite satisfied.

Some law enforcement officers who started their careers in detention or corrections recount beginning there as the best decision they ever made. One of the main reasons is that the overall experience taught them (or improved) their "gift of gab," or "verbal judo," as it's known in the police world. They feel the experience made them better interviewers and safer officers.

The Communication Gap

To survive in the prisons, either you learn how to communicate with criminals or you are dreadfully miserable at work. Convicted criminals will take advantage of a reticent officer. They respond well to firmness, as long as it is accompanied with respect. The prison environment introduces employees to a whole new vocabulary. You will learn terms such as *agitator*, *bean slot*, *blue bag*, *clavo*, *cat head*, *cho cho*, *dap*, and *fat back*. If you do use corrections as a ladder rung to law enforcement, you might be a good candidate for undercover work, buying and selling drugs. Talking the talk is the difficult part. Anyone can grow long hair, add a tattoo or two, and not shave or shower.

The Dangers for Correctional Officers

After time, many police officers get lackadaisical in their jobs when it comes to officer safety. Those with military or correctional backgrounds are the least likely to experience this injudicious relaxation on the job. Police officers have the privilege of working with law-abiding citizens as well as the criminal element of society. Correctional officers don't enjoy the same variety. They spend their shifts overseeing convicted criminals and those awaiting trial to ensure their safety and overall cooperation. They enforce facility rules and prevent inmate escapes. This requires a good deal of observation and patrolling and a lot of paperwork when security is breached. Correctional officers search convicted criminals at intake and at various other intervals during their sentences. Correctional officers are always at risk of being assaulted, either hand to hand or by having items thrown at them, such as food, urine, and feces.

In policing and corrections, the awareness level of an officer facing various stimulants is often categorized by color: condition white, condition yellow, or condition red. The color analogy applies to everyone, but most citizens aren't routinely preoccupied with safety and victimization concerns.

Condition white is used to represent a safe, relaxed frame of mind. This is usually the mentality people have when they are at home (not alone), in church, or engaged in other activities in a safe environment. White represents very low stress. Our bodies need to be "in white" periodically so as not to release too many stress hormones unnecessarily. Constant stress can lead to harmful effects in the body. Police officers and correctional officers need to learn how to relax at appropriate times because much of their lives is filled with stress and adrenaline rushes.

Condition yellow represents a stage of enhanced awareness. Being "in yellow" prepares a person for what could happen. There are times when a person needs to be in yellow. Anytime a person is vulnerable, such as being outdoors or home alone, she would be wise to be in condition yellow. A teenage girl walking home from school in white (thinking about what she will do when she gets home) might not notice a man who just drove past her for the third time. For police officers and correctional officers, it is common to start transitioning into yellow while putting on the uniform. Being in yellow means that you do not have tunnel vision. You are cognizant of all the activity around you. Police officers and correctional officers do not have the luxury of being in white while on duty. This is especially true for correctional officers.

Condition red is the "fight or flight" stage, when adrenaline is released. Adrenaline is a powerful hormone the body releases in response to excitement and emergency situations. The heart rate increases, the blood vessels contract, and the airways dilate. Speed and strength are increased, and at the same time, there is a decrease in the perception of pain. When a person enters the red zone, it is difficult to rationalize. It is normal for a person to go into panic mode. This is especially true if a person was in white instead of yellow when the stimulus presented itself. When panic sets in, the body reacts the way it normally does because you have less control of your thinking. This is why it is important to mentally prepare and physically train for what you want your normal response to be. If a person normally freezes and screams when a spider appears, this is likely how that person will respond to a kidnap attempt. "It is better to prepare and prevent than to repair and repent." For this reason, law enforcement personnel repeatedly practice their firearms and self-defense tactics to instill the proper, normal reaction during panic mode. Firearms instructors attempt to set up scenarios as realistically as possible, imitating incidents that would likely cause an adrenaline release. It is not uncommon for officers to accidentally fire their weapons during training (sometimes resulting in injuries or fatalities) because of a well-planned course that puts the officers in red. This type of training (done repeatedly) instills a new norm for the officers. In theory, they develop new habits and will, therefore, react the way they do in training when they are too keyed up to think clearly.

GUEST SPEAKER

BRIAN COLE, DIRECTOR OF CORRECTIONS

I started in 1989 and was hired as a corrections specialist with the Shawnee County Department of Corrections, Adult Detention Center. In December of 2012, I was appointed director of corrections. My duties include, but are not limited to, the following:

Under the administrative director of the Board of County Commissioners, this position administers the entire operation of the adult and juvenile detention programs of Shawnee County, Kansas; ensures offenders placed in custody are housed in a safe, secure manner and that offenders receive appropriately fair and humane treatment by staff; monitors the overall security of the centers and regularly tours the facilities to ensure the highest security standards are maintained; proactively seeks to improve offender processes to enhance the security and efficiency of the agency; creates and expects a staff culture of integrity when reporting misconduct by other staff and offenders; visits offender living units and speaks with offenders to gain sense of morale; and is active in the community to build positive partnerships.

This position requires a degree from an accredited college or university with major course work in corrections, criminal justice, public administration, behavioral science, or a related field. You must have at least four years of progressively responsible experience in planning, organizing, and directing major phases of the operations and programs of a correctional institution. Applicants must be at least 21 years of age, with no felony convictions and proof of a valid driver's license.

In October of 2012, our current director of corrections retired and I was appointed interim director. At this time I was advised that Shawnee County was carrying out nationwide recruitment for the permanent appointment. Once the top three applicants were chosen, we each went through an interview process. After a process lasting approximately two months, I was appointed director of corrections.

Working in the field of corrections takes committed people. On a daily basis, you will work with incarcerated individuals who have made (in some cases) some very bad life decisions. You have to be able to separate emotion from your job and understand you are managing people and their problems. You have to appreciate the environment you are working within. This is a "thankless" job that not many want or can do. However, this is a rewarding job!

Corrections can be a career, not just a stepping-stone or "another job." You make decisions each day that can mean the life or death of inmates, staff, and the community. You cannot take short cuts. Each day, learn as much as you can about your agency, the field of corrections, and where the field is trending. Learn the philosophy and culture that the leader of the organization has put in place. Corrections can provide a lot of opportunity and the ability to help others, work as a team, and truly better your community.

It is extremely difficult to keep a level head when one jumps from white to red. Perpetrators count on this advantage when they use the element of surprise. Robbers and rapists are thrilled when their victims freeze just as they are commanded to. Correctional officers can't afford to be caught in white while at work. They naturally remain in yellow while in public, especially when driving to and from work, because of the nature of their training. By being in yellow at the onset of a dangerous experience, less drastic shock to the body is the likely outcome. When correctional officers decide to transfer to police work, they have a huge advantage in the academy over other recruits who have little or no experience with life's perils.

Alternative Correctional Careers

Within the correctional system, there are some positions that are, to some extent, less dangerous than being a correctional officer and potentially as rewarding, especially for those leaning toward the helping professions. These alternative positions include probation officer, parole officer, corrections advisor, treatment officer, corrections counselor, juvenile review and release specialist, community corrections officer, and warden. We will cover some of these job descriptions in Chapter 8.

A popular position tied to corrections is that of probation officer. The workload is enormous, and the pay is subpar, but that is quite common in most government work. Probation work is a great ladder rung, offering valuable experience and a challenging career for the right type of person, and it is a typical second career for those exiting or retiring from law enforcement. What is the right type of person to successfully work with criminals in such an intimate capacity?

Juvenile probation work is generally more sought after than adult work, but it really depends on the person seeking the job. If you choose to work with juveniles, it is to be hoped that it is because you want to help rehabilitate them. Those who are very good at exhibiting power (such as a drill sergeant or an academy trainer) might be a better fit to work with adults than "touchy-feely" individuals. The roles of an adult probation officer and a juvenile probation officer are actually quite similar, but the methods used are fundamentally different. In other words, rehabilitation and low recidivism are common goals for adults and juveniles alike, but how the two types of probation officers approach their handiwork is fittingly diverse. Saying that adults need a firm hand and juveniles need a soft touch would be an inaccurate depiction of what really goes on in the probation office or at a probationer's home. Like police officers and lawyers, probation officers see new cases and new faces every day. They need to have flexibility and a remarkable ability to wear different hats.

Probation officers have immense power in their role. They act as representatives of law enforcement and as judges. Like police detectives, they are assigned more cases than they can feasibly control, and unless an arrest forces their hand, they work their caseloads at their own pleasure, with a constant fear that their competence may be second-guessed if something goes wrong. If a probationer violates the conditions of probation, a probation officer has the discretion to either issue a violation on the client or offer a second chance. Just as in police work, there are no specific and concrete words written somewhere explaining what discretionary choices a probation officer is permitted to make or prohibited from making. They learn from their coworkers and supervisors what is acceptable and what is not.

Probation officers constantly face dangers in their everyday contacts with their clients. Few probation officers are required to carry weapons, but for many it is offered as a choice to do so. It is common for probation officers to travel to intimidating neighborhoods to visit probationers in their homes. Many agencies have protocols for working in pairs during home visits, but not all employees like to work with partners or are willing to pull others from their own caseloads to serve as backup.

THE REALITIES OF WORKING IN CRIMINAL JUSTICE

Being realistic and being negative aren't the same thing. Some children start playing peewee football and decide that they want to play in the National Football League (NFL) when they grow up. If they stand on the sidelines during middle school or high school football games and watch the starters play, they begin to get more realistic about their futures. If high school starters are good enough to play for major colleges, they are normally given an eye-opening orientation at the outset of their college careers. In that orientation, they are told that their education is the most important part of their college experience because the odds of playing for the NFL are slim. According to the NFL (2013), in 2012, only 253 college players were drafted to the NFL. Only 256 were drafted in 2011.

Too many students beginning their criminal justice degrees have the goal of working for federal agencies such as the Federal Bureau of Investigation (FBI) or the U.S. Marshals Service. The reality is that of the 10,000 applicants to the FBI each year, only 500 to 750 are hired (FBI, 2013). Those who are hired as agents rarely reach that rung of the ladder right out of college. Many of those without boosters have worked in law enforcement or the military. They climbed the ladder one step at a time.

CHANGE

"Nothing can stop the man with the right mental attitude from achieving his goal and nothing on earth can help the man with the wrong mental attitude." What is the right mental attitude? Consider these quotations:

- God grant me the serenity to accept the people I cannot change, the courage to change the one I can, and the wisdom to know it's me. (Anonymous)
- When you are through changing, you are through. (Bruce Barton)
- Stubbornness does have its helpful features. You always know what you are going to be thinking tomorrow. (Glen Beaman)
- To exist is to change, to change is to mature, to mature is to go on creating oneself endlessly. (Henri Bergson)
- Those who expect moments of change to be comfortable and free of conflict have not learned their history. (Joan Wallach Scott)

- Continuity gives us roots; change gives us branches, letting us stretch and grow and reach new heights. (Pauline R. Kezer)
- If you would attain to what you are not yet, you must always be displeased by what you are. For where you are pleased with yourself there you have remained. Keep adding, keep walking, keep advancing. (Saint Augustine)
- Our only security is our ability to change. (John Lilly)
- The only man I know who behaves sensibly is my tailor; he takes my measurements anew each time he sees me. The rest go on with their old measurements and expect me to fit them. (George Bernard Shaw)

These are all positive and motivational thoughts that elucidate how we should approach our strategies for change. Expect change to be difficult and uncomfortable, similar to dieting to shed 10 to 15 pounds. Do you know what you get if you keep doing what you've always done? If you want to become better at public speaking, speak in public, but with a renewed purpose. Approach those things that are out of your comfort zone as practice, but make it perfect practice. If you are one of those students who stands in front of the class and reads every word from a PowerPoint presentation in a monotone voice, you will probably be doing the same thing next year. To improve, you must practice doing it the right way, which will likely be uncomfortable. If you are lacking in your written communication skills, take a writing class on the side. Go back and learn those things you missed in middle school and high school when you didn't have the motivation. Remember, criminal justice agencies are also working toward improvement. They want to hire someone who can potentially make them better. Stay focused on that! Are you capable of becoming that person? If your answer is yes, you are correct. If your answer is no, you are correct.

THE SEARCH FOR HAPPINESS

One approach to setting goals is to choose a place where you want to end up and then work as hard as you can to get there. You may never reach your goal, but you will likely make positive strides along the way. An alternative approach is like that of a sophomore pole vaulter. A pole vaulter's goal is to beat her personal record. Each time she performs a vault, she is seeking to better herself. She doesn't really risk that insidious feeling of failure because regardless of how she does today, she still holds the record. If she compares herself with the juniors and seniors who vault higher, she is prone to improve, but she might never reach her goal. With "doing your best" as the primary goal and "being the best you can be" as the long-range goal, there is a high likelihood of success and happiness.

Consider the old saying, "The grass is always greener on the other side of the fence." It only makes sense that someone younger or less fortunate than you is standing at his fence looking into your yard. If you do jump the fence to greener pastures, bask in the success before you look over the next fence and find an even greener hue. Remember, you eventually need to lay down your blanket and enjoy your picnic before it gets dark and the color of the grass doesn't matter anymore.

SUMMARY

Career development is a process. Without some kind of help, one needs to plan on climbing the ladder of success one rung at a time. Expecting to skip rungs of the ladder can potentially result in a feeling of failure and unhappiness. The two factors that affect your happiness most are your relationships and your job. They have an effect on each other. People tend to like doing what they are good at and excel at things they like to do. Therefore, becoming good at what you choose to do for your job correlates with being happy in your career.

People want choices, but to create choices, you need goals. To reach your goals and expand your choices you need assets, and the more the better. Some of the most important assets are your talents and skills. You should assess the talents and skills you already have and those you need for the career you are interested in. You then need to be realistic about your goals.

Improving skills and abilities often means stepping outside your comfort zone. Sometimes it involves altering your way of thinking first. The Serenity Prayer, which is used in Alcoholics Anonymous programs, gives perspective to our way of thinking. Most of our skills are improvable with practice. Some skills are more important than others in different careers.

You should learn as much as possible about the job you are seeking in order to know what kinds of skills are needed. You should also be realistic about whether a particular dream job is a good fit for you.

One of the skills necessary for police work is being a good actor. Some characteristics of police work to consider are the ambiguity of the rules, the stress from internal and external factors, and the potential for use of force against citizens and their use of force against you. There are some disqualifiers from police work, such as prior drug use and a criminal history.

The legal field is very competitive. The skills needed to succeed in law include the ability to persuade and influence, assertiveness, good communication skills both verbal and written, and being a hard worker. To be a lawyer, you must complete 3 years of law school after obtaining a bachelor's degree and then pass a bar exam to allow you to practice in your chosen state.

The workings of criminal court can be compared to a game of poker. The prosecutor and defense attorney use their influential skills to win their cases. They both attempt to persuade the jury to lean their way. Their success ultimately depends on the strength of their cases, but their litigation skills also come into play. Prosecutors and defense attorneys get more court experience than most other lawyers and are also under very close scrutiny. Working in law can be a lucrative career.

Corrections can be an enjoyable and challenging career, but it is not for everyone. An important skill needed for working in corrections is the gift of gab. Convicted criminals will take advantage of an introverted officer who doesn't know the lingo. They respond well to authoritative firmness, as long as correctional officers show respect. Correctional officers encounter less variety than those in police work and are also paid less, but it is easier to get hired, and the academy training is much shorter.

Correctional officers must be continuously alert during their shifts because of the nature of their work. Just like police officers, they must be mentally and physically ready for incidents that create panic. The color-coded mindset explains the mental state of a correctional officer throughout the day. White represents a relaxed mental state, such as being at home watching television. Yellow represents an enhanced state of awareness in which tunnel vision goes away and a person is more cognizant of what is going on around her. A correctional officer starts transitioning into yellow as she puts on her uniform to go to work. Red represents a state of panic and adrenaline release, also known as the fight-or-flight response, in which a person faces a potentially dangerous situation. A correctional officer would quickly move to red when attacked by a prisoner or just hearing a loud alarm go off. It is easier to move to red if a person is already in yellow. Going from white to red will create a greater deal of panic and may make it harder to react appropriately.

You need to be realistic in setting goals. It is unrealistic to expect to go straight from college into your dream career. There may be other steps of the ladder to achieve first. Change and improvement are always possible, but patience and effort are required. The main things to change are your own perspective and attitude. To be happy, you need to eventually be okay with the color of the grass you stand on and not continue looking over other fences.

DISCUSSION QUESTIONS

1. Do you agree with the statement "The two factors that affect your happiness most are your relationships and your job"? Why or why not?
2. Do you agree with Campbell's ranked order of assets? What, if anything, would you change?
3. How can a person who is fearful of public speaking become skilled at it?
4. How does it affect your view of police to know that deception is an important part of police work?
5. When is it okay for a police officer to lie?
6. What mental attitude does one need to effect change?
7. Of the two options listed in the section "The Search for Happiness," which approach to setting goals do you most relate to? Why?

REFERENCES

Bostain, J. (2006). Use of force: Are continuums still necessary? *FLETC Journal*, *4*(2), 33–37.

Campbell, D. (2007). *If you don't know where you're going, you'll probably end up somewhere else: Finding a career and getting a life*. South Bend, IN: Sorin Books.

Federal Bureau of Investigation. (2013). *Careers*. Retrieved from https://www.fbijobs.gov/index.asp

Graham v. Connor, 490 U.S. 386 (1989).

International Association of Chiefs of Police. (2001). *Police use of force in America 2001*. Retrieved from http://theiacp.org/Portals/0/pdfs/Publications/2001useofforce.pdf

National Football League. (2013). *Draft: History*. Retrieved from http://www.nfl.com/draft/history/fulldraft

Scaramella, G. L., Cox, S. M., & McCamey, W. P. (2010). *Introduction to policing*. Thousand Oaks, CA: SAGE.

Tennessee v. Garner, 471 U.S. 1 (1985).

SECTION 2

PURSUING

3 LAW ENFORCEMENT

INTRODUCTION

Law enforcement refers to the agencies and individuals responsible for maintaining public order and public safety and enforcing criminal laws. It includes the detection, prevention, and investigation of crime as well as the apprehension and detention of those who are suspected of violating the laws. *Local law enforcement* refers to city and county agencies, which make up 77% of the nation's police employees. Another 14% work in various federal agencies, and only about 9% work for state governments. According to the Bureau of Justice Statistics (Reaves, 2015), local law enforcement consists of approximately 1,134,000 employees, with about 765,000 of those being sworn. Being hired initially by a local agency is much likelier than starting a career with a federal agency, mainly because of the number of opportunities available. Being hired by any law enforcement agency is extremely difficult and may seem impossible to some who have already tried, but the opportunities increase if a person is willing to apply where the openings are and not look solely at his or her hometown.

Sworn employees of city agencies are called "police officers." Those working for county agencies are called "deputies," and sworn state employees are referred to as "officers" or "troopers." Sworn federal employees are commonly referred to as "agents." Police officers, deputies, and state troopers handle a larger variety of incidents than federal agencies. There are more city codes and state statutes to enforce than federal laws. Additionally, local and state agencies are "first responders" and thus are at citizens' beck and call for whatever need arises. Federal agencies are more specialized, and only some are first responders and wear uniforms. As enforcers of laws pertaining to federal crimes, they handle such things as terrorism; illegal immigration; bank robberies; drug enforcement; organized and white-collar crime; crimes involving alcohol, tobacco, firearms, and explosives; and interstate crimes. Specialization is also available in state and local agencies where one can choose to excel and work primarily in a particular area of expertise, such as traffic enforcement, accident investigation, burglary, robbery, child crimes, missing persons, sex crimes, K9, drug enforcement, school resource, special tactics and weapons, and auto theft. There is less variety within each federal agency, but there are more opportunities for travel, including international placement.

In this chapter, we will explore local, county, and state law enforcement as well as some of the more prominent federal agencies, including job descriptions and hiring information.[1] We will also touch on some of the support positions for those who are not interested in carrying a gun and handcuffs.

LOCAL LAW ENFORCEMENT

Police departments range in size from one sworn officer to thousands. The top 10 largest police agencies in the United Sates are listed in Exhibit 3.1. For basic hiring and pay scale information, as well as a general job description for police officers, we will use Mesa, Arizona, as our reference. This information is similar across the country, including county and state law enforcement. Mesa is the 40th largest city in the United States, with a population just under 500,000. The estimated median household income in 2016 was $49,453. The full-time police force in June, 2017 was 1,211 employees, with 782 of those sworn (Mesa Police Department, 2017).

A police recruit attends the police training academy to learn to perform the responsibilities of an entry-level law enforcement officer, which include interacting with a culturally and socially diverse population; using discretion in solving problems; maintaining public order; preventing crime; enforcing laws and ordinances; conducting investigations; making arrests; issuing summonses, citations, and warnings; and assisting the public. Upon successful completion of academy instruction, a recruit receives further training in the Field Officer Training Program.

The academy is a wide-ranging training course that prepares recruits for protective service work in their respective jurisdictions. Recruits receive instruction and training in the areas of patrol methods, causes of criminality, courtroom procedures, fingerprinting, community relations, and other law enforcement topics that prepare the recruit for a full-time position with the police department. After successful completion of the academy and the post-academy field training, a police recruit is ready to work solo as a first responder (patrol officer). Being a first responder means you are likely to be among those who arrive first at crime and emergency scenes, such as accidents, assaults, homicides, robberies, sexual assaults, fires, and multicasualty incidents such as active shooters and terrorist attacks.

Exhibit 3.1 ■ Top 10 Largest Police Agencies in the United States by Number of Full-Time Personnel

Department	Population	Agency Sworn	Per 10,000	Agency Total	Per 10,000
New York City	8,336,697	34,454	41	49,089	59
Chicago	2,714,856	12,042	44	12,864	47
Los Angeles	3,857,799	9,920	26	12,791	33
Philadelphia	1,547,607	6,515	42	7,343	47
Houston	2,160,821	5,295	25	6,640	31
Washington, D.C.	632,323	3,865	61	4,327	68
Dallas	1,241,162	3,478	28	4,022	32
Phoenix	1,488,750	2,952	20	4,004	27
Baltimore	621,342	2,949	47	3,256	52
Miami-Dade County	1,243,623	2,745	22	3,908	31

Source: Reaves (2015).

The new "rookie" officer is assigned to a particular shift with a particular sergeant who assigns the new officer to a specific beat. The new officer's methods and skills are checked and measured through personal inspections, discussions, and careful reviews of written reports. If the academy did its job well, a new officer will be able to make it through the probationary period without getting sued, seriously injured, or worse.

Typical police duties involve an element of personal danger. Officers must regularly take action without direct supervision, exercising independent judgment in meeting routine and emergency needs of citizens. Police work requires occasional physical exertion under adverse circumstances, such as foot chases and physical struggles. Officers are subject to rotating shifts, including weekends and holiday work. The minimum qualifications for most large police departments are broken down in Exhibit 3.2.

Exhibit 3.2 ■ Minimum Requirements for Most Large Police Departments

Category	Minimum Requirement	Rationale
Age	Twenty-one years of age upon graduation from the police academy. Usually no upper age limit.	The age at which people are considered mature enough to handle the responsibilities associated with the job.
Height/Weight	Generally no minimum standards.	To avoid discrimination, applicants need only to be able to perform the duties of the job. Appearance, however, plays a part in hiring decisions.
Health	Vision must be correctable to 20/50. Hearing aids are usually allowed to bring hearing into the standard range. Must pass a doctor's physical exam.	Police work is a dangerous and physically demanding job. Police are responsible for their own safety as well as that of others. Agencies hire those who can do every aspect of the job.
Fitness	Varies, but all departments have physical fitness tests with minimum standards to demonstrate that applicants can do ordinary police duties. Tests can include running, jumping, push-ups, sit-ups, stretching, and pulling.	Officers must be able to defend themselves and others, consistently performing at a high level of stress for extensive periods of time. Conditioning can save lives.
Education	High school diploma or General Educational Development (GED) certificate	About 18% of departments require some college at the entry level, but degrees are usually required only for promotions. This issue remains controversial. Having a degree is helpful for hiring considerations, even if it is not required. Studies show that more education (generally) produces better officers.
Skills and characteristics	Maturity, intelligence, critical thinking, problem solving, high ethical standards, and emotional intelligence. The abilities to read, write, memorize, reason, and communicate.	Some say you must "walk on water" to be hired for police work. Naturally, agencies want the best of the best. Tests and interviews are created to explore these minimum traits.

(Continued)

Exhibit 3.2 ■ (Continued)

Category	Minimum Requirement	Rationale
Background	Investigation includes past employment, medical records, school records, relationships, military records, credit check, driving record, and criminal history.	Ninety-eight percent of agencies perform some level of background check to determine the character of an applicant that isn't apparent through written tests, interviews, and polygraph tests.
Criminal history	No felony convictions. Misdemeanors may not automatically disqualify applicant unless the circumstances warrant disqualification. The majority of large agencies administer polygraph tests. The commission of certain crimes will disqualify an applicant regardless of conviction.	Departments recognize that citizens make mistakes in their younger years, but police also must respect and adhere to the laws of society. Agencies look at the seriousness of crimes committed as well as the number of crimes and the amount of time since crimes were committed.
Drug history	Varies widely. Generally 3 to 5 years since marijuana was used, and it must have been experimental use only. Generally 10 years since harder drugs were used.	As with criminal activity, many citizens experiment with drugs at younger ages. By being more liberal, the agency's candidate pool is increased without necessarily opening up to unsuitable candidates. Agencies perform random drug tests to ensure the continuity of policy adherence.
Psychological health	Generally, candidates must pass an exam or be recommended for employment by an expert designated by the department.	This appraisal of applicants helps identify individuals who may not function well in the police environment. The assessment explores personality disorders, self-management skills, abilities for team functioning, intellectual strength, impact of prior trauma, and anger management.

Because of the confidential and sensitive nature of the information police officers encounter, the successful completion of a background investigation and polygraph test is required. Candidates who are given conditional job offers are also required to pass preemployment medical exams, psychological test batteries, and drug screening. To ensure the safety and security of the public, officers are generally subject to random alcohol and drug testing from right out of the academy through retirement.

Completion of college-level courses is rarely required but is always desirable. Communication skills, in person and via radio, are essential functions. Police officers mediate disputes and conduct interviews while performing routine patrol activities and investigations. Police officers present testimony and evidence in both civil and criminal court proceedings. They also record information and prepare detailed reports of investigative findings.

Police officers operate patrol vehicles, pursue offenders in their vehicle and on foot, stop offenders, subdue resisting offenders using force where appropriate (including deadly force), and arrest offenders. An officer searches persons, places, and things. She seizes and impounds property and evidence, transports persons and property, performs crowd and riot control activities, issues summonses, and maintains proficiency in operating a variety of law enforcement tools, including weapons, vehicles, and computers. A police officer observes criminal behavior and conducts law enforcement investigations, which includes protecting crime and traffic accident scenes; measuring and diagramming crime and traffic accident scenes; seizing and processing evidence; administering first aid to sick and injured persons for a wide variety of illnesses and injuries; assisting distressed motorists; directing traffic; assisting and referring mentally ill, indigent, and other persons in need; performing evacuations; and moving persons, vehicles, and other property from unsafe locations.

To enforce the laws, a graduate of the academy will be expected to comprehend and make inferences from written materials, including federal and state statutes, city codes and ordinances, and departmental policies and operating procedures. An officer must maintain composure and operational efficiency in high-stress situations and learn job-related details through verbal instruction; observation on the job; structured lectures in a classroom setting; and reading with regard to police procedures and methods, case law, federal and state statutes, and departmental policies and procedures.

An applicant for the police department needs knowledge of general social problems, basic writing skills, and proficiency in the English language. An officer is expected to acquire a working knowledge of police methods, practices, and procedures and apply it to specific situations; learn departmental rules and regulations; acquire a working knowledge of state and city laws and enforce, interpret, and explain the same; learn the geography of the city and the locations of important buildings; acquire a working knowledge of crime patterns and trends in an assigned area; work effectively with all segments of the public; be courteous but firm with people; follow directions; meet specific attendance and scheduling requirements; use good judgment and make effective decisions under pressure; evaluate situations and take appropriate action; observe and recollect details; perform all of the physical requirements of the job; and establish and maintain effective working relationships with other public employees.

The pay scale for police officers in Mesa starts at a salary of $50,960. The top pay for police officers can reach $72,862. Lateral officers are those who are already working as police officers at other agencies and then transfer to different agencies. Their starting salary is between $50,960 and $78,790.40 (Mesa Police Department, 2017), Police work, like any full-time government job, offers vacation pay, sick pay, and usually overtime pay or other forms of compensation for working extra hours.

States have standards and training boards that set the guidelines all law enforcement agencies must adhere to in order to certify their officers. The Arizona Peace Officer Standards and Training Board (AZPOST) establishes the qualifiers and disqualifiers for certification in the state of Arizona. Basic requirements include minimum age, physical fitness, and the polygraph test. Disqualifiers include drug use and criminal history. To be AZPOST certified, you cannot have used marijuana more than for experimental purposes, which has been determined not to exceed 20 uses in a lifetime, with no more than 5 of those uses being at age 21 or older. As far as criminal history goes, AZPOST looks at a person's conduct rather than the arrest record to determine suitability to be a law enforcement officer. It is the commission of crimes that concerns AZPOST, not just convictions. Commission of crimes demonstrates a willingness or propensity to do illegal things. This shows a lack of respect for the law. Applicants are asked to list all police contacts, whether as suspects, witnesses, or otherwise. Applicants are asked to disclose all undiscovered crimes, including those nobody but the applicant knows about. Complete disclosure and truthfulness on these questions are usually more important than what is disclosed. The only absolute disqualifier for certification is a felony conviction. Other offenses are reviewed on a case-by-case basis to see how the conduct reflects on the public trust in the profession and the ability of an individual to perform the duties of a law enforcement officer, such as to testify credibly in court. Applicants' answers to all background questions are tested and verified by polygraph tests (Arizona Peace Officer Standards and Training Board, 2017).

As you can see by the multitude of skills required for police work, as well as the disqualifiers, it is no wonder why some claim that you need to "walk on water" to be hired as a police officer. If you want to work in law enforcement badly enough, all your efforts to get hired will prove worth it. A career in law enforcement is exciting, challenging, and rewarding. Every shift is like a box of chocolates. Unlike jog-trotty jobs where you continuously check your watch to see when your workday will be over, you will find yourself anxiously anticipating the beginning of each shift.

There are other types of law enforcement agencies to work for besides the state, county, or local police. We will explore some of these agencies and include a variety of states to give a broader coverage of what might be available in different geographical areas. Keep in mind that entering law enforcement may require an applicant to consider moving to where the positions are. Limiting your search to the city or county in which you live might significantly delay your career.

Game and Fish Warden

Game warden positions are generally with state agencies. This position offers a challenging career with a wide array of job duties while working with a diverse and abundant wildlife resource. The Wyoming Game and Fish Department currently employs more than 82 game wardens, wildlife investigators, game warden trainees, and wildlife technicians all over the state. Wardens in Wyoming act as liaisons between the public and the department. They enforce fish and wildlife laws, deal with human–wildlife conflicts, and play an active role in managing Wyoming's wildlife. Game wardens receive department housing and a competitive salary with state employment benefits. One of the most rewarding aspects of a warden's job is preventing or solving some of the most egregious wildlife crimes. Wanton destruction (illegally killing a big game animal, often to take only the horns or antlers) is one of those violations. Being able to successfully prosecute violators and keeping them from acting again is extremely gratifying.

Wardens also create big game seasons. An effective big game season can increase opportunities for sportsmen and alleviate game damage problems while keeping animals and their habitats in a healthy condition. Other duties a game warden performs include enforcing trapping and boating laws. To effectively perform these tasks, a warden must spend time in the field. Depending on the circumstances, getting to the field involves the use of trucks, snowmobiles, boats, horses, four-wheelers, or boots. Wardens also collect biological data on the game herds they manage. Wardens often fly over areas in fixed-wing aircraft or helicopters. Other shifts might be spent in a truck looking through binoculars and spotting scopes. Wardens work with landowners to gain access for hunters and fishermen. Landowners may also experience damage to their crops from big game animals or loss of livestock to trophy game animals. It is the warden's duty to respond to these calls, sometimes having to trap the offending cougar or bear or chase deer and elk off agricultural land. Responding to calls regarding injured and nuisance wildlife is another important duty. These calls are often in highly visible areas and in the public eye. These situations call for quick, diplomatic, and accurate decision making by the warden.

Nearly a third of a game warden's job is directly related to law enforcement. Another third deals with taking an active role in wildlife management. Wardens collect and analyze biological data for use in managing fish and wildlife populations. A warden is also the "public face" of the Wyoming Game and Fish Department and is the person most likely to meet and work with the public. Game wardens routinely deal with human–wildlife conflicts and provide vital customer service to their local communities. Game wardens also enjoy the opportunity to work with young students and to give public presentations.

Job prerequisites include passing a competitive examination, which is offered each year to qualified applicants with bachelor's degrees in biology, natural resources,

GUEST SPEAKER
JAN STRAUSS, RETIRED POLICE CHIEF

I started as a police officer in 1970 and retired from police work in 2002. I retired as chief of police after having served in every rank in my police department. The majority of my time was spent as a detective working sex crimes and crimes against children. I also worked patrol, hiring, training, and the juvenile detail.

Being a female officer in the 1970s was not easy. There were few women in police departments, and very few working in patrol divisions. Most departments were reacting to affirmative action lawsuits when they began hiring officers in the early 1970s. The rank and file as well as the command staff were mostly resistant to women in police work and felt that it was only a temporary inconvenience. Because of this resistance, it was very difficult to fit in as a fellow officer. Women who were pioneers in police work definitely had to work harder, as they were constantly under scrutiny by others in the department.

When I began, women were not allowed to work patrol. Although women attended the same academy and received the same training as their male counterparts, they were routinely assigned to desk duty or juvenile detail. My uniform upon graduating from the police academy was a white shirt, a tight black skirt, 2-inch black heels, and a purse designed to carry a gun and handcuffs. By the mid-1970s, I had been assigned to the patrol division. The uniform stores did not carry female-specific uniforms, so the male uniforms had to be tailored to fit women. By the late 1970s, women were being hired at most major police departments, and the assimilation process was well under way.

I encourage anyone with a sincere interest to pursue a career in law enforcement. Despite the early difficult trials I faced, I never regretted my decision. Police work is a wonderful occupation full of challenges, excitement, and potential for advancement. It may sound trite, but "making a difference" is very true when it comes to law enforcement. Few days will go by that an officer doesn't have an impact on someone's life in a positive way.

There are few careers that offer more diversity than law enforcement. A person can remain on patrol his or her entire career, or choose to work as a detective working a variety of details. Specialty assignments in narcotics, special weapons and tactics teams, or hostage negotiation are also options. Opportunities for promotion are available, from sergeant up to chief of police.

or closely related fields. The examination includes a written test of basic wildlife management knowledge, followed by oral interviews and psychological testing. Candidates are ranked throughout the selection process, and jobs are offered as they become available (Wyoming Game and Fish Department, 2017).

Gaming Officer

Other than Nevada, where gambling is wholly legal, the states that allow casino-style gambling generally restrict it to small geographic areas or to American Indian reservations. Most states currently have Indian gaming and state gaming agencies. The Arizona legislature passed laws in 1995 expanding the Arizona State Gaming Agency, which became the Arizona Department of Gaming. The department partners with Arizona's Indian tribes to oversee Indian casinos. Gaming in Arizona is governed by the Arizona Tribal-State Gaming Compacts between the state and 21 Arizona tribes.

Arizona gaming employs a variety of positions, including AZPOST-certified law enforcement officers, financial investigators and auditors, certified fraud examiners, slot machine technicians, and administrative staff. The Gaming Vendor Certification Unit (GVCU) determines the suitability of companies and individuals doing business with casinos in Arizona. The GVCU is composed of special agents, financial investigators, a compliance auditor, and intake officers. Each company, principals of a gaming company, and key personnel providing gaming products or services must undergo a thorough background investigation. The GVCU certifies all vendors providing financing to tribes for gaming facilities, all management contractors engaged by a tribe to assist in the management or operation of a gaming facility, all manufacturers and distributors of gaming devices, and all companies providing services to casinos in excess of $10,000 in any single month. A special agent's primary function is to conduct investigations to ensure compliance with the Arizona Tribal-State Gaming Compacts, as well as state and federal laws. This includes the following:

- Writing comprehensive reports
- Reviewing regulatory, criminal, and financial documents
- Conducting interviews
- Participating in surveillance and undercover operations
- Preparing search warrant affidavits
- Securing evidence
- Testifying at hearings and in court proceedings

Special agents must possess sufficient knowledge of the Arizona criminal code, basic computer search skills (to conduct open-source intelligence searches), and the necessary knowledge to prepare criminal intelligence files. Special agents have a starting salary of just over $50,000.

Financial investigators do not need to be AZPOST certified, but they do need bachelor's degrees in accounting or 5 years of professional financial investigative experience or closely related experience. An advanced degree may substitute for

6 months of the required experience. You will find that many agencies will allow substitutions between education and experience. Financial investigators are paid about the same as special agents. The job description for financial investigators includes conducting forensic financial audits and investigations of all sensitive management position applicants; examining financial and income tax records; conducting in-depth interviews; preparing comprehensive reports of findings; coordinating and conferring with appropriate managers, attorneys general, and tribal entities; presenting testimony in administrative hearings and other courts of law; and acting as the lead investigators in financial investigations (Arizona Department of Gaming, 2017).

Campus Police

Campus police perform a variety of duties related to the protection of life and property, enforcement of criminal and traffic laws, prevention of crime, preservation of the public peace, apprehension of criminals, and calls for service. They perform basic police services in accordance with the missions, goals, and objectives of universities and in compliance with governing federal and state laws.

Here are some major responsibilities of police officers at the Georgia Institute of Technology in Atlanta:

- Engaging in law enforcement patrol functions by foot, bike, or vehicle, including rotating shifts and physically checking the doors and windows of buildings to ensure that they are secure; conducting visual and audio surveillance
- Operating law enforcement vehicles both day and night in emergency situations involving speeds in excess of posted limits in congested traffic and in unsafe road conditions caused by factors such as fog, smoke, rain, ice, and snow
- Effecting arrests, forcibly if necessary, using handcuffs and other restraints, and subduing resisting suspects using maneuvers and weapons, resorting to hands and feet and other approved weapons in self-defense
- Exercising independent judgment in determining when there is reasonable suspicion to detain, when probable cause exists to search and arrest, and when force may be used and to what degree
- Preparing investigative reports, including sketches, using appropriate grammar, symbols, and mathematical computations
- Performing rescue functions at accidents, emergencies, and disasters, including directing traffic for long periods of time; administering emergency medical aid; lifting, dragging, and removing people from dangerous situations; and securing and evacuating people from particular areas
- Mediating disputes and advising citizens of rights and processes
- Gathering information in criminal investigations by interviewing and obtaining the statements of victims, witnesses, suspects, and confidential informers; detecting and collecting evidence and substances that provide the basis of criminal offenses and infractions

With a few exceptions, the basic qualifications to work at Georgia Tech are the same as those for most municipal agencies. Georgia Tech requires 1 to 3 years of job-related experience. They prefer applicants to have bachelor's degrees, 3 to 5 years' experience in a police department, and Georgia Peace Officer Standards and Training Council certification.

The selection process for Georgia campus police includes a thorough background check covering education, employment, criminal history, driving history, and credit history; psychological and medical evaluations; drug screening; and successful completion of the police academy entrance examination. The availability to work any day, any shift, and overtime as required. The pay scale for campus police is usually slightly lower than for municipal police (Georgia Institute of Technology, Office of Human Resources, 2017).

Reserve Officer

A great way to get a foot in the door at a police department is to work as a reserve officer (RO). An RO is a citizen volunteer who wears the same uniform and performs the same duties as a regular police officer, but on a part-time, volunteer basis. ROs receive compensation for court appearances and other specific assignments approved by their supervisors. ROs are a valuable resource to both the community and the police department. Although this is generally a volunteer position, it can be a paid position in some departments. Agencies that use ROs normally require a minimum number of hours each month. Some students who don't feel they are ready to work full-time will become an RO with the long-range goal of being hired full time. Some professionals become ROs just for the experience but continue working in their full-time careers.

ROs for the Glendale Police Department in California participate in pre-academy training and the actual police training academy in preparation for performing all the normal functions of a full-time, paid, sworn officer. ROs are beloved by the troops because they fill slots that are empty due to emergencies or sick officers, which can leave the squads with more work than they can handle. Paid officers can get vacation time approved much more easily if they find ROs to substitute for them.

The minimum age to be an RO in Glendale is 20 years. ROs need high school graduation or a GED certificate or California High School Proficiency Examination equivalent. Applicants must be of good moral character, with no felony convictions or misdemeanor convictions involving moral turpitude. Candidates must be U.S. citizens or be permanent resident aliens who are eligible for and have applied for citizenship. Desirable qualifications include college-level course work in written and oral communications, police science, or a related field; knowledge of computers; and bilingual abilities.

All candidates in Glendale must pass a preplacement medical examination and a psychological evaluation. Hearing and vision must be at acceptable city standards. Applicants' weight must be in proportion to height according to medical standards. There is a written test, graded on a pass/fail basis, that may assess general abilities and aptitude for police work. The process also includes a physical agility test consisting of a 1.5-mile run, a 99-yard obstacle course, a 165-pound body drag, climbing a chain-link fence, climbing a 6-foot solid fence, and a 500-yard run.

Qualified applicants are invited to take an oral examination to evaluate their experience, education, and personal fitness for the position. Candidates who are successful in the examination process will be subjected to a comprehensive background investigation and then a polygraph test. Candidates hired for this position are required to live within a 40-mile radius of the Glendale Civic Center (City of Glendale, CA, 2017).

Nonsworn Opportunities

Law enforcement agencies have nonsworn positions for support personnel, such as property clerk, evidence technician, records clerk, traffic accident investigator, crime analyst, and dispatcher. Some of these positions pay very well.

A property clerk has duties similar to those of any warehouse employee. The clerk controls the inventory of police supplies, such as radios, firearms, helmets, riot gear, flashlights and batteries, pens and pads, badges, bulletproof vests, and so on. Property clerks normally perform the following functions:

- Checking incoming material for quality and quantity against invoices, purchase orders, packing slips, contract order release forms, or other documents
- Stocking shelves and keeping stock in order
- Making simple mathematical computations to reconcile physical count with inventory records and order requests
- Issuing general and specialized goods and supplies
- Inputting and retrieving inventory information using a remote computer terminal and/or microcomputer

To work for the Clearwater Florida Police Department as a property clerk, you would need 1 year of experience in the receipt, storage, and issuance of property and maintaining property control. Other combinations of experience and education that meet the minimum requirements may be substituted. The Salary for property clerk is $25,729.12–$39,495.48. (City of Clearwater, FL, 2017).

To work for a police department as an evidence technician, you would normally perform these duties:

- Processing invoices and logging in property received from law enforcement personnel
- Safeguarding and maintaining proper integrity and chain of evidence
- Loading and transporting property impounded from outlying stations or precincts
- Preparing impounded property for distribution and/or auction as authorized
- Tagging, marking, packaging, and storing property and evidence received
- Destroying impounded property as required by law or regulation

- Responding to inquiries from law enforcement personnel and citizens concerning property in custody
- Maintaining appropriate release records and records of disposition of property and evidence
- Making accurate comparisons of items from serial numbers or other descriptive features
- Maintaining and securing biological evidence contained in refrigerators and freezers requiring strict temperature control
- Verifying stolen weapons through the use of national and state crime information computer systems
- Transporting evidence for analysis
- Receiving vehicles impounded as evidence only and various gasoline-powered equipment
- Demonstrating superior, seamless customer service; integrity; and commitment to innovation, efficiency, and fiscally responsible activity

To work in Texas for the College Station Police Department as an evidence technician, you must have a high school diploma or GED equivalent and a valid Texas driver's license. You need to have knowledge of different digital storage hardware and software. Many police departments require polygraphs for all hiring, but College Station PD does not require a polygraph exam for the position of evidence technician. The pay range for an evidence technician at College Station is $29,140.80–$32,052.80 (City of College Station, TX, 2017).

Police departments store vast amounts of records, and in large departments, several clerks are needed to enter data and provide records to officers. Records clerks handle all the reports officers turn in. When officers (or the public) need to obtain a police report, a records clerk locates it, prints it, and sends it to the requestor. The job description in Topeka, Kansas, includes creating, revising, and reviewing criminal history documents and entering information into electronic format, including dictaphone and computer databases. The minimum requirements include a high school diploma or equivalent, the ability to type at least 40 words per minute, and successfully passing a basic Microsoft Word test. You must have at least 1 year of clerical work experience and you must pass an extensive background check and polygraph exam. The pay is $14.65–$15.15 per hour, depending on work shift (City of Topeka, KS, 2017).

Many police departments have civilianized the position of traffic accident investigator. The Yuma Arizona Police Department employs civilian traffic investigators whose basic duties include the following:

- Investigating traffic accidents and hazardous incidents not requiring a sworn police officer
- Interviewing drivers, passengers, and witnesses and taking detailed notes
- Maintaining traffic control at accident scenes and other hazardous incidents

- Preparing comprehensive accident reports, including diagrams, photographs, and measurements
- Testifying and presenting evidence in court
- Maintaining absolute confidentiality of work-related issues and city information

To work in this position for Yuma PD, you need a high school diploma or GED equivalent and 1 year of accident investigation, accounting, or law enforcement experience, or any combination of these. you would need a valid Arizona driver's license and completion of CPR and first aid training within 6 months of hire. The salary is $39,694.30–$55,571.98 (City of Yuma, AZ, 2017).

A position that has become more popular in recent decades is that of crime analyst. Police departments historically have been slow to change their tactics and philosophies. But innovative research such as the Kansas City Preventive Patrol Experiment (Caro, 1977) resulted in departments becoming more open to trying new things. One beneficial addition to many larger police departments is a staff of crime analysts who aid departments in crime prevention, among other tasks. These crime specialists take crime data and manipulate the information to be able to identify areas where more (or fewer) officers are needed. They work closely with staff, creating charts and graphs for staff meetings, which help clarify the crime picture. Decisions are based on actual statistics instead of best guesses.

A crime analyst in Harford County, Maryland, analyzes police reports to identify crime patterns, including suspect characteristics and demographic information as they relate to certain crimes. Crime analysts prepare statistical reports and various correspondence for management, and they communicate crime trends, suspect characteristics, and intelligence data to operational components of the police department. Crime analysts also input data into computer program systems to prepare reports, graphs, and maps for presentations to management concerning crime trends and necessary corrective actions. Crime analysts recommend staffing patterns to management to anticipate and combat criminal activity, enter crime data into a computer using mapping and spreadsheet software, prepare special information bulletins and direct patrol requests using crime statistics, and then disseminate that information to appropriate personnel. Crime analysts contact governmental agencies to gather criminal statistical data and compare crime analysis methods; research federal and state laws and local ordinances; respond to special crime information requests; and operate computers with databases, spreadsheets, and word processing software to generate presentations and reports.

The minimum qualifications include a bachelor's degree in statistics or a closely related field, 3 years of experience in criminal intelligence and/or crime analysis, and thorough knowledge and ability to perform the collection, collation, and analysis of the intelligence process. The pay is $22.85 an hour (Harford County, 2017).

An essential person in police work is the dispatcher. A large part of police work is responding as first responders to calls for service. The dispatcher is the officer's lifeline. A dispatcher needs the skills of an officer and more. The police dispatcher may be the most underappreciated position in police work.

To work as a dispatcher for the College of Charleston, South Carolina, your duties would include receiving emergency and nonemergency calls from the public requesting police, fire, or other emergency services; determining the nature and locations of emergencies; determining their priority; referring calls as necessary and in accordance with established procedures; responding to field unit requests involving other law enforcement agencies; relaying information and assistance requests involving other law enforcement agencies; monitoring alarms received through automatic alarm systems; dispatching emergency units as appropriate; and making inquiries and interpreting responses from Teletype networks relating to wanted persons, stolen vehicles, vehicle registration, and stolen property. Dispatchers test and inspect equipment as required, and they establish and maintain daily logs of all field calls and units dispatched. They record, classify, and maintain records of communications; operate a variety of communications and office equipment; and perform related duties as assigned or required by the position.

Minimum requirements include a high school diploma and entry-level work experience with voice communications systems or central switchboard operations. An associate degree in a technical communications discipline may be substituted for the required experience. You would need knowledge of FCC rules and regulations, and you must be SLED/NCIC certified in Teletype procedures or receive certification within 6 months of appointment. Previous dispatching experience in a police environment is a plus. The salary is $28,336–$38,460 (College of Charleston, 2017).

FEDERAL LAW ENFORCEMENT

FBI

A job with the FBI is one of the positions most sought after by students entering their degree programs in criminal justice. The FBI isn't a national police force, as some might misconstrue. The agency is actually more of a national security organization that partners with countries all over the globe to combat serious security threats. As of September 2012, the FBI had a total of 36,074 employees, including 13,913 special agents and 22,161 support professionals, such as intelligence analysts, language specialists, scientists, information technology specialists, and other miscellaneous professionals. The duties are prioritized as follows:

1. Protecting the United States from terrorist attack
2. Protecting the United States against foreign intelligence operations and espionage
3. Protecting the United States against cyber-based attacks and high-technology crimes
4. Combating public corruption at all levels
5. Protecting civil rights
6. Combating transnational and national criminal organizations and enterprises

7. Combating major white-collar crime
8. Combating significant violent crime
9. Supporting federal, state, local, and international partners
10. Upgrading technology to successfully perform the FBI's mission

Although combating terrorism is a priority for the FBI, it isn't necessarily where most of the workforce is utilized. Agents enforce many different federal laws and perform various roles in the bureau. Most work is done in the United States, involving U.S. victims and U.S. perpetrators. As mentioned earlier, FBI agents do work that is similar to that of a detective in a police department. An agent in a field office, for example, could be testifying in federal court one day and executing a search warrant and gathering evidence the next. Over the course of a week, an agent might meet with an informant to gather intelligence on illegal activities, arrest a suspect, and then head back to the office to talk with her squad members and catch up on some paperwork. Some agents work in specialized areas across the FBI, such as training, fingerprinting, lab services, and public affairs, while many serve as supervisors or managers.

Special agents are always on call and could be transferred at any time, according to the needs of the FBI. The work is challenging and exciting. Although their workload is heavy, special agents still find opportunities to spend quality time with their families. The FBI has a greater variety of laws to enforce (200 categories of federal laws) than most federal agencies, such as the DEA and the Bureau of Alcohol, Tobacco, Firearms, and Explosives (ATF). The FBI also participates in "task forces" with local and state agencies.

As an FBI agent, you would be responsible for conducting sensitive national security investigations and enforcing federal statutes. You might work on matters including terrorism, foreign counterintelligence, cybercrime, organized crime, white-collar crime, public corruption, civil rights violations, financial crime, bribery, bank robbery, extortion, kidnapping, air piracy, interstate criminal activity, fugitive and drug-trafficking matters, and other violations of federal statutes.

To be hired as an FBI agent, you must be a U.S. citizen or a citizen of the Northern Mariana Islands. You must be at least 23 years of age to apply and younger than 37 years of age upon your appointment as a special agent. Age waivers may be granted to preference eligible veterans who are older than 37. You must have a 4-year degree from a college or university accredited by one of the regional or national institutional associations recognized by the U.S. secretary of education. You need at least 3 years of professional work experience. You must have a valid driver's license and be available for assignment anywhere in the FBI's jurisdiction.

All applicants for the position of special agent must qualify through one of five special agent entry programs: accounting, computer science and information technology, language, the law, and diversified fields. After qualifying for one of the five entry programs, applicants are prioritized in the hiring process on the basis of certain skills for which the FBI is recruiting. Since June 2013, the FBI has been recruiting candidates with one or more of the following critical skills:

- Accounting
- Military experience

- Finance
- Computer science and information technology expertise
- Law experience
- Engineering expertise
- Foreign language proficiency
- Physical sciences (e.g., physics, chemistry, biology) expertise
- Intelligence experience
- Law enforcement and investigative experience
- Diversified experience

Candidates with these skills are essential to addressing the FBI's complex responsibilities. Those with one or more of these skills are prioritized in the hiring process. A common practice has been to put a higher priority on applicants with military experience.

Applicants must be in excellent physical condition, with no disabilities that would interfere in firearm use, participation in raids, or the use of defensive tactics. All applicants must be able to pass physical tests to gain admittance to the FBI Academy in Quantico, Virginia. The tests consist of four mandatory events, generally handled in the following order:

1. Maximum number of sit-ups in 1 minute
2. Timed 300-meter sprint
3. Maximum number of push-ups (untimed)
4. Timed 1.5-mile run

FBI work is very sensitive in nature, so all positions require top-secret security clearance. Once you have received a conditional offer of employment, the FBI will initiate an intensive background investigation that you must pass before your hiring is official. The investigation includes a polygraph examination to investigate illegal drug use, credit and records checks, and extensive interviews with former and current colleagues, neighbors, friends, professors, and others. Besides the requirements that all candidates must meet, there are also some disqualifiers to be aware of:

- Felony conviction
- Use of illegal drugs in violation of the FBI Employment Drug Policy
- Default on a student loan (insured by the U.S. government)
- Failure of an FBI-administered urinalysis drug test
- Failure to register with the Selective Service System (for men only)

The hiring process for special agent consists of the following steps:

1. **Application:** Done online
2. **Phase I and Meet and Greet:** Takes approximately 3 hours to complete. Consists of three different multiple-choice tests that measure the kind of thinking and reasoning skills required to perform the special agent job, as well as background experiences that indicate whether or not the special agent work environment would be a good fit.
3. **Phase II testing:** Takes approximately 2.5 hours to complete. The test is split into two parts: an oral interview and a written exam. The oral interview lasts 1 hour and is administered by a panel of three special agents. The panel uses standardized scoring criteria to measure the special agent core competencies as well as your honesty and integrity. Here are some helpful tips:
   - Be yourself.
   - The evaluators will be taking notes during the interview to assist them in documenting the results. Do not let this distract you.
   - Provide detailed information when answering the interview questions. Do not be modest in your responses. To provide the best examples of your skills and abilities, draw from all of your life's experiences.
   - Remember that the interview panel knows no information about you beyond your name.
   - Keep your answers concise and specific—answers that are too lengthy will detract from your ability to complete the interview within the required time frame.
   - Do not make assumptions about what the evaluators are seeking. The interview instructions are straightforward. There are no "trick" questions.
   - Study your résumé and be able to speak about how your experiences match with the special agent core competencies.
   - Practice the sample test (https://www.fbijobs.gov/sites/default/files/SpecialAgentPhaseISampleTest.pdf).

The written segment of the Phase II test is a 90-minute exam that tests an applicant's ability to analyze data and prepare a sample report. At the start, applicants will be given a set of background materials to use. There is no preparation manual for the writing exercise, but here are some tips:

- Read instructions carefully and make sure you understand what the exercise requires.
- Be detailed and thorough in your report.
- Use only the facts provided—do not make up additional facts.
- Follow grammatical rules and spell words correctly.
- Write legibly.

4. **Background Investigation:** All applicants must be eligible to receive an FBI top secret security clearance in order to become a special agent. This investigation looks at an applicant's actions, relationships, and experiences over the last 10 years. It includes a medical examination, drug testing, and a polygraph test.
5. **Basic Field Training Course (BFTC):** Those who have been successful to this point will receive orders to report to the FBI Academy in Quantico, Virginia, to begin their 21-week training as new agent trainees (NATs). Candidates are typically notified 2 to 4 weeks in advance of their class date. NATs must successfully complete all portions of the BFTC. During the academy, you live on campus and participate in a variety of training activities. Classroom time consists of a wide range of academic and investigative subjects. The FBI Academy's curriculum includes intensive training in physical fitness, defensive tactics, practical application exercises, and firearms training. Several tests are administered in all of these areas to monitor progress.
6. **Graduation:** Upon successful graduation from the BFTC, special agents report to their assigned field office. Special agents must undergo 18 months of probation during which they gain hands-on experience working in different specialties within the FBI's jurisdiction.

As a trainee at the Academy, you would be administered the physical fitness test during the 1st, 7th, and 14th weeks of your training. Those trainees who fail the test during the first week would be placed in a remedial program and would be subject to certain restrictions. These restrictions include no overnight leave from the Academy until they pass the test. Those who fail the first week's physical fitness test and the seventh week's test would be dismissed from training. You must pass all training requirements to graduate. Special agent trainees start out with a salary of $62,878 (Federal Bureau of Investigation, 2017).

Because of the scope of the FBI's responsibilities, you could also enter the FBI in other fields, such as intelligence analysis, laboratory sciences, linguistics, security, information technology, human resources, general management, and more. In addition to any current job postings for full-time positions, the FBI offers a paid internship program as well as an unpaid volunteer internship program. Student internship opportunities include the Laboratory Division's Visiting Science Program. Students with backgrounds in science, engineering, or technology disciplines are invited to apply. Watch for career fairs and other recruiting events where you may have a chance to meet an FBI employee and learn more about job opportunities.

DEA

The DEA was created through an executive order in July 1973 to establish a single, unified command to combat drugs. At the beginning, the DEA had 1,470 special agents. Today, the agency employs nearly 5,000 special agents. The DEA has 221 domestic offices in 21 divisions throughout the United States and 90 foreign offices in 69 countries. Jobs with the DEA include special agent, diversion investigator, forensic scientist, intelligence researcher, and professional and administrative positions.

The first step in the application process is to contact your local DEA recruitment office. The DEA encourages applicants to attend a special agent applicant orientation session. You can find information about the orientation on the DEA website (https://www.dea.gov). On that website you can also take a short eligibility quiz to see if you qualify. The first time you try to reserve a seat for an orientation, it may be full, requiring you to wait for the next session. Casual business attire is the appropriate dress. A valid driver's license or military identification may be required for entry. If you live far from the local recruitment office, the office could opt to conduct a phone screening and orientation in lieu of a face-to-face meeting.

To become a special agent, you must successfully complete all phases of a thorough and in-depth hiring process. This process may take up to a year or longer and includes the following phases:

- Qualifications review
- Written assessment and panel interview
- Drug test
- Medical examination
- Polygraph examination
- Psychological assessment
- Full-field background investigation
- Final hiring decision

The DEA has a strict drug use policy. The agency requires that all applicants complete a drug questionnaire as part of the application process. Applicants who are found to have experimented with or used narcotics or dangerous drugs, except those medically prescribed, will not be considered for employment with the DEA. Exceptions to this policy may be made for those who admit to limited youthful and experimental use of marijuana. Such applicants may be considered for employment if there is no evidence of regular, confirmed use and the full-field background investigation and results of the other steps in the process are favorable.

In 1999, the DEA Training Academy opened on the Marine Corps base at Quantico. DEA trainees live on site and attend classes at the DEA Training Academy, but the facilities for firearms training, physical fitness and defensive tactics training, defensive driving training, and all practical application exercises are held at the FBI Academy. To graduate from the 18-week academy, students must maintain an average of 80% on academic examinations, pass the firearms qualification test, successfully demonstrate leadership and sound decision making in practical scenarios, and pass rigorous physical tests. Upon graduation, students are sworn in as DEA special agents and assigned to DEA field offices located across the United States, at a starting salary around $58,000 (U.S. Drug Enforcement Administration, 2017).

ATF

The Bureau of Alcohol, Tobacco, Firearms, and Explosives (ATF) was transferred under the Homeland Security Act of 2002 to the U.S. Department of Justice in 2003. The ATF investigates and prosecutes terrorist acts and violent crimes that involve explosives, arson, firearms, repeat and violent offenders, criminal gangs, the illegal use and trafficking of firearms and explosives, and the illegal diversion of alcohol and tobacco products. There are positions for special agents, investigators, and attorneys; professional and technical positions; and internships. Working as an ATF special agent is a unique job and one of the most challenging in federal law enforcement.

The ATF has field offices throughout the United States and its territories. As of fiscal year 2015, ATF has 5,026 employees, including 2,618 special agents who are responsible for investigating violations of federal laws relating to firearms, explosives, arson, and alcohol and tobacco diversion. Investigations involve surveillance, interviewing suspects and witnesses, making arrests, obtaining search warrants, searching for physical evidence, preparing concise criminal investigative case reports, testifying for the federal government in court or before grand juries, gathering and analyzing evidence through investigative leads, seizures, arrests, execution of search warrants, and a variety of other tasks.

To be a special agent you must be tough physically and mentally. You would need to handle rigorous training, personal risks, irregular hours, and extensive travel. Special agents are subject to reassignment to any ATF office in the United States, including any U.S. territory or ATF overseas assignment. To be a special agent, you would need to meet the following criteria:

- Be a U.S. citizen
- Possess a current and valid automobile operator's license
- Complete the ATF special agent applicant questionnaire
- Take and pass the ATF special agent exam
- Take and pass the ATF special agent applicant assessment test
- Take and pass the ATF pre-employment physical task test
- Appear for and successfully complete a field panel interview (a writing sample will be required)
- Be in compliance with the ATF's drug policy for special agent applicants
- Take and pass a medical examination by an authorized government physician and meet medical requirements
- Weight must be in proportion to height
- Take and pass a drug test
- Take and successfully complete a polygraph examination
- Successfully complete a background investigation for a top secret security clearance

The starting salary for special agents ranges from $34,865 to $57,093. As a special agent, you would receive an additional percentage of your base salary, depending on your location. You would also receive 25% law enforcement availability pay, which is added to locality pay.

The DEA also has investigators who are the backbone of the ATF's regulatory mission. To work as an investigator, you would primarily investigate, routinely have contact with, and interview individuals from all walks of life and all levels of industry and government. To be an investigator, you must meet similar criteria as listed for special agents. The basic training for investigators involves an 8.5-week academy. The salary ranges from $28,262 to $55,666 and also includes locality pay. There is a strict drug use policy, which includes no marijuana use in the past 3 years and never more than experimental use (Bureau of Alcohol, Tobacco, Firearms, and Explosives, 2017).

U.S. Border Patrol

U.S. Customs and Border Protection's (CBP) top priority is keeping terrorists and their weapons from entering the United States. While welcoming legitimate travelers, CBP officers and agents enforce all applicable U.S. laws. CBP prevents narcotics, agricultural pests, and smuggled goods from entering the United States and also arrests those with outstanding criminal warrants. On a typical day, CBP makes more than 900 apprehensions and seizes more than 9,000 pounds of illegal drugs (U.S. Customs and Border Protection, 2017).

With more than 60,000 employees, the CBP is the largest federal law enforcement agency in the United States. The CBP is under the arm of the Department of Homeland Security (DHS). Its agents are mobile and uniformed. The CBP has grown quickly since 9/11, when it employed only 9,821 agents. Besides the normal agents, there are also three specialty teams that are trained for activities normally outside the scope of the agency. These specialty units are the Border Patrol Tactical Unit; the Border Patrol Search, Trauma, and Rescue Unit; and the Border Patrol Special Response Team.

When most law enforcement agencies slowed or stopped hiring in 2007, the Border Patrol remained consistent in its hiring practices. In 2017, President Donald Trump called for an additional 5,000 border agents as part of his plan to control the borders. There have been only minor changes in the hiring process to help expedite this unprecedented order. Unlike other federal law enforcement agencies, the CBP will hire Border Patrol agents as old as 39. The polygraph test remains a requirement, but any candidate who previously took a federal polygraph exam can request reciprocity.

Here are some of the requirements for Border Patrol agents:

- U.S. citizenship
- Referral for selection before a candidate's 40th birthday
- Pass a polygraph test
- Pass a background security investigation
- Residency in the United States for the past 3 years
- No convictions, including for misdemeanor crimes of domestic violence
- Eligible to carry a firearm

If the Border Patrol hires you, you would likely be stationed at the southwestern border of the United States. You must be willing to accept placement anywhere along that border. You can identify one regional preference for placement (South Texas, West Texas and New Mexico, Arizona, or California), but this does not guarantee placement in that region. Your primary responsibilities would be the detection, prevention, and apprehension of undocumented aliens and smugglers of aliens at or near the borders by maintaining surveillance from covert positions; following up leads; responding to electronic sensor alarms and infrared scopes during night operations; monitoring low-light television systems; checking aircraft sightings; and interpreting and following tracks, marks, and other physical evidence. You would also perform farm and ranch checks; traffic checks; traffic observation; city patrol; transportation checks; and administrative, intelligence, and antismuggling activities.

To work as a Border Patrol agent, you would need to meet some experience requirements, educational requirements, or a combination of both. You can get detailed information about these requirements at USAJOBS (http://www.usajobs.gov). The application process includes an entrance examination. This examination tests general abilities, logical reasoning, and language ability. A free 60-page preparation manual is available for download from the CBP website (https://www.cbp.gov/sites/default/files/documents/prep1896_3.pdf).

You apply for the Border Patrol online at USAJOBS (https://www.usajobs.gov). The high demand for employees may force changes in the future, but as of June 2017, there were nine steps in the hiring process:

1. Apply
2. Take the Border Patrol Entrance Exam
3. Qualifications review
4. Background investigation
5. Medical exam
6. Fitness test
7. Structured interview
8. Polygraph exam
9. Drug test

There is a mandatory basic training program for Border Patrol agents. Soon after entering duty, you would be sent to the U.S. Border Patrol Academy in Artesia, New Mexico, for 19 weeks of intensive instruction in immigration and nationality laws, law enforcement and Border Patrol–specific operations, driving, physical techniques, firearms, and other courses.

To be a Border Patrol agent, you must speak and read Spanish. The Spanish taught at the Border Patrol Academy is specialized. The staff provides an 8-week language training program that is focused on critical Border Patrol–specific tasks. Soon after arriving for basic academy training, all students are tested on their language abilities. Those who fall below a benchmark score are assigned a Spanish class that will begin upon successful completion of the standard academy program. Proficient Spanish speakers will report directly to their duty stations to begin post-academy training.

Upon successful completion of the academy training (and language training), all Border Patrol agents begin the field training program and the post-academy training program at their stations and sectors. The field training program will consist of on-the-job, hands-on training with an experienced agent. The salary range for Border Patrol agents is $51,424.00 to $82,945.00 (U.S. Customs and Border Protection, 2017).

ICE

ICE, Immigration and Customs Enforcement, is the principal investigative arm of the DHS and the second-largest investigative agency in the federal government. ICE has more than 19,000 employees in offices in all 50 states and 47 foreign countries. Jobs within ICE include deportation officer (DO), detention and deportation officer (DDO), special agent, immigrations enforcement agent (IEA), intelligence positions, and investigative support positions.

DOs conduct legal research to support decisions on deportation and exclusion cases and assist attorneys in representing the government in court actions. DOs work with other federal law enforcement officials to identify, locate, and arrest aliens and are responsible for ensuring the physical removal of aliens from the United States. DOs also prepare, present, and defend deportation or exclusion proceedings. As a DO, you would be working with both criminal and noncriminal aliens at various stages of their deportation and exclusion proceedings. Additional responsibilities include conducting complex investigations, conducting surveillance work, preparing investigative reports, and assisting in seizures.

DDOs are responsible for directing, coordinating, and executing detention and removal activities. DDOs recommend administrative procedures and policies; participate in long-range planning; and provide guidance on detention and removal operations, policies, and requirements. Additional responsibilities may include developing budget estimates and justifications, analyzing programs to recommend improvements, and assisting in investigations. Criminal investigators, also referred to as special agents, conduct criminal and civil investigations involving national security threats, terrorism, drug smuggling, child exploitation, human trafficking, illegal arms export, financial crimes, identity fraud, benefit fraud, commercial fraud, and more.

IEAs are the uniformed presence of immigration enforcement within the United States. IEAs perform enforcement functions related to the investigation, identification, arrest, prosecution, detention, and deportation of aliens and the apprehension of absconders from removal proceedings. IEAs assist in the processing and removal of aliens to their countries of citizenship.

Intelligence officers' responsibilities include analyzing and evaluating information and preparing intelligence products, along with interfacing with other ICE components and the larger intelligence community, providing on-site intelligence input to field offices involved in major criminal investigations, and coordinating and monitoring ICE intelligence operations.

Intelligence research assistants' responsibilities include technical and administrative support and assistance for intelligence operations through a wide range of procedural work and data gathering. Intelligence research specialists' responsibilities include analyzing and evaluating information and coordinating and preparing intelligence products.

Management and program analysts' and mission support specialists' responsibilities involve administrative and management services essential to the operations of the office, including management and information systems, telecommunications, budget, finance, procurement, human resources, training, logistics, property, space, records and files, printing and graphics, mail, travel, and office equipment.

If you worked as an auditor, you would plan, perform, and advise on a variety of external audit assignments in connection with financial and work site enforcement audits of suspected criminal organizations and businesses. You would provide technical assistance and analysis to criminal investigators and others as required in the course of investigations, including participating in on-site reviews of financial documents and employment documents. You would support the other offices by working directly with criminal investigators and other auditors in financial investigations and identifying unauthorized workers in both critical and noncritical sectors during administrative and criminal work site investigations. You would be responsible for conducting highly complex financial audits of criminal organizations and business entities. You would use a variety of audit procedures, statistical techniques, and data analyses to assemble and develop findings.

As a criminal research specialist, you would perform a wide range of duties on criminal, civil, and administrative investigations relating to financial crimes, smuggling, public safety, critical infrastructure, national security, arms and strategic technology, and human smuggling. You would provide briefings, advice, and assistance to management on government-wide intelligence operations for the promotion and implementation of a criminal analysis program. On the basis of reports, assessments, and statistical summaries, you would be responsible for planning, conducting, and coordinating complex, multifaceted analytical assignments and research projects in support of diverse investigations on matters involving DHS investigations.

If you were hired as an investigative assistant, you would provide a wide range of technical, administrative, and clerical support to the investigations program. This includes gathering data and conducting limited inquiries regarding individual case assignments; assisting in and accomplishing case research and trial preparation; and researching, assembling, compiling, and tabulating information and figures for agents' use in investigations, seizures, and evidence in various cases. During mobile investigative activity, you would monitor the base station's radio, coordinate and relay information among agents when radio transmissions are hampered, respond to requests by agents for investigative information (which may be of an urgent nature), and use personally developed contacts from other law enforcement agencies and state government agencies to obtain the required information. In addition, you would compile reports on the progress of various cases, seizures, and arrests and perform a variety of clerical duties for the office and the agents, including typing, receiving and screening mail, and acting as the office timekeeper.

Mission support specialists coordinate and perform a wide variety of administrative and management services essential to the operations of the office, including management and information systems, telecommunications, budget, finance, procurement, human resources, training, logistics, property, space, records and files, printing and graphics, mail, travel, and office equipment. They serve as advisors to management on assigned administrative matters. In addition, as a mission support specialist, you would conduct or participate in the evaluation of administrative programs, systems, and methods and identify ways to improve the efficiency and effectiveness of these services at the local level. You would also represent the office in dealings with vendors and organizations within the agency that have primary responsibility for these services.

As a technical enforcement officer, you would participate with criminal investigators and other law enforcement officers in active criminal investigations and apply advanced investigative techniques to gather evidence and intelligence that facilitate the prosecution of violations of criminal laws of the United States. You would have an extensive working knowledge in the use, instruction, installation, maintenance, troubleshooting, and integration of the full range of electronic surveillance devices, including telephone, video, audio, tracking, radio-frequency technologies, and associated unique surveillance systems. You would provide extensive expertise in the planning and execution of the electronic surveillance phases of major investigative and enforcement operations. You would serve on high-risk special operations teams. You would make covert court-ordered entry into the property of targets of criminal investigations to install equipment for collecting evidence. You would also serve as a technical authority and provide training and guidance to journey-level technical enforcement officers, special agents, and other law enforcement officers engaged in electronic surveillance and investigative work, ensuring that mission requirements are fulfilled.

For all positions, except special agent, you would use an automated, online application system. You can search USAJOBS for openings. Some positions are open to the general public, and others are open only to current government employees. Applications for special agent positions are accepted during an open vacancy announcement. During an open announcement period, applicants will be required to submit résumés with their original applications. Applicants must be at least 21 years of age. The day immediately preceding an individual's 37th birthday would be the last day to be referred for selection consideration. You cannot have a domestic violence or a felony conviction.

Once officially selected as a special agent, you would be required to attend 22 weeks of paid training at the Federal Law Enforcement Training Center (FLETC) in Brunswick, Georgia. The training program is a formalized course of required basic technical instructions that must be successfully completed according to the standards of ICE. Failure to successfully complete the training would be grounds for mandatory removal from the position. ICE agents' salaries vary widely depending on their areas of assignment. An ICE agent could earn $40,000 to $68,000 (Immigration and Customs Enforcement, 2017).

U.S. Secret Service

The U.S. Secret Service was created on July 5, 1865, in Washington, D.C., to suppress the creation and circulation of counterfeit currency. The Secret Service's responsibilities were later broadened to include the detection of persons perpetrating frauds against the government. This resulted in investigations into the activities of the Ku Klux Klan, nonconforming distillation, smuggling, mail theft, land fraud, and a number of other infractions against federal laws. As the years passed, the Secret Service increased its responsibilities to include protecting the president, president-elect, and former presidents and their spouses and family members, as well as investigating espionage, crimes against federally insured financial institutions, identity theft, telemarketing fraud, computer crimes, and counterfeiting.

Positions with the Secret Service include special agent, uniformed division officer, special officer, administrative personnel, and technical and administrative and clerical support. There are opportunities for women, veterans, students, and those with disabilities.

To be considered for a special agent position, you must be a U.S. citizen and meet the following additional criteria:

- Be at least 21 years of age and younger than 37 at the time of receipt of a conditional offer of employment to continue in the application process
- Have (a) a bachelor's degree from an accredited college or university, (b) 3 years of work experience in the criminal investigative or law enforcement fields that require knowledge and application of laws relating to criminal violations, or (c) an equivalent combination of education and related experience
- Have uncorrected vision no worse than 20/60 binocular, correctable to 20/20 in each eye
- Be in excellent health and physical condition
- Pass a written examination
- Qualify for top secret clearance and undergo a complete background investigation, including in-depth interviews, drug screening, and medical and polygraph examinations
- Certify that you have registered with the Selective Service System or are exempt from having to do so, if you are a male applicant born after December 31, 1959

The Secret Service prohibits employees from having visible body markings (including tattoos, body art, and branding) on the head, face, neck, or any area below the wrist bone. If you have visible body markings, you will be required to medically remove such visible body markings at your own expense prior to entering duty with the Secret Service.

Special agent trainees and new uniformed division officer trainees undergo months of intensive training through established programs at the FLETC. For officers, this is followed by a 14-week specialized training program at the Secret Service's training facilities outside Washington, D.C. Training includes coursework in police procedures, firearms, physical fitness, psychology, police-community relations, criminal law, first aid, laws of arrest, search and seizure, physical defense techniques, diplomatic immunity, and international treaties and protocol. On-the-job training and advanced in-service training programs complement the classroom studies.

Upon successful completion of the Criminal Investigator Training Program at FLETC, special agents continue with the 18-week Special Agent Training Course at the Secret Service's training academy. This course focuses on specific Secret Service policies and procedures associated with the dual responsibilities of investigations and protection. Trainees are provided with basic knowledge and advanced application training in counterfeiting, device fraud, and other financial criminal activity; protective intelligence investigations; physical protection techniques; protective advances; and emergency medicine. The core curriculum is augmented by extensive training in marksmanship, control tactics, water survival skills, and physical fitness.

Secret Service agents and officers receive continual advanced training throughout their careers. In part, this training consists of regular firearms requalification and emergency medicine refresher courses. Agents with protective assignments also participate in unique crisis training simulations that present agents with a variety of "real world" emergency situations. Agents assigned to offices in the field have the opportunity to acquire advanced training in the area of criminal investigations and are also encouraged to attend training sessions sponsored by other law enforcement agencies. As with other federal law enforcement jobs, the pay scale varies with experience and location. The salary ranges from $44,000 to $89,000 per year (U.S. Secret Service, 2017).

USMS

The offices of U.S. marshals and deputy marshals were created by the first U.S. Congress in the Judiciary Act of 1789. The USMS is the nation's oldest and most versatile federal law enforcement agency, occupying a uniquely central position in the federal justice system.

The USMS is the enforcement arm of the federal courts, involved in virtually every federal law enforcement initiative. Presidentially appointed, U.S. marshals direct the activities of 94 districts, one for each federal judicial district. Approximately 3,709 deputy U.S. marshals and criminal investigators form the backbone of the agency. Among their many duties are the following: they apprehend more than half of all federal fugitives; protect the federal judiciary; operate the Witness Security Program; transport federal prisoners; conduct body searches; enforce court orders and orders of attorneys general involving civil disturbances and acts of terrorism; execute civil and criminal processes; and seize property acquired by criminals through illegal activities (U.S. Marshals Service, 2017).

Career opportunities with the USMS include deputy positions, administrative positions, and detention and aviation enforcement positions. Experienced former law enforcement officers, having served in various capacities and specialties throughout their careers, comprise the agency's court security officer (CSO) program. These contracted CSOs receive limited deputations as special deputy marshals and play a vital role in courthouse security. Using security-screening systems, CSOs detect and intercept weapons and other prohibited items that individuals attempt to bring into federal courthouses. Senior inspectors, deputy marshals, and CSOs provide security at facilities that house court operations. The agency also oversees each aspect of courthouse construction projects, from design through completion, to ensure the safety of federal judges, court personnel, and the public.

To work for the USMS, you must be a U.S. citizen and meet the following additional criteria:

- Be at least 21 and no older than 36 years (must be appointed before 37th birthday)
- Have a bachelor's degree, 3 years of qualifying work experience, or a combination of education and experience equivalent to the GL-07 level
- Successfully complete a structured interview, background investigation, and other assessments
- Pass medical exam and be in excellent physical condition
- Pass a rigorous 17.5-week basic training program at the USMS Basic Training Academy in Glynco, Georgia

The hiring process for the USMS may take from 9 to 12 months, depending on the various assessment phases. If you are hired, you may be placed in any of the 94 districts throughout the continental United States. Deputies are assigned to their first duty stations at the need of the USMS. All candidates are required to remain at their initial duty stations for a minimum of 3 years. A mobility agreement and memorandum of understanding must be signed prior to employment. The pay scale is similar to other federal jobs. You would start at between $38,000 and $48,000 (U.S. Marshals Service, 2017).

Nonsworn Positions

Just as with local and state police, all federal law enforcement agencies are composed of sworn and nonsworn employees. With rare exceptions, if sworn employees take polygraph tests, civilians, interns, and volunteers will also be required to take them. Some nonsworn positions offer higher pay than the sworn assignments. Some positions can offer challenges and excitement without the person ever carrying a gun. The application process differs somewhat for each type of job. At a minimum, most nonsworn hiring processes involve a résumé review, an interview, a background check, and a polygraph test. Nonsworn positions are just as hard to earn as sworn jobs, but you may find a better fit for your interests and skills outside of enforcement responsibilities. It is easier to move around in federal jobs once inside than it is to enter a federal job initially.

DIVERSITY IN LAW ENFORCEMENT

Some people question the motives of state, county, and municipal police departments in their efforts to hire more minorities and women, but the truth is, police agencies genuinely need diversity. Police departments learned this a long time ago. The Caucasian male police officers of today weren't around when gender and racial bias were the quintessence of police forces. Now the presence of minorities and women in police work is the norm. Diversity is advantageous in any job but especially in law enforcement. As with the blind men and the elephant (Chapter 1), the more opinions and life experiences an agency can draw from, the better the outcome will be. Minorities and women who are the right fit will find police work today inimitably copacetic.

Police departments wisely persuade minorities and women to work in hiring units in the hope of encouraging skeptics to apply. Having a diverse recruiting staff at job fairs presents the proper image for police departments and allows women and minorities to ask questions about equality, harassment, and bias issues. Minorities and women in hiring units are also part of the interviewing team for applicants. It is wise for minorities and women to look into the atmosphere of the departments they are applying to. If you can feel good about the attitude of a department, you will go into an interview with a better mindset. Remember, you want to show your personality. Try to eliminate any doubts and thoughts that might hinder your performance in the interview.

Likewise, federal law enforcement agencies need representation from all cultures, races, and genders. According to the Bureau of Justice Statistics (Reaves, 2012), women accounted for 15.5% of federal officers with arrest and firearm authority in 2008. This was a slightly lower percentage than in 2004 (16.1%) but higher than in 1996 (14.0%). About a third (34.3%) of federal officers were members of racial or ethnic minorities in 2008. This was only a slight increase compared with 2004 (33.2%) but more substantial compared with 1996 (28.0%). The increase in minority representation from 1996 to 2008 is primarily attributable to an increase in the percentage of Hispanic or Latino officers, from 13.1% to 19.8%. The percentage of African American or black officers in 2008 (10.4%) was lower than in 2004 (11.4%) or 1996 (11.5%).

Nowadays, women and minorities are likelier to hold leadership positions. Until May 2015, the DEA was under the direction of Administrator Michele Leonhart, the first female career law enforcement officer to lead a federal law enforcement organization. Janet Napolitano was the first woman to serve as the U.S. Secretary of Homeland Security. Former president Barack Obama was the first African American to hold the office of president of the United States, and Hillary Clinton was the first female presidential nominee from a major political party. Great things are happening in our country in the area of diversity. Don't let the fear of discrimination hold you back from your dream job!

EXPERIENCE

Common requirements among federal law enforcement jobs are a college degree and experience. Most students can obtain a degree, but getting the required experience is a tougher hurdle. When trying out for a federal position, you will be going up against those who have experience. It is highly unlikely that a federal agency would hire you fresh out of college with no experience in a related field. If you focus on getting the experience during and after college, the climb toward the long-range goal of a federal job will be much smoother. Consider either military or local police experience as part of your ladder. If the public sector is not hiring at the time you graduate, consider working in the private sector in loss prevention, risk management, or corporate security. Settle for earning your way to the top and not counting on a boost. Get the experience! If you resolve to climb each rung of the career ladder, you are likelier to make the right decisions at the right time.

SUMMARY

There are law enforcement opportunities in municipal, county, state, and federal agencies. The largest concentration of law enforcement employees is at the municipal and county levels, which are also referred to as local law enforcement. Local and state law enforcement offers a greater variety of work experiences than federal agencies. To work as a police officer, you need to meet the minimum requirements established by your state's standards and training board for police officers. The requirements and expectations for police work are enormous. The hiring process is very tedious for applicants and expensive for agencies. Opportunities for employment in state, county, and local law enforcement include state fish and game departments, Indian and state gaming agencies, and campus police. Many agencies also have opportunities for those who want to be reserve officers. These positions are usually unpaid, but it is a great way to get a foot in the door of law enforcement.

State, county, and local law enforcement agencies have nonsworn positions for support personnel, such as property clerk, evidence technician, records clerk, traffic accident investigator, crime analyst, dispatcher, and reserve officer. Some of these positions pay hourly wages, and some may pay better than sworn officer positions.

Federal law enforcement is prestigious work and therefore very competitive. Most federal law enforcement is similar to detective work in local agencies in which no uniform is worn and employees specialize in areas of expertise, without much variation in their fields of work. As enforcers of federal crimes, they handle such things as terrorism; illegal immigration; bank robberies; drug enforcement; organized and white-collar crime; crimes involving alcohol, tobacco, firearms, and explosives; and interstate crimes.

Opportunities to work in federal law enforcement include the Federal Bureau of Investigation Drug Enforcement Administration; Bureau of Alcohol, Tobacco, Firearms, and Explosives; U.S. Border Patrol; Immigration and Customs Enforcement; Secret Service; and U.S. Marshals. There are also nonsworn positions at federal law enforcement agencies. Some nonsworn positions are just as challenging and pay as well as (or better than) sworn law enforcement positions. Minorities and women are needed in all areas of law enforcement. Agencies often encourage women and minorities to work in the recruiting realm. Recruiters work at job fairs answering questions, and they also interview applicants. Women and minorities are well represented in federal jobs and are continuously being recruited. Students who want to work for the federal government should gain experience first to increase their chances of being hired.

DISCUSSION QUESTIONS

1. Do you feel that the educational requirements for police officers are too lenient? Why or why not?

2. Are there any requirements for law enforcement employment you don't agree with? Explain.

3. Law enforcement is one of the only professions that routinely administer polygraph tests to applicants. Do you feel that this is unfair? Why or why not? How about police employees who are not sworn?

4. Do you feel that law enforcement needs to be diverse, hiring more minorities and women? Why or why not?

5. What civilian jobs are interesting to you? Why?

6. In states where marijuana is legal, do you feel that police departments should weaken or

eliminate their drug policies and allow officers to use the substance? Why or why not?

7. Should all federal law enforcement agencies standardize and use the same requirements for all positions? Why or why not?
8. Should state and local police be held to the same standards for hiring as federal law enforcement (education, experience, drug use, etc.)? Why or why not?
9. Do federal law enforcement (sworn) employees have more authority than state and local police? Explain.
10. Do any of the requirements for federal law enforcement employment seem unnecessary or too strict? Explain.
11. Which federal agency interests you the most? Why?

NOTE

1. Throughout the book (primarily in Chapters 3 through 9), information is provided on specific employment opportunities with local, state, and federal agencies, as well as public and private institutions. Citations refer the reader to the general "careers" or "employment" pages at these entities' websites, but job postings change frequently, so the reader shouldn't necessarily expect to find that the jobs described are presently available. The intent is to provide a sense of the requirements and realities of the various positions described.

REFERENCES

Arizona Department of Gaming. (2017). *Human resources & employment opportunities*. Retrieved from http://www.azgaming.gov/content/hr

Arizona Peace Officer Standards and Training Board. (2017). *Welcome*. Retrieved from http://www.azpost.state.az.us/

Bureau of Alcohol, Tobacco, Firearms, and Explosives. (2017). *Careers*. Retrieved from https://www.atf.gov/careers

Caro, F. G. (Ed.). (1977). *Readings in evaluation research*. New York, NY: Russell Sage Foundation.

City of Clearwater, FL. (2017). *Police property clerk*. Retrieved from https://www.governmentjobs.com/jobs/1755773-0/police-property-clerk

City of College Station, TX. (2017) *Career opportunities*. Retrieved from http://agency.governmentjobs.com/cstx/default.cfm

City of Glendale, CA. (2017). *Job descriptions and salaries*. Retrieved from http://agency.governmentjobs.com/glendaleca

City of Topeka, KS. (2017). *Current openings*. Retrieved from https://www.topeka.org/careers

City of Yuma, AZ. (2017). *Civilian accident investigator*. Retrieved from https://www.governmentjobs.com/jobs/1545791/civilian-accident-investigator/agency/yuma/apply

College of Charleston. (2017). *Police dispatcher*. Retrieved from https://jobs.cofc.edu/postings/6272

Federal Bureau of Investigation. (2017). *Careers*. Retrieved from https://www.fbijobs.gov/career-paths

Georgia Institute of Technology, Office of Human Resources. (2017). *Careers@Tech*. Retrieved from http://careers.gatech.edu

Harford County, MD. (2017). *Crime analyst*. Retrieved from http://agency.governmentjobs.com/harford/default.cfm

Immigration and Customs Enforcement. (2017). *Careers*. Retrieved from http://www.ice.gov/careers

Mesa Police Department. (2017). *Recruiting news.* Retrieved from http://www.mesaaz.gov/pdjobs/

Reaves, B. A. (2015). *Local police departments, 2013: Personnel, policies, and practices.* Retrieved from https://www.bjs.gov/content/pub/pdf/lpd13ppp.pdf

U.S. Customs and Border Protection. (2017). *Careers.* Retrieved from http://www.cbp.gov

U.S. Drug Enforcement Administration. (2017). *Careers: Occupations.* Retrieved from http://www.justice.gov/dea/careers

U.S. Marshals Service. (2017). *Career opportunities.* Retrieved from http://www.usmarshals.gov/careers/

U.S. Secret Service. (2017). *Employment opportunities.* Retrieved from http://www.secretservice.gov

Wyoming Game and Fish Department. (2017). *Game and fish career home.* Retrieved from http://wgfd.wyo.gov/gameandfishjobs

4 FORENSIC SCIENCE

INTRODUCTION

Having a witness to a crime is valuable for the successful prosecution of a case. Gaining a confession from a suspect is another key component. However, neither of these on its own is good enough to convict a defendant of a crime. The days of routinely convicting innocent people have been over for quite some time. As we develop more technology and discover better methods of manipulating evidence, more is expected. Today, the successful prosecution of a case depends largely on physical evidence that is properly collected, tested, and presented.

DNA (deoxyribonucleic acid) technology has become one of the most effective forensic tools law enforcement uses to convict suspects of certain crimes. DNA can be found in blood, semen, hair, saliva, sweat, skin cells, vomit, tears, earwax, and feces. A drop of blood the size of a pinhead is enough to identify a suspect. Because such small samples can be used, crime scenes must be cautiously searched and the evidence properly collected to preserve any evidence available. Once collected, the materials must be properly tested. A record of all those who have handled the evidence must be documented. If comparisons are successful, the evidence must then be presented in court, along with testimony from those who took part in each step of the process. The jury would need to be educated by the expert witnesses so that they would understand what the evidence corroborates, proves, or disproves.

Fingerprints remain among the most common and consistent means for identifying suspects. They are infallible, because the crucial features never change, barring any surgeries, injuries, or diseases. A lot of fingerprinting technology has been computerized, including a national computerized system that allows identity matches to be completed in minutes. However, the use of powders, sprays, tape, ink, and paper continues to be a necessary part of fingerprint collection and identification. The fingerprint expert who sits at a desk with a magnifying glass and fingerprint cards continues to be an essential employee at many law enforcement agencies.

Until technology advances its methods, there will be a need for compound microscopes, comparison microscopes, stereoscopic microscopes, polarizing microscopes, microspectrophotometers, and scanning electron microscopes. Vials, test tubes, syringes, catheters, electrocardiographs, blood gas analyzers, ophthalmoscopes, chromatographs, endoscopes, and ultracentrifuges remain important tools in forensic work. Until scientists work miracles in the area of robotics, there will always be a need for human beings to operate the equipment, perform necessary tasks, and testify in court.

The television show *CSI* may mislead viewers somewhat on the realities of forensics and crime scene work. Nevertheless, the actual present-day capabilities of what can be accomplished at a crime scene and in the lab are astounding. Like a family sitting at a card table assembling a 500-piece puzzle, crime scene technicians (CSTs) and other forensic experts are part of the criminal justice family, contributing vital pieces to the successful outcomes of multifaceted cases.

Forensic science is the use of science and technology to investigate and establish facts in criminal or civil courts of law. There is a variety of criminal justice–related positions in forensics, including criminalist, pathologist or biologist, computer forensics specialist, CST, forensic nurse examiner, toxicologist, entomologist, accident reconstructionist, odontologist, anthropologist, and psychiatrist. Some jobs, such as medical examiner, require expertise in more than one of these areas of science.

The criminal justice system consists of several separate entities working together for a common purpose. The more each component knows about the other working parts, the better the overall quality of the output. Detectives need to know what prosecutors require to prosecute cases. Prosecutors need to know the protocols of police work so that they can intelligently formulate their questions during trials. First responders, detectives, crime scene techs, and prosecutors need to understand the procedures involved in lab work to know what to look for, where to find it, how to preserve it, how and when to collect it, how to package it, and how to store it. CSTs need to understand the rules of evidence, how to work a crime scene, and how to testify properly in court. Because of the wealth of knowledge needed to be effective in criminal justice jobs, there is more than one path to getting there. Working in a forensics-related field is no exception; there are numerous avenues one can take. As with any other job, the more you have on your résumé, the likelier you are to get an interview.

The first step of the ladder for a forensics career would be a volunteer or internship program. Students are likeliest to enter the field as a crime scene technician, which is sometimes attainable without completing a bachelor's degree. To eventually land a high-paying job in the forensics arena, students should consider classes and/or degrees in chemistry, biology, math, and English. Many major colleges offer classes (and degrees) in forensics. Legitimate programs are accredited through the Forensic Science Education Programs Accreditation Commission.

Throughout the rest of this chapter, we will look at some of the forensic jobs one can strive for, including the qualifications, requirements, and salaries. We will explore job descriptions and requirements at various agencies to encompass a broad spectrum of information. You can search government job websites periodically for additional information and available positions. We will also discuss some of the preparations that can be done now to brighten your résumé and portfolio.

CRIME SCENE TECHNICIANS

A crime scene technician (CST) is almost always a civilian. CSTs perform a variety of analytical examinations. They process crime scenes using chemicals, light source enhancement, and other methods. They reconstruct crime scenes, preserving marks or impressions made by shoes, tires, or other objects with plaster or moulage casts. They sketch and draw details of crime scenes; collect and package evidence for presentation in court; prepare reports or presentations of findings, methods, and techniques used to support conclusions; and complete photograph referrals, blood draws, photographs, and prints of dead persons at the morgue.

CSTs are responsible for executing competent forensic processing during calls for service. Often calls develop into complex investigations involving high-profile matters and sensitive information. CSTs gather and ensure the integrity of physical evidence or subsequent scientific evaluation for court presentation. They sometimes conduct laboratory examinations of physical evidence using a variety of forensic applications and instrumentation. CSTs prepare detailed investigative and supplemental case reports and communicate with follow-up investigators regarding observations and processing actions. They also identify, collect, preserve, package, and present biological evidence, latent fingerprints, tire impressions, shoe impressions, tool marks, and other physical evidence. They can act as liaisons among crime laboratories, investigators, prosecutors, and defense attorneys, and confer with experts in relevant specialties as necessary. This position also requires court testimony about work performed.

An applicant for the position of CST generally needs to be 21 years of age; to have a bachelor's degree in natural science, forensics, or a related field; and have 5 years of evidentiary or crime scene experience. However, some agencies around the country make available volunteer programs in which no degree or experience is required.

GUEST SPEAKER
SHAYLEEN EASTMAN, CRIME SCENE SPECIALIST III

Growing up I thought about becoming an attorney or a police officer. However, my route in life took a turn and I returned to college to attain a job in some aspect of the criminal justice field.

In 2002, I enrolled at Phoenix College. While taking up to 28 credits at one time, working 40 hours a week, and caring for three children and a husband, I also volunteered with the Chandler Police Department. I graduated in 2003 with high honors and an associate's degree in evidence technology and another associate's degree in administration of criminal justice. I applied for a position with the Phoenix Police Department and after a competitive testing process, including a background check and polygraph test, I was hired.

To become better qualified for advancement, I enrolled at ITT in 2008 in the criminal justice bachelor's degree program. Upon graduation in 2010 as valedictorian, I began teaching criminal justice courses for ITT while maintaining my position with the Phoenix Police Department.

As a crime scene specialist, I respond to crime scenes and take photographs, identify and collect evidence, sketch and diagram the scene, and write detailed reports. In addition I perform various tests and analysis, testify in court, and participate in numerous public relations events. I have worked many death and homicide scenes as well as other violent crimes and high-profile cases.

This type of work is stressful and physically taxing. Having a supportive network and finding avenues to release the stress are essential. It is extremely satisfying to know that because of the hard work I do, I make a difference. I view the job as a challenging puzzle that needs to be pieced together (without a picture as a guide) using investigative skills while thinking outside the box. Self-motivation and excellent interpersonal skills are crucial.

My advice to those interested in this career is to volunteer, get a formal education, have a strong work ethic (and a strong mind and stomach), and develop excellent communication and writing skills.

This type of program offers the opportunity to gain the experience that so many agencies require. Forensic laboratory experience can also be substituted for the required bachelor's degree. A polygraph test, agency proficiency test, and interview process constitute the normal protocol for applicants seeking this position. The pay scale for CSTs is approximately $28,000 to $48,000.

FORENSIC SCIENTIST

Forensic scientists work with law enforcement at the federal and state levels and in large cities. Smaller agencies that can't afford their own crime labs contract with other cities or their state labs. To be a forensic scientist with the Illinois State Police, you need an undergraduate degree in forensic science or one of the natural sciences. Commonly recognized natural sciences include disciplines such as agricultural science, animal science, biochemistry, botany, biology, chemistry, medical technology, geology, preliminary medicine, physics, and zoology. Trainees get paid while learning their new profession.

A new hire with the Illinois State Police would be trained in one of several specialties, which include forensic biology and DNA, drug chemistry, latent prints, firearms and tool marks, microscopy, questioned documents, forensic toxicology, and trace evidence. Forensic scientist trainees receive comprehensive instruction in the use of the most advanced scientific technology and procedures for analyzing evidence. The length of training programs varies with the forensic disciplines. The length of a person's training will depend on his or her ability to progress through a program. The average training times tend to be as follows:

Forensic biology: 18 months (stain identification for 5 months, DNA for 13 months)

Documents: 36 months

Drug chemistry: 12 months

Firearms and tool marks: 24 months

Latent prints: 24 months

Microscopy: 18 months

Toxicology: 18 months

Trace chemistry: 23 months (instruments and arson for 14 months, glass for 4 months, explosives for 4 months, and paints and polymers for 1 month)

In Illinois, under normal circumstances and if there are no major quality issues, a trainee would be promoted to a Level I forensic scientist after 1 year. Trainees are paid in the range of $45,000 to $67,000. An applicant must undergo a written exam and score an A. The next phase is an interview, and the last phase is a background check. The pay scale for forensic scientists ranges from $52,000 as a trainee to $105,000 as a Level III scientist (Illinois State Police, Division of Forensic Services, Forensic Sciences Command, 2017).

MEDICAL EXAMINER

As a medical examiner in Maricopa County, Arizona, you would perform autopsies to determine the cause and manner of death. You would review items related to autopsies, such as hospital charts, medicolegal death investigator reports, law enforcement agency reports, and postmortem results. You would also investigate unnatural deaths by performing scene investigations, gathering information, and responding to hospitals. You would serve as an expert witness in depositions, grand jury sessions, trials, and conferences with attorneys. You would also provide expert witness capabilities for all forensic criminal and civil actions associated with cases investigated and any other forensic needs within Maricopa County. You would participate in conferences with family members, law enforcement representatives, attorneys, and other individuals to provide information on investigations and autopsies. You would train personnel such as forensic technicians, investigators, photographers, and others assisting in autopsies. You would also be expected to provide assistance and guidance to organ donor centers and participate in mass fatality planning, training, and other relevant exercises as needed. You would possibly be asked to present lectures for students, officers, and the general community. You may need to provide information to citizens, groups, the news media, and the general public. You would write scientific papers and presentation materials, attend seminars and lectures for continuing education in forensic medicine, and provide training and observation opportunities to selected students during autopsy examinations.

Requisite qualifications for medical examiner in Maricopa County include graduation from an accredited school of medicine and possession of a current license to practice medicine in the state of Arizona as required by the Arizona Department of Professional Regulations. You would need to display knowledge of the principles and practices of forensic pathology, and the laws, rules, and regulations governing forensic services. You would need the ability to operate a personal computer, including experience with Microsoft Office programs. You would need to be able to communicate effectively orally and in writing. You would need to establish and maintain a positive working relationship with members of law enforcement agencies, as well as prosecuting and defense attorneys, and to conduct research in forensic pathology. You must be board certified in anatomic or clinical pathology and in forensic pathology by the American Board of Pathology.

The hiring process for Maricopa County medical examiner involves an online application, after which the agency fills positions as needed through interviews, background checks, and polygraph tests. As part of the online application process, you are required to answer these four questions:

1. Are you currently licensed to practice medicine in the State of Arizona?
2. Are you able to work with decedents and malodorous conditions?
3. Are you certified in forensic pathology by the American Board of Pathology?
4. Are you a graduate from an approved school of medicine?

The hourly pay range for Maricopa County medical examiner is $81.26 to $101.50 (Maricopa County Human Resources, 2017).

INVESTIGATIVE TECHNICIAN

The position of investigative technician in San Diego, California, is a job within the Trial Support Services Unit within the Bureau of Investigation, allocated only to the district attorney's office. Investigative technicians provide audiovisual, fingerprint, and graphic design support for the district attorney's staff. This position is law enforcement related; investigative technicians perform criminal investigations of alleged violations of criminal and civil laws.

If you were hired as an investigative technician in San Diego, you would perform the following essential functions:

- Create court exhibits, such as photo boards, maps, and timelines
- Photograph crime scenes, items of evidence, lineups, and other items of evidence
- Edit, duplicate, convert, and enhance audio and/or video recordings and files
- Provide testimony in court
- Consult with attorneys concerning the production and presentation of evidence
- Operate photographic, audiovisual, computerized, and trial presentation software in producing trial exhibits
- Videotape and document courtroom proceedings, lineups, and crime scene activities
- Provide courteous, high-quality service to members of the public by personally responding to requests for service or making appropriate referrals
- Record, categorize, and file rolled, inked, and electronic 10-print fingerprint cards
- Compare and classify fingerprints using recognized techniques, reprinting suspects if necessary, and establishing or eliminating the identity of specific individuals by visually inspecting, examining, and matching inked or electronic fingerprints

The knowledge base and skills you would need for a position such as this include knowledge of operating and using computers and computer-aided design systems; skills in investigating methods and techniques, including the collection and preservation of data, presentation methods, and techniques for court appearances; understanding chain-of-evidence procedures; comprehension of basic photographic film processing and procedures, the operation and use of photographic, audiovisual, and computer equipment; and expertise with audio and video equipment, fingerprinting, closed-circuit television systems, and video and digital-image compression techniques to maintain evidence integrity.

All agencies look for employees who communicate effectively, are knowledgeable workers, are customer focused, value and respect others, have the drive to excel, are good at teamwork and collaboration, are open to continuous learning, demonstrate ethical behavior, and are supportive of change.

The desirable education for this position includes an associate's degree from an accredited U.S. college or university or a certified foreign studies equivalency in evidence technology or a related field from an accredited institution or a federal, state, or local agency. You also need 1 year of full-time work experience comparing and identifying fingerprints to determine the prints' usability in the areas of civil and criminal investigations and providing technical investigative support to law enforcement personnel, attorneys, or other investigative personnel, which must have included designing and producing a variety of exhibits presented in court. An alternative to an associate's degree would be 3 years of full-time work experience.

San Diego performs a thorough background check as part of the hiring process. You must have a reputation for honesty and trustworthiness. Misdemeanor or felony convictions could be disqualifiers depending on type, number, severity, and how recent they are. The annual salary for this position ranges from $56,971 to $70,054 (County of San Diego, 2017).

CRIMINALIST

DNA Analyst

The position of DNA analyst is a technical and advanced professional-level laboratory position in a specialized field of biology involving work with DNA evidence from cases. Working in this position in Houston, Texas, involves the application of laboratory techniques, materials, equipment, and instruments used in various physical and chemical analyses of evidence obtained at crime scenes or elsewhere and the presentation of findings for investigative and prosecution purposes. The work is performed in accordance with standardized laboratory methods and controls to ensure accurate and verifiable analyses of specimens. If you had this position in Houston, you would be required to conduct complex analyses requiring subjective opinions. You would need the ability to work with minimal instructions and the ability to use complex instrumentation. Under the supervision of the forensic director, you would perform scientific examinations and analysis of biological evidence collected in connection with criminal and death investigations. Because of the nature and complexity of DNA casework, you would need to meet the minimum requirements, which are the following:

- Bachelor of science degree in biology, chemistry, forensic science, or a related field in physical science
- One year of experience working in a laboratory using recent technology, including the use of a variety of microscopes
- Visual acuity sufficient to perceive minute differences and detail and to withstand the strain of continued close work
- Manual dexterity to perform assigned laboratory tasks as determined by the forensic genetics laboratory director

- Successful passage of a test for color blindness
- Ability to lift a minimum of 45 lbs.
- Ability to sit and stand for long periods of time
- A valid driver's license and ability to safely operate a motor vehicle

As a long-range goal, a master's degree in biology, chemistry, forensic science or a related field of physical science would be a great help in landing a high-paying job in forensics. Other helpful qualifications include laboratory experience conducting DNA tests in a forensic DNA laboratory and experience with evidence screening, DNA extractions, quantifications, and PCR amplification of STR fragments. It would be a plus to have computer literacy in the use of Microsoft Office applications and to be familiar with database applications. Knowledge of the polymerase chain reaction (PCR), short tandem repeat (STR) analysis, and capillary electrophoresis methods would also be desired. The pay for a DNA analyst in Houston is dependent on qualifications, but this position pays very well anywhere you get hired (Harris County, Texas, 2017).

Toxicologist

As a toxicologist, you would analyze blood and urine evidence using established procedures and guidelines, keep precise records, and develop scientific conclusions. Some agencies combine toxicologist work with other chemistry tasks. If you worked in Austin, Texas, you would perform chemical and physical analysis and examination of evidence using qualitative and quantitative techniques in one or more of the following disciplines: drug, clandestine laboratory, blood, alcohol, and breath alcohol testing.

Austin, Texas, requires its toxicologists to have graduated from an accredited 4-year college or university with major course work in chemistry, natural science, or a field related to the job, including 28 hours of physical chemistry. Applications are submitted online at the city's website (http://www.austintexas.gov/department/forensic-science-division). The salary for a toxicologist in Austin is comparable with other large agencies (City of Austin, 2017).

FORENSIC NURSE EXAMINER

A forensic nurse examiner is specially trained to provide all-inclusive care to adults, adolescents, and children who have been victims of sexual assault, intimate partner violence, child abuse, elder abuse, or human trafficking. If you worked for the University of Colorado Hospital in Aurora, you would be responsible for staffing the forensic nurse examiner team, providing medical/legal exams to patients of the University of Colorado health care system, and maintaining the chain of custody with medical/legal documentation and storage. You would also be responsible for testifying as an expert witness in court and providing education/outreach to the community at large. As a forensic nurse examiner clinician, you would interface with medical professionals, law enforcement agencies, criminal justice, victim advocacy, and external support agencies that provide services to victims of crime and violence. You would perform forensic examinations of individuals who have been sexually assaulted and provide related patient care and referrals.

The minimum requirements include graduation from an accredited registered/professional nursing program and completion of sexual assault nurse examiner training within 3 months of hire. You would also need to be licensed as an RN and have three years of RN experience in an acute care/hospital setting. You would need to be willing to work all shifts and live within a 30-minute drive of the hospital. The pay for this position is comparable with all other forensic nurse positions (University of Colorado Hospital, 2017).

FORENSIC PSYCHIATRIST

Forensic psychiatry combines psychiatry with the subfields of forensics and criminology. A student interested in this field would need to go through all the necessary training and certification to become a psychiatrist and, at the same time, learn sufficiently about the criminal justice system. Those who put in the effort and the years of schooling necessary can find themselves rewarded with a job that pays very well and offers a variety of interesting work on a regular basis.

A forensic psychiatrist provides diagnostic assessments about people's mental state and then develops a treatment plan to overcome their problems. The assessments are then used by the courts in making decisions about clients' fitness to stand trial or maybe the validity of insanity pleas.

Forensic psychiatrists are utilized to evaluate people in order to determine their mental state prior to trial.

The forensic psychiatrist may also be called upon to determine what the mental state of a suspect was at the time the crime was committed.

To become a forensic psychiatrist, you need to first go to medical school and earn an MD or DO (doctor of osteopathic medicine). From there, you would need to specialize in psychiatry by entering a residency in that field. Once the residency is complete and you receive your accreditation, you would likely continue by completing a one-year fellowship in forensic psychiatry.

An example of a job in this field is in Atlanta, Georgia, at Emory University (EU) in the Department of Psychiatry and Behavioral Sciences. If you worked at EU, about 30% of your time would be dedicated to supervising psychiatry residents and other trainees; conducting individual, group, family, and couples therapy; performing assessments; and seeing individual psychotherapy patients.

About 70% of this job would entail the necessary duties as the program manager of the Fulton County Jail Competency Restoration Program (FCJCRP). The goal of the FCJCRP is to expedite the movement through the legal system of criminal pretrial defendants in Fulton County who are thought to be incompetent to stand trial, utilizing direct treatment, appropriate treatment planning, and interfacing with attorneys and courts to arrange appropriate legal dispositions. The manager's job is to develop, supervise, and provide the administrative structure necessary to achieving this goal. In addition, the program manager provides some mental health treatment and conducts forensic evaluations and assists in the academic and research efforts of the program. Duties include the following:

1. Managing daily operations of an in-jail program that treats mentally ill criminal defendants
2. Conducting program development, including appropriate procedures and written policies
3. Arranging transfers on and off the program to other areas within the jail as well as to outside agencies such as Georgia Regional Hospital and specialty outpatient programs
4. Tracking the process and obtaining data to "sell" court hearings
5. Being willing to work and have an office in a somewhat chaotic high-security jail environment with mentally ill and often violent inmates
6. Helping develop and oversee an outpatient competency restoration program for incompetent defendants who are out on bond
7. Assisting in developing research projects on the program
8. Facilitating the collection of tracking and research data regarding program clients
9. Providing clinical mental health services to program inmates
10. Conducting forensic evaluations and writing reports to court

The following are the preferred qualifications for employment with EU:

1. Academic qualifications necessary for Emory faculty appointment in the Department of Psychiatry and Behavioral Sciences
2. Licensed in the state of Georgia in the relevant discipline
3. Advanced training and experience in forensic psychology or psychiatry
4. At least 3 years' experience working on units that serve mentally ill defendants and/or insanity acquitees
5. Detailed understanding of legal issues and processes regarding how the legal system handles mentally ill defendants who are likely incompetent to stand trial
6. Demonstrated expertise in working with attorneys, judges, hospital admissions workers, and mental health professionals to help develop treatment and management plans, including risk management plans, for criminal defendants
7. Existing working relationships with Fulton County attorneys and judges strongly preferred

The annual salary for forensic psychiatrists ranges from $150,000 to $250,000 (Emory University, 2017).

FORENSIC INTERVIEWER

The position of forensic interviewer is common in law enforcement and advocacy centers. Forensic interviewers generally have the responsibility of interviewing children and adolescents ages 2 through 17 and vulnerable adults who are alleged to be victims of, or eyewitnesses to, abuse or violence. An experienced forensic interviewer uses research-based interview protocols and techniques in a developmentally appropriate manner to elicit factual information.

An example of an agency that employs a forensic interviewer is Childhelp, in Phoenix, Arizona, a leading national nonprofit organization dedicated to helping at-risk children and victims of child abuse and neglect. Childhelp focuses on advocacy, prevention, treatment, and community outreach. Childhelp's programs and services also include residential treatment services, children's advocacy centers, therapeutic foster care, group homes, and child abuse prevention, education, and training.

The essential responsibilities at Childhelp are as follows:

- Schedule and coordinate joint forensic interviews of alleged child, adolescent, and vulnerable adult abuse victims with multidisciplinary team members
- Conduct forensic interviews of alleged victims and witnesses of abuse on behalf of multidisciplinary team members
- Maintain and update case files, case lists, video logbooks, and statistical tracking
- Provide written documentation pertaining to interviews conducted for case review purposes
- Participate in weekly case reviews, including coordinating case review information with multidisciplinary team members
- Participate in defense interviews
- Testify in civil and criminal court proceedings regarding general interview processes, techniques, and interviews regarding individual cases as appropriate and requested
- Remain current on research involving forensic interviewing and abuse investigations
- Participate in monthly interview program peer review sessions, providing training regarding interview protocols and child developmental levels
- Consult with members of a multidisciplinary team as requested or deemed necessary

Minimum requirements at Childhelp include the following:

- A master's degree in social services or other related fields
- Five years' experience working in a multidisciplinary environment with child protective services, law enforcement, and human services

- Ability to communicate effectively with children and adolescents, ranging in age from 2 to 17 years, to solicit sensitive case information pertaining to abuse or eyewitness accounts of abuse
- Fluency in both English and Spanish (preferred but not required)
- Academic training or practical experience in developmental stages of children and the dynamics and effects of intra- and extrafamilial child abuse
- Familiarity with and a disposition toward the multidisciplinary team approach regarding the investigation and prosecution of child abuse cases
- Ability to communicate effectively in writing and orally to a variety of individuals and groups (Childhelp, 2017)

Women are normally preferred as forensic interviewers, but you might not see that elsewhere in print. Forensic interviewers may be needed with adult victims, but they primarily interview children about sexual molestation and physical abuse. Although some children will open up to a skilled male interviewer without too much apprehension, more often than not, it was a male perpetrator who harmed the child. There may be a lack of trust, which is a huge stumbling block. Women also play a nurturing role in children's eyes, which aids in building rapport.

There is more to interviewing children than being friendly. A trained interviewer knows how to build rapport, how to ask questions, and how to interpret a child's answers and body language. Building rapport with children can be challenging. Children usually know why they are being interviewed and may have their defenses up. If the perpetrator is a family member, a child might be afraid of having to face the abuser again. You must be careful not to make promises you can't keep. You can't give children treats or gifts prior to an interview, for a defense attorney will use that information to convince a jury that the child was influenced to say what the interviewer wanted to hear. The key is to know about the development of children at all stages.

Once rapport has been established, a skilled interviewer will transition into the fact-finding portion of the interview, with questions that are as nonleading as possible. An example of a leading question is "Did he touch you in your private area?" A nonleading question would be "What happened?" A skilled interviewer knows how to listen without interrupting, so as not to disturb the steady flow of a narrative. A trained forensic interviewer knows how to go back and clarify statements that may seem unclear to a prosecutor and jury. An expert interviewer is constantly aware of a child's choice of words and body language. One of the signs of a true statement is when a child's narrative is complete and includes information that happened before, during, and after the incident. A pretender will usually not offer any more information than necessary, resulting in shorter answers.

To become a forensic interviewer, you can take one of several routes. One path would be to earn a degree in child psychology, with a minor in criminal justice. Another option is to become a police officer, transfer to detective work in the area of child crimes, attend all available trainings offered by forensic interviewers, and get a degree in child psychology. You could also consider working or volunteering for child protective services or a domestic violence shelter to add child interviewing and group work experience to your résumé. Once you have some training, experience, and credentials, you can seek opportunities for further experience in your quest to become an expert.

Forensic interviewers are often paid very well, depending on credentials, experience, location, and whether the positions are grant funded. Those working in police departments earn about as much as lieutenants. Salaries can range from $45,000 to $90,000. Forensic interviewers can also work under contracts with several agencies at a time. They may set up offices with interview rooms that are wired for video recording (hidden) and decorated in a child-friendly manner. If you went this route, you would work under an appointment system and bill the department on the basis of the interview time and any follow-up court testimony. This type of setup is perfect for someone who doesn't want to work full time or wants to work extra jobs.

FORENSIC ENTOMOLOGIST

Forensic entomologists are typically employed by academic institutions, not law enforcement agencies, but they can provide valuable information and work for law enforcement, medical examiners, and coroners in establishing a portion of the postmortem interval (PMI). Entomologists are experts at determining the ages of insects on human remains. Such information can be extremely valuable when law enforcement investigators are attempting to establish a time frame to support or refute suspect or witness statements.

Approximately 8,000 women and men work as professional entomologists in the United States, which includes teaching, working as extension entomologists, raising bees, enforcing quarantines and regulations, performing insect survey work, consulting on integrated pest management topics, selling insecticides, controlling pests, and conducting research on insect classification, taxonomy, biology, ecology, behavior, and control. A great number of entomologists work in some aspect of economic or applied entomology that deals with the control of harmful insects.

Many police agencies, coroners, medical examiners, and federal agencies throughout the United States are now relying on forensic entomologists to assist in answering vital questions concerning death investigations. Although forensic entomologists are often called upon by attorneys, law enforcement agencies, and medical examiners to analyze entomological evidence, few are employed full time by law enforcement agencies. Many board-certified forensic entomologists are employed by institutions of higher education.

The specific area of entomology called upon by law enforcement is medicocriminal forensic entomology. It is generally criminal in nature, focusing on the insects that colonize human tissues in the PMI. It has been assumed that forensic entomologists estimate the PMI. However, forensic entomologists actually estimate the ages of the insects developing on human (or animal) remains and therefore actually estimate the time of colonization. This is the time at which eggs or larvae are deposited on the remains. The adult arrival time is also added to the time of colonization, and thus a forensic entomologist can derive the time since colonization of the remains. More specifically, forensic entomologists often determine the minimum time since colonization.

Medicocriminal entomology is a powerful tool for forensic scientists, medical examiners, coroners, and law enforcement. It has been used for the following purposes:

- Estimating a portion of the PMI
- Establishing the geographic location of death
- Associating the victim and suspect with each other and with the scene
- Identifying possible sites of trauma
- Acquiring alternative toxicological samples
- Providing alternative DNA samples
- Resolving traffic accidents resulting from panic due to stinging insects in an automobile
- Resolving aircraft incidents in which entomological evidence was found to be a contributing factor
- Identifying criminal misuse of insects that are induced to bite or feed upon a victim
- Resolving child neglect and elder abuse cases

The requirements to be a forensic entomologist are as follows:

- A master's degree or doctorate in entomology
- Graduate coursework with a specialization and area of concentration in the forensic application of entomology
- Five years of relevant case experience
- Five case exemplars to submit to the American Board of Forensic Entomology
- Ability to score 80% or higher on a written examination
- Ability to score 80% or higher on a practical examination and case workup on a mock case

If you are interested in becoming a forensic entomologist, you may consider a degree in biology or zoology. Finding an undergraduate degree in entomology would be difficult. You may find employment at a large law enforcement agency, at which you would also take on other responsibilities depending on the needs and your expertise. Entry-level salaries can be as low as $29,000 per year, but experienced forensic entomologists working in government jobs can make more than $71,000 annually (North Carolina Association for Biomedical Research, 2017).

DIVERSITY IN FORENSIC SCIENCE

Underrepresentation of women and minorities is not an issue in the forensic field. In fact, according to Associated Press writer Dena Potter (2008), an AP review of accredited forensic science programs in the United States found that about 75% of graduates are women, an increase from about 64% in 2000. Furthermore, it is estimated that employees in the nation's forensic labs are 60% female. One example of this is Virginia's Department of Forensic Science, where 36 of 47 scientists hired since 2005 were women.

SUMMARY

Forensic science is the use of science and technology to investigate and establish facts in criminal or civil courts of law. As technology develops and better methods of manipulating evidence are discovered, more is expected. Today, the successful prosecution of a case depends largely on physical evidence that is properly collected, tested, and presented. DNA technology has become one of the most effective forensic tools used by law enforcement to convict suspects of certain crimes. DNA can be found in blood, semen, hair, saliva, sweat, skins cells, vomit, tears, earwax, and feces. Fingerprints remain among the most common and consistent means of identifying suspects. They are infallible because the features never change, barring any surgeries, injuries, or diseases.

The criminal justice system consists of several separate entities working together for a common purpose. The more each component knows about the other working parts, the better the overall quality of the output. Prominent forensic jobs in the criminal justice system include CST, forensic scientist, medical examiner, investigative technician, DNA analyst, toxicologist, forensic nurse examiner, forensic psychiatrist specialist, forensic interviewer, and forensic entomologist.

There is a specific need for women as forensic interviewers because this position deals primarily with children. Children often respond to women more easily than to men. The position of forensic interviewer requires less schooling than some of the other positions in the field of forensics and pays very well. Women and minorities are more prevalent in the forensic field as a whole.

DISCUSSION QUESTIONS

1. Many jobs in the forensic world require experience. How can a person get the minimum experience? Explain.
2. Agencies such as Childhelp that work closely with child victims generally prefer their forensic interviewers to be women. Should this type of job bias be allowed? Explain.
3. What job in the forensic arena sounds most interesting and enjoyable to you? Why?
4. What job in forensics appears to be the most difficult to attain? Why?
5. At one time, we didn't have the DNA analysis capabilities we now enjoy. Nonetheless, our courts flourished with trials, and juries convicted criminals. As technologies have been invented and improved, expectations have also been raised. Do you feel that it is fair for prosecutors to be expected to provide more and better evidence than what was acceptable in the past? Why or why not?

REFERENCES

Childhelp. (2017). *Employment opportunities.* Retrieved from http://www.childhelp-usa.com/pages/employment

City of Austin. (2017). *Careers.* Retrieved from http://www.austintexas.gov/department/forensic-science-division

County of San Diego. (2017). *Job postings.* Retrieved from http://agency.governmentjobs.com/sdcounty

Emory University. (2017). *Careers.* Retrieved from http://hr.emory.edu/careers/index.html

Harris County, Texas. (2017). *Career opportunities.* Retrieved from https://www.governmentjobs.com/careers/harriscountytx/jobs/1746221-0/dna-analyst-iii-serology

Illinois State Police, Division of Forensic Services, Forensic Sciences Command. (2017). *Employment.* Retrieved from http://www.isp.state.il.us/Forensics/html/Employment.html

Maricopa County Human Resources. (2017). *Home page.* Retrieved from http://agency.governmentjobs.com/maricopa/default.cfm

North Carolina Association for Biomedical Research. (2017). *Bioscience careers: Entomologist.* Retrieved from http://www.aboutbioscience.org/careers/entomologist

Potter, D. (2008, Aug 15). More women choosing careers in forensic science. *Fox News.* Retrieved from http://www.foxnews.com/wires/2008Aug15/0,4670,ForensicScienceWomen,00.html

University of Colorado Hospital. (2017). *Careers.* Retrieved from https://careers.uchealth.org/Nursing-Professional-jobs

VICTIM SERVICES

INTRODUCTION

The Crime Victims' Rights Act of 2004 forced many changes in the criminal justice system. The onus was put on all city and state governments to ensure that victims received the rights promised them by the legislation. These rights included the following:

- The right to notification
- The right not to be excluded from proceedings
- The right to protection from the accused
- The right to speak at criminal justice proceedings
- The right to restitution
- The right to consult with the prosecuting attorney
- The right to proceedings free from unreasonable delay
- The right to be treated with fairness and respect for the victim's dignity and privacy

Seeing these rights that are now mandated, you may be surprised that they had not already been awarded to victims. Why hadn't these amenities been offered to victims all along? Before the economy crashed in 2007, some would have answered that it was a lack of money and resources. However, since 2007, we have seen agencies work with less because they have to. Police departments and courts have had to rethink and alter how they accomplish their everyday tasks. If anything good came out of the financial crisis, it was these forced improvements. Better victim service is just one of many transformations in recent years. Some of the new victim service responsibilities were given to police departments, and some were given to the courts.

It should be pointed out that the deficit of efficient services for victims wasn't due to a lack of concern on the part of police and courts. It is difficult to change paradigms in any occupation, but it is especially hard in law enforcement. While assistant chiefs and captains were dealing with departmental issues, police chiefs handled outside political issues, which included pleading with city management for more staff. Justifying a need for patrol officers was always much easier than selling new programs, such as victim services. Even if administrators of police departments had recognized the need for better treatment of victims, the idea of trying to change officers' approach to their job would have been a huge undertaking, if even possible. Placing an emphasis on victims of crime isn't what many police officers signed up for (prior to 2004). Even today, the victim-focused mentality isn't found among all police employees, but more and more, hiring units are looking for just that type of mindset.

There have been huge changes in intimate partner violence laws all across the country, and many veteran officers have had to be taught new procedures for handling domestic disputes. In the early 1980s, an officer would have to ask the victim of domestic violence whether she (or he) would prosecute the perpetrator. Often the victim would be afraid to follow through because of fear of the perpetrator or lack of trust in the criminal justice system. Frequently, a victim would tell the on-scene officer that she (or he) just wanted the offender to leave for the night. The officer would make the offender leave but would sometimes make the victim feel bad for wasting his time. The offender would leave; the officer would leave; the offender would return; the victim would receive more bruises; the police would never know.

The crime victims' movement intensified during the mid-1980s, and many agencies received funding to facilitate better treatment of victims. The Victims of Crime Act (VOCA) of 1984 was the catalyst. Over $1 billion has been spent on victim assistance programs since the start of VOCA funding. This funding has come from numerous contributors besides the government. Many community leaders have also stepped up and persisted in keeping the vision alive. Instead of the crime victims' movement being just a temporary fad, it has become one of the most successful and supported movements in recent history. Today, thanks to more than 30 years of perpetual change and improvement, we have witnessed the emergence of enhanced victim-centered protocols and the creation of new jobs associated with victim advocacy.

Today, many victim advocacy positions are funded by state and federal grants, but city governments remain accountable to support the programs. For this reason, police departments and courts look for victim services personnel who are grant savvy. Many victim services specialists are self-supporting, writing their own grant requests to retain their positions in the agencies for which they work. City governments sometimes have to budget for victim services positions when grant funding isn't available. Today it is common to find victim service personnel working for state coalitions, police departments, prosecutor's offices, courts, hospitals, and a variety of privately owned facilities and government supported programs. We will explore some these positions around the country and give general examples of job descriptions and requirements.

DOMESTIC VIOLENCE COALITIONS

Advocacy is significant in domestic violence cases. Victims of domestic violence stay in abusive relationships for a variety of reasons. The main reasons are fear, economic dependency, belief that the abuser will change, isolation, cultural influences, immigration status, religion, low self-esteem, and concern for children. Advocates play a multifaceted role with these types of victims. Advocates educate victims to help them understand their abusers better and learn what resources are available. They develop safety plans with victims. Advocates find shelter for victims and help them acquire financial help to travel and eat. Advocates become liaisons between victims and the criminal justice system to help ensure that their cases are investigated properly and that abusers receive prompt consequences. Advocates accompany victims to court to obtain orders of protection and then follow through with the police to make sure the orders are served.

Law enforcement and attorneys benefit by having someone take the victim by the hand. If a victim retains confidence in the criminal justice system, it is likelier that she will follow through with her part in a case. Even though a victim no longer needs to say, "I'll prosecute," a case is unlikely to be successful if the victim refuses to testify in court.

Fixty-six state coalitions, as well as the National Coalition Against Domestic Violence, target domestic violence prevention. You can find a list of the state coalitions (and their contact information) at http://ncadv.org/stay-connected/state-coalitions. These coalitions work closely with the state governments from which they often receive much of their funding. The Arizona Coalition to End Sexual and Domestic Violence (ACESDV) was organized in 1980. It was formed so that professionals and concerned citizens statewide could unite, increase public awareness about the issue of domestic violence, enhance the safety of and services for domestic violence victims, and reduce the incidence of domestic violence in Arizona families. ACESDV is based in Phoenix and has a significant statewide presence. It is a nongovernmental, nonprofit membership organization that works with more than 170 formal members and allies to carry out its mission and objectives (Arizona Coalition to End Sexual and Domestic Violence, 2017).

Those working within the realm of ACESDV include victim advocates, legal advocates, system advocates, and trainers. ACESDV hosts a number of volunteer opportunities to bring concerned leaders, citizens, and communities together to solve some of the most pressing issues facing domestic violence victims and the domestic violence community. Some of the volunteer opportunities are with the Legislative Advisory Committee, Legal Committee, Domestic Violence Programs Committee, Women of Color Committee, and SHARE Survivors Advisory Committee (Arizona Coalition to End Sexual and Domestic Violence, 2017).

There are similar volunteer opportunities in all 56 state programs. Volunteering with a domestic violence coalition would add a great bullet point to your résumé. Some coalitions have volunteers doing the bulk of the work. The Nebraska Domestic Violence Sexual Assault Coalition is a statewide advocacy organization committed to the prevention and elimination of sexual and domestic violence. Its aim is to enhance safety and justice for victims of domestic violence and sexual assault by supporting and building upon the services provided by the network of local programs. For its first 10 years, the coalition was a volunteer organization with no paid staff and no office. In 1987, the coalition received funds from the Department of Social Services to open an office and hire a staff person (Nebraska Domestic Violence Sexual Assault Coalition, 2017).

The Oregon Coalition Against Domestic and Sexual Violence is a statewide nonprofit corporation composed of 48 member programs. It offers support services to providers and community partners, including systems advocacy; development and distribution of funds, information, referrals, and technical assistance; training and education; and shaping public policy around intimate partner violence, sexual assault, and stalking. The coalition was formed to support efforts at passing legislation important to the antiviolence movement, such as the landmark Oregon Abuse Prevention Act and the Rape in Marriage Law. The coalition was incorporated in 1978 and continues to strengthen support systems in favor of victims of domestic and sexual violence.

With some advocacy experience, you could transition into other positions within a coalition or its partner organizations. One example is the position of social media and events coordinator for the Oregon Coalition Against Domestic and Sexual Violence. This individual provides a wide array of event, administrative, technical, and office coordination. This position is responsible for the overall coordination of the agency's regional conferences, annual conference, technology infrastructure, integration of software applications, and training regarding technology use.

The minimum qualifications for the position of social media and event coordinator are the following:

- An understanding of, and agreement with, the coalition's mission statement and philosophy regarding the elimination of sexual violence, empowerment, inclusiveness, and social change
- Two to 5 years' experience working with domestic or sexual violence survivors
- Three years of experience providing internal technology support
- Proficiency in database and website administration
- Demonstrated understanding of social media activities and use
- Very high attention to detail and excellent verbal and written communication skills
- An associate's degree in computer systems administration or the equivalent of education and experience
- Ability to travel statewide on some overnight and weekend trips

The position of social media and event coordinator pays between $36,000 and $40,000 (Oregon Coalition Against Domestic and Sexual Violence, 2017).

The Tennessee Coalition to End Domestic and Sexual Violence is a statewide nonprofit organization that provides training, technical assistance, policy work, and legal services to victims of domestic violence, sexual assault, stalking, and trafficking. The coalition employs a sexual assault victim advocate for its sexual assault legal clinic. The goal of the clinic is to provide comprehensive and holistic legal representation in civil matters for victims of sexual assault. The funding for these services allows the coalition to provide representation to clients in 34 counties.

The sexual assault victim advocate for the Tennessee coalition is responsible for assisting the staff attorneys in representing sexual assault victims. Specific duties include the following:

- Conducting intake for referred clients and performing safety needs assessments
- Making referrals for resources needed to increase victim safety

- Working directly with sexual assault programs to obtain documents necessary for legal representation
- Assisting in collecting and managing data related to clients

The qualifications and desired qualities for this position include knowledge of and experience with sexual assault victims, excellent communication skills, fluency in languages other than English, cultural knowledge, familiarity with Microsoft Word, and the ability to work with people from diverse backgrounds. As with most advocate positions, the salary is between $30,000 and $44,000 (Tennessee Coalition to End Domestic and Sexual Violence, 2017).

The position of prevention specialist exists at the Florida Coalition Against Domestic Violence. Working for the Florida coalition in this position, you would provide training and technical assistance to Florida's 42 certified domestic violence centers and allied partners. You would need knowledge of the root causes of violence against women and oppressed groups, proven training experience, an ability to multitask, and a consistent employment history. You would need extensive knowledge of primary prevention for domestic violence; experience planning, implementing, and evaluating prevention programs; experience working with youth and engaging youth leadership; experience with the coordinated community response to domestic violence; and a proven history of successful organizing for social change. You would need a high school diploma or equivalency and 4 years' relevant experience or a bachelor's degree in a related field and 3 years' relevant experience.

Another position with the Florida coalition is statewide domestic violence hotline advocate. In this job you would provide crisis intervention, information, referral, and ongoing advocacy to survivors of domestic violence who call Florida's toll-free statewide domestic violence hotline. When not answering the hotline, you would provide administrative support for the program department, build upon the existing hotline resources, review hotline data, assist with developing hotline training and corresponding curricula, and support the direct supervisor with other duties and assignments (Florida Coalition Against Domestic Violence, 2017).

To be a statewide domestic violence hotline advocate, you would need to possess a high school diploma or equivalent and have 4 years' relevant experience or a bachelor's degree in a related field and 3 years' relevant experience. As a hotline advocate, you must have extensive knowledge of the dynamics of domestic violence and a history of successful advocacy on behalf of survivors. Experience working at a certified domestic violence center is preferred.

The Washington Coalition of Sexual Assault Programs employs training specialists, a common position in most states. Training specialists develop, implement, and evaluate and facilitate training and events related to the continuum of sexual violence and sexual assault services. Washington prefers employees from historically marginalized communities (Washington Coalition of Sexual Assault Programs, 2017).

Generally, a training position requires the same skills as an advocacy position. Individuals who can present in front of large groups are also sought. Job interviews for training positions usually involve giving a short presentation in front of the staff to demonstrate your abilities. Spanish fluency is a plus for any advocacy position but especially for trainers. Often a grant will specify that the employee hired under the grant be bilingual.

The National Resource Center on Domestic Violence, located in Washington, D.C., employs training and resource development specialists who are responsible for coordinating domestic violence training, specialized technical assistance, and resource development on a wide range of subjects and issues that intersect with domestic violence dynamics, prevalence, intervention, prevention, and public awareness. The training, technical assistance, and resource development are guided by high-quality research, analysis, information, and resources on domestic violence and are provided to individuals and local, state, tribal, and federal entities throughout the United States.

A training and resource development specialist requires a bachelor's degree or equivalent from an accredited 4-year college or university and a minimum of 5 years' experience in work directly pertaining to domestic violence, social justice, systems advocacy, or social change or any equivalent combination of education and experience. Direct domestic violence service experience is strongly preferred. For this position, you would need to demonstrate knowledge and experience of planning, developing, and implementing technical assistance and training specifically related to domestic violence. You would need to assess the development and delivery of resources, consultation and services, and follow-up and evaluation (National Resource Center on Domestic Violence, 2017).

Because victim advocates are often paid by grants, the victim advocate or victim services supervisor is usually responsible for writing the grants. Having grant-writing experience is not always vital for advocate positions, but it can propel you ahead of other candidates for practically any position in government work for which grant writing is a preferred skill. Grant-writing training is offered all over the country. You can go online and find an affordable training course in your area, which will offer a certificate upon completion. In some areas, you can find training for as little as $100. Once you receive your certificate, you can list "grant writing certified" on your résumé. The ideal situation for a victim advocate is a job in which the city sponsors the position and includes all the usual benefits, such as sick pay, vacation time, and health insurance. The salary for most advocacy positions ranges from $24,000 to $44,000.

Victim advocacy is usually a female-dominated field, but there are some advantages to having men involved in the work. Victims of theft or burglary rarely need as much intervention as those of family deaths, sexual assault, or domestic violence, but in many government agencies, victim advocacy is available for victims of all types of crimes. Most advocacy work is short term. Advocates help victims get through the initial crises and refer victims to counselors if necessary, but they seldom perform counseling themselves.

POLICE DEPARTMENTS

Many medium and large police departments have their own victim service program, with advocates who handle all different types of victimization. There is usually a coordinator who oversees the entire program, which often includes grant writing, staffing and training advocates, and supervising volunteers and interns. The coordinator and staff are usually housed in an accessible location near the detectives who handle child crimes, sex crimes, and domestic violence. This type of proximity facilitates a convenient working relationship between the police department and the victim services personnel. It is common for a detective to be assigned a case and immediately walk over to the victim services area and ask the coordinator to assign an advocate to accompany the detective to the hospital or victim's home. If possible, victim service units are housed away from areas frequented by uniformed first responders. The presence of uniforms can be intimidating to victims, especially children. It is also a common practice to keep victims and witnesses separate from where suspects are commonly held. Some of the larger police departments have their own center that houses detectives, victim services, attorneys, child protective services, and an on-call doctor. The centers that are at a separate location from the main station are preferred.

There is a Victim Advocate Services Program (VASP) in New Mexico with the Department of Public Safety (DPS). Working as the VASP coordinator with DPS is a critical position with the Office of Legal Affairs. You would be responsible for launching and overseeing the Victim Advocate Services Program and would act as a liaison between victims of crime and law enforcement agents with the Investigations Bureau. You would be responsible for providing a broad range of social work services to and on behalf of crime victims, in accordance with the Victims of Crime Act (VOCA), including emergency, crisis, and other short-term counseling and assistance services; providing crime victims with information on DPS investigation updates, available shelters, advocacy programs, and financial assistance; helping victims with application forms; initiating appropriate referrals and coordinating direct services; and transitioning victims to available crime victim services

GUEST SPEAKER
GINA MCALISTER, VICTIM SERVICES SPECIALIST

In 1986, I began working at the San Bernardino County District Attorney's Office as a victim compensation advocate. I assisted victims of crime in recouping out-of-pocket losses incurred due to their victimization. I had the opportunity to work with victims of Richard Ramirez, the "Night Stalker" in Southern California and with Doris Tate, the mother of the late actress Sharon Tate, murdered by the Charles Manson family.

After several years, I left to care for a seriously ill infant daughter. After staying home for 6 years, I realized I would need a bachelor's degree to get back to the work I love. After completing my associate's degree in administration of justice, I was hired by the Presentence Division at Maricopa County Adult Probation in Arizona. I obtained my bachelor's degree in justice studies and was hired by the Mesa Arizona Police Department as a victim services specialist. I subsequently completed a master's degree in education and am working on a second in administration.

My daily duties can involve caring for child abuse victims; visiting residences of domestic violence victims; and responding to homicides, suicides, aggravated assaults, robberies, and other situations in which help is needed. I am fortunate that I love reporting to work each day. I feel I make a difference. I work at the Mesa Family Advocacy Center, a national model of multidisciplinary services.

My advice: Communication and writing skills are paramount! Internships, offered by most human service agencies, provide inimitable experience and expose you to the real world of victimization, helping you decide if this is the career for you.

through the courts. You would also promote and maintain a victim assistance services program that complies with statutory requirements, program guidelines, and regulations. Preference is given to candidates who are bilingual English/Spanish speakers. The salary for this job with DPS is $31,782.40 to $55,307.20 (State of New Mexico, 2017).

The Dutchess County Sheriff's Office (DCSO, 2017) in New York has a victim advocate position. If you held this position with DCSO, your duties would be as follows:

- Provide casework services to clients, including crisis counseling, safety planning, advocacy, information and referrals, emergency financial assistance, and claims filing
- Complete and maintain training certification as NYS DOH Rape Crisis counselor
- Act as the liaison with law enforcement with colocation at the police department
- Accompany victims of crime to hospitals, police departments, and court while providing crisis counseling, information and referrals, assistance with crime victims' compensation claims, criminal justice advocacy, and personal advocacy
- Provide information and referrals to all clients in need following agency and department protocols
- Evaluate and dispense emergency financial assistance to victims as needed
- Assist with fundraisers and special events
- Maintain statistics and prepare reports as needed

This position requires a bachelor's degree in a human services field from an accredited university or college. You would need to be flexible in your working hours. The pay is comparable with similar positions at other agencies.

In Colorado, in 2014, the City of Brighton and Commerce City merged victim services units. Through a cooperative effort and the approval of staff and city council from both communities, the units were combined and have since gained support from the program's volunteer victim advocates. The Brighton and Commerce City Victim Services Unit is administrated out of the Brighton Police Department. However, staff is located at the Commerce City Police Department as well to serve victims at both locations.

Victim advocates with this unit focus on the victims to help them (and their family) cope with the crisis resulting from victimization. If you worked with this victim services unit, you would be on call 24 hours a day, 7 days a week, to respond immediately to the scene of a crime, accident, or victim's home at the request of a police officer. As an advocate, you would not only support victims through the immediate trauma; you would also provide follow-up with referral information to further aid victims and their families through the healing process. The pay is comparable to other victim advocacy positions (Brighton, Colorado, 2017).

COURTS AND PROSECUTORS' OFFICES

Victim advocates are often employed in courts and prosecutors' offices. An example is the position of victim witness coordinator for the Wahkiakum County Prosecuting Attorney's Office in the state of Washington. The person holding this position provides and coordinates the services within the prosecuting attorney's office that support state-mandated services to victims and witnesses of crimes, such as advocacy, restitution, assistance, and referrals to support and services. The coordinator assures these services are offered from the time of incident through disposition of the case and release of the defendant. The coordinator also provides support to attorneys throughout the court process. Some paralegal and administrative support duties are required. The coordinator's job also includes the coordination of witnesses for trial and case and statistic collection.

The minimum qualifications are as follows:

- College degree or credits in legal, social, or other related field or 2 years' experience as a prosecution or community-based victim advocate or closely related field
- Knowledge of the criminal justice system, legal protocol, and court rules
- Experience in social services and contemporary social issues, including domestic violence, sexual assault, stalking, and elder abuse
- Experience with office applications, including Microsoft Office, Excel, and PowerPoint.

The job is grant funded and pays $16.00 per hour plus full insurance and retirement benefits (Wahkiakum County, 2017).

Some agencies partner with the courts and receive funding from the government and other donors from the community. One such nonprofit organization is Edwin Gould Services for Children and Family (EGSCF), which is located in Brooklyn, New York. As a provider of services to battered women defendants, EGSCF partnered with the Center for Court Innovation to develop a project at the Midtown Community Court (MCC), providing on-site, intensive services to people arrested for prostitution and other offenders, sensitive to this population's experience of trauma, including domestic violence, sexual assault, and transgender and homophobic violence. The MCC is a public-private partnership and a project of the Fund for the City of New York. Its mission is to respond constructively to quality-of-life crimes and to work to prevent further crimes. It accomplishes these goals by sentencing persons arrested for misdemeanors in the court's catchment area to a range of community service and social service sentences, including drug treatment, job training, and counseling. As an advocate for this organization, you would have responsibilties that include the following:

- Completing intake and psychosocial assessments and keeping accurate records
- Providing individual counseling and case management to both mandated and voluntary clients

- Facilitating therapeutic groups for women, transgender individuals, and men and developing the group curricula
- Developing and conducting training for court stakeholders
- Developing a directory of resources for program participants
- Drafting court compliance memoranda
- Providing statistical and narrative reports covering services provided on a monthly basis
- Attending casework supervision and clinical training at MCC
- Participating in weekly case conferences, clinics, and staff meetings at MCC

Qualifications and skills that are required for this job include the following:

- A bachelor's degree in social work or a related field
- Experience working with victims of trauma, including domestic violence and sexual assault
- Experience working within the criminal justice system and understanding of mandated programs
- Experience working with the lesbian, gay, bisexual, and transgender communities
- Spanish fluency (preferred)
- Knowledge and understanding of trauma, specifically domestic violence and sexual assault

The salary for an advocate at MCC ranges from $35,000 to $40,000 (Edwin Gould Services for Children and Families, 2017).

The Arizona Attorney General's Office, Criminal Division, Office of Victim Services has an advocate program specialist. This individual performs casework, human services, and administrative duties of moderate difficulty. An advocate program specialist assists victims through the complex criminal justice system, providing quality crime victim services, including both mandated and nonmandated services, as cases progress through the judicial pretrial or postconviction process, handling often high-profile and complex cases such as multiple-victim white-collar crimes, elder exploitation, and death penalty cases. Casework includes victims' rights notification activities, monitoring and advocating for compliance with court orders for restitution, and the promotion of victims' interest and participation in the criminal justice process. Advocate program specialists provide services in the form of crisis counseling and intervention and follow-up services to victims, such as referrals to community agencies for assistance, court orientation and escort, and personal and legal advocacy. Advocates implement program policies and procedures, operation manuals and protocols, and serve as resources on victims' rights issues. They facilitate attorney-victim meetings and serve as liaisons between victims and prosecutors, courts, the criminal justice system, and community agencies statewide. They are also responsible for the completion and accurate case documentation of activities and services; assisting in the selection, training, and monitoring of volunteer interns; providing coverage for other advocates; and completing periodic assignments from the advocate program manager and the director of the Office of Victim Services. Ideal candidates have bachelor's degrees from accredited universities with an emphasis on social science and/or extensive experience in victim services or a related field (Arizona Attorney General, 2017).

The courts in Augusta, Georgia, have a victim advocate position. Advocates provide direct services and information to victims of misdemeanor crimes within the guidelines of the Criminal Justice Coordinating Council, local government, and department policies. Advocates report to the chief assistant solicitor general, the domestic violence prosecuting attorney, the victim-witness manager, or another designated person, and they work with governmental and victim-related agencies, crime victims, and the public to provide administrative support.

The principal duties of court advocates include the following:

- Attending court sessions and assisting in providing crime victims with information regarding victims' rights pursuant to the Crime Bill Act of 1995
- Assisting in notification procedures for victims regarding the criminal justice process
- Working as liaisons among victims, social services, and government agencies
- Assisting victims of domestic violence with victim compensation forms
- Assisting in documenting data of victim contacts and notices, recording court dispositions, and maintaining data for monthly and yearly reports
- Responding to requests for information from officials, employees, other staff members, the public, and other individuals
- Preparing grant and funding proposals and statistical reports to meet grant requirements
- Interviewing victims
- Serving as resources to subordinate personnel

The requirements for educations and skills include the following:

- A bachelor's degree in psychology or social work
- At least 5 years in a similar position or sufficient experience to perform principal duties and responsibilities, usually associated with the completion of an apprenticeship or internship
- Considerable knowledge of Georgia laws pertaining to misdemeanors and victims' advocacy
- Familiarity with county and departmental rules and regulations and the criminal justice system

- Proficiency in implementing program activities, interpersonal relations, public speaking, and time management

This position pays between $31,283 and $49,783 (Augusta, Georgia, 2017).

HOSPITALS

Hospitals also employ victim services personnel. White Plains Hospital in New York has clinical social workers who provide social work services to patients and families, including obtaining, analyzing, and evaluating data relating to medical and psychosocial programs. Clinical social workers formulate and carry out treatment plans and initiate and follow through in a cooperative effort with other members of home care interdisciplinary teams to enable patients to be maintained safely in the community or discharged to appropriate facilities.

The requirements for education and skills include the following (White Plains Hospital, 2017):

- A master's degree in social work from a school of social work accredited by the Council on Social Work Education
- Licensed master social worker or licensed clinical social worker approval from the State Education Department of the University of the State of New York
- Two years' experience in an acute care hospital or related setting

The Grady Health System in Atlanta, Georgia, has victim/witness advocates (VWAs). VWAs work directly with sexually assaulted patients, primarily in emergency rooms, women's urgent care centers, and rape crisis centers. VWAs work closely with the center's manager to coordinate services to victims in the hospital and in the courtroom; serve as liaisons with police, the courts, and district attorneys regarding sexual assault case management; and provide community education in Fulton and DeKalb counties (Grady Health System, 2017).

The qualifications for the position of VWA are a bachelor's degree in counseling, social work, criminal justice, or a related area and a minimum of 1 year of related experience. For this job, you must have skills and experience to work effectively with the police, the courts, community agencies, hospital staff, volunteers, center staff, patients, and their families. You must also have skills to effectively handle persons under emotional stress and be able to problem solve. The pay is comparable to all other advocate jobs.

OTHER VICTIM SERVICE PROGRAMS

There are also opportunities to work at private shelters or other types of victim service facilities. These agencies are connected to the overall network of victim services in their states. The majority are nonprofit agencies that receive funding from the government and numerous private partners. One such facility is Harbor House in New Philadelphia, Ohio, which is a domestic violence shelter and substance abuse halfway house serving Tuscarawas and Carroll counties in Ohio. As a division of Personal & Family Counseling Services of Tuscarawas Valley, Inc. (an affiliate organization of OhioGuidestone), Harbor House is dedicated to serving both victims of domestic violence and their children, as well as women who are recovering from substance abuse.

Harbor House has residential advocates (RA) who provide direct client support by monitoring the household and supervising a client's activities, in addition to crisis intervention. RAs help clients adjust to shared family living while being responsible for their safety and well-being. RAs monitor medications, complete necessary paperwork, answer the crisis line, and assess callers' appropriateness for admission to the program. To work as an RA, you would need an associate's degree or enrollment in college with a major in sociology, psychology, or criminal justice (or a related field) and you must have completed a minimum of 12 hours of course work in your major field or have work or life experience. Four months to 1 year of applicable employment experience at a residential facility is strongly preferred (Personal and Family Counseling Services of Tuscarawas County, 2017).

There is a position for sexual assault/abuse advocate at The Nord Center in Lorain, Ohio. This is a full-time employee who reports to the Children's Advocacy Center and Lorain Crisis Resource Center coordinator. This individual has the general responsibility for providing direct services to survivors and secondary survivors of sexual assault and abuse. This includes during exams, forensic interviews, scheduled appointments, and the 24-hour hotline and on-call schedule. Sexual assault/abuse advocates are responsible for providing services that meet the needs of survivors (both children and adults), constituents, and the community in compliance with program standards.

The minimum requirements for this position in Ohio include a bachelor's degree in social work or a related field. An associate's degree in social work or a related field may be considered with previous experience working with children and adults who have experienced sexual assault and abuse. You would need to be able to work well under pressure and demonstrate good time management and organizational skills for this position. Certification through the Ohio Advocate Network is preferred. Previous crisis intervention and diversity training is desired. The necessity for travel requires that the employee possess a valid driver's license, have proof of automobile insurance, and have use of a personal vehicle. Favorable references or evaluations are also required (The Nord Center, 2017).

At any given time, you can find 200 to 300 job openings (online) for advocate-type positions around the country. Regardless of the state you live in, there is an abundance of volunteer opportunities, internships, and paid positions. Common requirements for a paid position are education and experience. Often the educational preferences fall within the areas of sociology, psychology, and criminal justice. You have some control of your education, but obtaining any experience working with victims is dependent largely on what opportunities are available in your area and what fits your schedule. It is easy to tell yourself that you are too busy to squeeze in any time to volunteer somewhere. It is sometimes just a matter of priorities. The key is to search out openings and grab the first opportunities that come along. The first agency you volunteer for is another step on the ladder and another bullet point on your résumé. You can keep looking for new and better breaks while you are doing your best where you are. Just remember that each agency you work at is another reference for a background check. Make each experience a positive one.

If criminal justice is currently your major, consider psychology or sociology as your minor. These fields can open up more doors than just criminal justice alone. As you saw with some of the job descriptions in this chapter, it is often necessary to have some knowledge of criminal justice as well as victimology or social work. Having a dual plan may bump you ahead of others for internships as well.

A remarkable master's degree that is relevant for all social work is in community counseling. This is a difficult 60-hour program with a 600-hour internship obligation. With this master's degree, you can test to become nationally certified as a counselor. You may decide to go on and become licensed, but just the degree and certification will satisfy the requirements for basic social work positions.

DIVERSITY IN VICTIM SERVICES

Naturally, victim advocacy is a woman's ambit. Fortunately, it is adequately represented by minorities as well. Although rare for most professions, the labor force and supervision in social work are predominantly female. Is there a place for men in this type of work? Absolutely! Especially in the area of domestic violence. An important goal of intervention and counseling is to empower victims. Many women suffer years of brainwashing from their male counterparts. Combining a male counselor with a female counselor can open up an opportunity for the male counselor to model proper relational etiquette. Although not necessary, men can assist skilled female counselors in restoring hope to battered, defeated survivors.

It is refreshing to women when men join the battle as advocates for women's rights. There are organizations for men who are against violence to women all over the country. Male patrol officers and detectives working in areas such as domestic violence, sexual assault, and crimes against children can also have a huge impact on victims' road to recovery. This can be done if they receive some training from experienced victim service specialists to improve their own skills working with victims of crime.

In some parts of the United States, particularly in California, Arizona, New Mexico, and Texas, there is an extra need for Hispanic and American Indian organizations and advocates. The Arizona governor's office spends millions of dollars annually to support domestic violence and sexual assault prevention programs. Some grants are specifically for improving services in underrepresented communities. Spanish fluency is a valuable asset for those who choose victim services as their career.

SUMMARY

Since the enactment of the Crime Victims' Rights Act of 2004, there have been a number of forced changes in the criminal justice system. The treatment of victims has improved thanks to these revisions. Police agencies and courts have created new positions, such as victim advocates, to carry out the imposed modifications. There have also been huge changes in intimate partner violence laws all across the country since the early 1980s. These laws have improved the way victims are treated, specifically in domestic violence investigations.

Victim advocacy positions are available in coalitions, police departments, prosecutors' offices, courts, hospitals, and various other private agencies. There are opportunities for volunteering, internships, part-time positions, and full-time careers. With experience, one can work in related positions in supervision or support. Volunteering is a great way to gain experience and another eye-catcher on the résumé. Many positions are grant funded, making grant-writing experience a big plus on the résumé as well.

Common degrees for victim assistance work are in sociology, psychology, and criminal justice. A notable master's degree to consider is in community counseling, which requires a 600-hour internship. Along with this degree, one can obtain a national certification.

Victim services is a career represented predominantly by women, and it is well represented by minorities as well. There is a need for Spanish speakers, especially in California, Arizona, New Mexico, and Texas.

DISCUSSION QUESTIONS

1. Why did it take legislation such as the Crime Victims' Rights Act of 2004 to compel police departments and courts to improve their treatment of victims of domestic violence?
2. What are some pros and cons of grant-funded positions?
3. What are some pros and cons to having men involved in victim services?
4. Should all officers receive mandatory academy training from victim services specialists? Should they receive more in-service training after the academy? Explain.

REFERENCES

Arizona Attorney General. (2017). *Employment.* Retrieved from https://www.azag.gov/employment

Arizona Coalition to End Sexual and Domestic Violence. (2017). *Home page.* Retrieved from http://www.azcadv.org

Augusta, Georgia. (2017). *Career opportunities.* Retrieved from http://agency.governmentjobs.com/augustaga/default.cfm

Brighton, Colorado. (2017). *Victim services.* Retrieved from http://www.brightonco.gov/312/Victim-Services

Dutchess County Sheriff's Office. (2017). *Employment opportunity.* Retrieved from https://workforcenow.adp.com/jobs/apply

Edwin Gould Services for Children and Families. (2017). *Job opportunities.* Retrieved from http://www.egscf.org/get-involved/job-opportunities/

Florida Coalition Against Domestic Violence. (2017). *Employment opportunities at FCADV.* Retrieved from http://www.fcadv.org/node/10

Grady Health System. (2017). *Careers.* Retrieved from http://grady.ttcportals.com/#

National Resource Center on Domestic Violence. (2017). *Home page.* Retrieved from http://www.nrcdv.org

Nebraska Domestic Violence Sexual Assault Coalition. (2017). *Employment and volunteer opportunities.* Retrieved from http://ndvsac.org/get-involved/employment-and-volunteer-opportunities/

The Nord Center. (2017). *Employment opportunities.* Retrieved from https://nordcenter.hua.mytalentlink.hrdpt.com/hrsmart/ats/Posting/view/307/0

Oregon Coalition Against Domestic and Sexual Violence. (2017). *Current job listings.*

Retrieved from http://www.ocadsv.com/take-action/current-job-openings

Personal and Family Counseling Services of Tuscarawas County. (2017). *PFCS employment*. Retrieved from https://recruiting.ultipro.com/OHI1003/JobBoard/4da200cc-2a1f-0d6e-6a26-433bb2d266af/?q=harbor+house&o=relevance

State of New Mexico. (2017). *Victim advocate services coordinator*. Retrieved from www.spo.state.nm.us/applicationguide

Tennessee Coalition to End Domestic and Sexual Violence. (2017). *Career opportunities*. Retrieved from http://www.tncoalition.org/careers

Wahkiakum County. (2017). *County job postings*. Retrieved from http://www.co.wahkiakum.wa.us/JobPostings.htm

Washington Coalition of Sexual Assault Programs. (2017). *Job opportunities*. Retrieved from http://www.wcsap.org/job-opportunities

White Plains Hospital. (2017). *Careers*. Retrieved from http://www.wphospital.org/Careers/Search-Jobs-and-Apply-Online

6 COURTS

INTRODUCTION

If you are considering a law career, there is good news and bad news. The good news is there are numerous branches one can specialize in. The bad news is you will be attending at least 3 more years of college after you receive your bachelor's degree. If you don't already possess the skills for analytical thinking, problem solving, being persuasive, and writing creatively, law school will groom you for employment. Just look at it as continuing into any master's degree program, though law school does have some logistical differences.

Law graduates can find careers in politics, business, publishing, real estate, education, the arts, social services, criminal justice, and more. Typical arenas for lawyers include law firms, corporations, private practice, and government agencies. Pursuing a law career is a two-step process: getting into a top law school and acquiring decent employment after graduation. This process begins yesterday; more important than in any other criminal justice career, you need to start as early as possible engineering your credentials. So naturally, the earlier you decide where you want to end up, the straighter your course will be getting there.

There is an old saying: People who get lost tend to walk in circles. A German psychologist named Jan L. Souman once did an experiment to find out if it was true. He had some volunteers participate in his research project in a large forested area and other areas in the Sahara Desert. The subjects were asked to walk in a straight line in an assigned direction, and a global positioning system was used to track where they went. Some of the participants walked on a cloudy day with the sun hidden and walked in circles, often crossing their own paths without realizing it. Others walked in the shining sun, which allowed them to use reference points off in the distance. Those with sunlight walked along straighter paths. Other like experiments have been done, with similar results (Souman, 2009). Absent visible landmarks, people tend to walk in circles. This is also true with the college experience. Without establishing your landmark, you could be squandering valuable time and resources going in the wrong direction.

What is your landmark? Those who are still trying to decide what they want to do will be losing ground (walking in circles) and trailing you in the job hunt. If your target is a law profession, the information in this chapter can help to point you in the right direction. This chapter is separated into three sections. The first part focuses on law school, the second on job search tips, and the third segment on law careers. The emphasis is on criminal justice–related jobs, but it is common for law graduates to navigate through a variety of jobs before settling into their long-term careers.

LAW SCHOOL

What is the difference between law school and other degree programs? In most master's degree programs, you specialize in a particular field. In law school, your curriculum is diverse. You then specialize in a particular area of law after graduation. Another difference is seen in the very 1st year of law school, the most challenging of the 3-year stretch, which exposes you to numerous courses and plenteous reading, but no periodic quizzes to assess your progression. Instead, your testing is done at the end of each semester, generally in the form of essay questions. The format in the classroom is also different from that of most other programs. Professors use the Socratic method, stressing student-professor interaction via open-ended questions, making it imperative that students attend all lectures and participate enthusiastically. To encourage student participation and ensure fairness, law schools typically use number systems on tests instead of students' names. This anonymity on assessments means students have fewer concerns about their exam grade being influenced by what they have said or done in the classroom.

Law schools are ranked by *U.S. News & World Report* using a number of criteria, such as peer reviews (deans and faculty members), lawyers' and judges' reviews, students' median Law School Admission Test (LSAT) scores, students' median grade-point averages (GPAs), acceptance rates, placement success rates, employment rates for graduates, bar pass rates for graduates, available faculty resources, ratios of teachers to students, and campus law libraries. The following law schools, with their annual tuitions, are ranked as the top 20 ("Best Law Schools," 2017):

1.	Yale University	$59,865 (full time)
2.	Stanford University	$58,236 (full time)
3.	Harvard University	$60,638 (full time)
4.	University of Chicago	$59,541 (full time)
5.	Columbia University	$65,260 (full time)
6.	New York University	$61,622 (full time)
7.	University of Pennsylvania	$60,988 (full time)
8.	University of Michigan–Ann Arbor	$55,012 (in state, full time)
9.	University of Virginia	$56,300 (in state, full time)
10.	Duke University	$59,912 (full time)
11.	Northwestern University	$59,850 (full time)
12.	University of California, Berkeley	$48,703 (in state, full time)
13.	Cornell University	$61,485 (full time)
14.	University of Texas at Austin	$33,995 (in state, full time)
15.	Georgetown University	$57,576 (full time)
16.	University of California, Los Angeles	$45,338 (in state, full time)

17.	Vanderbilt University	$53,150 (full time)
18.	Washington University in St. Louis	$53,506 (full time)
19.	University of Southern California (Gould)	$60,339 (full time)
20.	University of Iowa	$24,930 (in state, full time)

I received the following e-mail from a former student:

> Mr. J,
>
> To add to the good news about classmates making progress toward their goals, I wanted to drop a line and say that it's true when family, friends, professors, and mentors say that hard work, dedication, sacrifice, and a little faith will pay off. I will be attending Georgetown Law this fall!
>
> Additionally, I found myself in a difficult position choosing between schools; I ultimately turned down seven other schools—including a couple that offered over $100,000 scholarships—to attend my "dream school" in the nation's capital where the laws are made.
>
> My best advice for those still in undergrad is to treat their studies like it's their career. Their performance now will make all the difference in what doors open down the road.
>
> Thanks for all of your help and best of luck to your continuing and incoming students!
>
> Semper Fi,
>
> Alex

This e-mail epitomizes what any law student would advise after experiencing the arduous law school search. The search and application process is time consuming, costly, and unavoidable. You will find yourself in a competition with other students across the country in which there are no winners or losers, but there are good, better, and best. As Alex implied in his e-mail, he was fortunate to be offered several choices. He opted for the number 15 school, which is considered one of the best. How did he accomplish this?

There are two primary criteria all law schools look at when reviewing applications: grades and LSAT scores. Because there are more applicants than available seats, law school admission committees inevitably draw on a variety of additional data and tools to select their law students. Other criteria that are considered include the following (Law School Admission Council, 2017):

- Letters of recommendation and evaluations
- Personal statements or essays (maturity, ability to communicate)
- Undergraduate courses of study
- Graduate work, if any
- College attended (quality and grading patterns)
- Improvement in grades and grade distribution
- Collegiate curricular and extracurricular activities

- Ethnic and racial background
- Individual character and personality (unique experiences, foreign languages)
- Writing skills
- Work experience or other postundergraduate experiences (service in the armed forces)
- Community activities (demonstrated commitment to service)
- Motivation to study and reasons for deciding to study law
- State of residency
- Obstacles that have been overcome (economic, discrimination, disabilities)
- Past accomplishments, leadership, honors, awards, and personal talents

What to do first? The best step you can take right now is to register with the Law School Admission Council (LSAC). Registration is free and can be done online in minutes at http://www.lsac.org. The LSAC is a nonprofit corporation that offers services and products that improve and ease the admission process for law schools and applicants. All law schools approved by the American Bar Association are members of the LSAC. There are nonmember law schools that make use of the LSAC's services as well. The LSAC administers the LSAT, processes academic credentials for as many as 60,000 law school applicants annually, provides necessary software and information for applicants and admission offices, conducts conferences for prelaw advisors and law school professionals, sponsors and publishes research, funds outreach grant programs, and publishes law school guides and LSAT preparation books (Law School Admission Council, 2017).

Creating your own account with the LSAC enables you to participate in its Candidate Referral Service (CRS), which enables you to provide information about yourself, thus making it easier for law schools to search you out and recruit you. Law schools may hunt for specific applicants on the basis of distinct characteristics, such as ethnicity, undergraduate major, law school preference, and other attributes. Candidates who generate LSAC accounts may authorize the release of their CRS profiles to all law schools participating in the CRS. Many potential candidates are contacted and ultimately recruited by law schools they might not have otherwise considered.

Signing up with the LSAC allows you to use the Credential Assembly Service so that you can request letters of recommendation and academic records just once to apply to multiple law programs, which you can do electronically. Being an LSAC member also enables you to search for law schools by location and interest. Regardless of where you are in your bachelor's program, navigating through the LSAC's website and exploring the different services it offers will provide you with the best landmarks.

One of the benefits of setting your sights on law school early is the added stimulus it gives you to improve your GPA. Students can be somewhat blasé in their efforts when they are going to school solely for a degree. Few jobs put as much weight on GPA as law careers. If you slack off for even one semester or try to take too many classes in a semester, it could drop you below those who are able to generate stellar GPAs. You can go to the LSAC's website and take a look at the correlation of GPA, LSAT score, and admission likelihood. This knowledge will give you a landmark that can help keep you focused each semester when you get tempted to blow off an assignment.

The LSAT is of utmost importance. It is a half-day, standardized tool administered four times a year at testing centers all around the world. It is designed to measure the essential skills needed to succeed in law school. The test consists of five 35-minute multiple-choice exams, of which only four contribute toward the final score. The four that count include a reading comprehension segment, an analytical reasoning segment, and two logical reasoning segments. A 35-minute writing exercise takes place at the end of the test. The writing section is not graded by the LSAC, but it is sent to the law schools to which you apply (Law School Admission Council, 2017).

You can find some free practice tests and sample questions at the LSAC's website, and you can purchase additional practice tests there as well. There are some great books that can help improve your scores as you take practice tests. Consider purchasing *The Logic Games Bible, The Logic Reasoning Bible, The Reading Comprehension Bible, The Official LSAT SuperPrep*, and *10 Actual, Official LSAT PrepTests*. You can also work logic problems from puzzle books while you are on the treadmill or stationary bike. Here is a sample question and answer from the LSAC site:

> Executive: We recently ran a set of advertisements in the print version of a travel magazine and on that magazine's website. We were unable to get any direct information about consumer response to the print ads. However, we found that consumer response to the ads on the website was much more limited than is typical for website ads. We concluded that consumer response to the print ads was probably below par as well.
>
> The executive's reasoning does which one of the following?

1. bases a prediction of the intensity of a phenomenon on information about the intensity of that phenomenon's cause.
2. uses information about the typical frequency of events of a general kind to draw a conclusion about the probability of a particular event of that kind.
3. infers a statistical generalization from claims about a large number of specific instances.
4. uses a case in which direct evidence is available to draw a conclusion about an analogous case in which direct evidence is unavailable.
5. bases a prediction about future events on facts about recent comparable events.

> Explanation:
>
> This question asks you to identify how the executive's reasoning proceeds. The ads discussed by the executive appeared in two places—in a magazine and on the magazine's website. Some information is available concerning the effect of the website ads on consumers, but no consumer response information is available about the print ads. The executive's remarks suggest that the ads that appeared in print and on the website were basically the same, or very similar. The executive reasoned that information about the effect of the website ads could be used as evidence for an inference about how the print ads likely performed. The executive thus used the

analogy between the print ads and the website ads to infer something about the print ads. (4), therefore, is the correct response.

Response (1) is incorrect. The executive's conclusion about the likely consumer response to the print ads does not constitute a prediction, but rather a judgment about events that have already transpired. Moreover, the executive's conclusion is not based on any reasoning about the cause of the consumer response to the print ads.

Response (2) is incorrect. The executive does conclude that certain events are likely to have transpired on the basis of what was known to have transpired in a similar case, but no distinction can be made in the executive's argument between events of a general kind and a particular event of that kind. There are two types of event in play in the executive's argument and they are of the same level of generality—the response to the website ads and the response to the print ads.

Response (3) is incorrect. The executive does not infer a statistical generalization, which would involve generalizing about a population on the basis of a statistical sample. The executive merely draws a conclusion about the likely occurrence of specific events.

Response (5) is also incorrect. The executive does use the comparability of the print and website ads as the basis for the conclusion drawn; however, as noted above, the executive's conclusion about the likely consumer response to the print ads does not constitute a prediction about future events, but rather a judgment about events that have already occurred.

This question is considered easy on the basis of the number of test takers who answered it correctly when it appeared on the LSAT. Each logical reasoning question involves a short passage, usually followed by one question (seldom two). The questions are intended to aid in assessing a wide range of skills associated with thinking critically, with an emphasis on legal reasoning.

Letters of recommendation are a necessary part of the admission process. It is recommended that you contact your professors early in the semester and ask if they would be willing to write you letters, provided you earn the favor. Sit near the front of the class, attend every lecture (promptly), participate earnestly, earn a high grade, and remind each professor periodically that you are hoping for a nice letter at the end of the semester. Collect a hard copy soon after the semester. You may not interact with particular instructors for a period of time, and you don't want to be forgotten. Later on, when you are ready to start your law school application process, the LSAC will send an e-mail to your references and ask them to submit their letters electronically. It is easier for an instructor at this point if the letter is already written and saved. You will be facing deadlines, so you want to make it as easy as possible to collect what you need.

Personal statements are another necessary part of the process. Excellent writing skills will boost you ahead of others who didn't take the time to have their statements proofread and fine-tuned. In law school, your assessments will almost always be contingent on your ability to write. You have your entire bachelor's degree to prepare yourself. Look at every essay and paper assignment as an opportunity for practice and feedback from knowledgeable professors. Contact your professors early in the semester and let them know that you would appreciate more than just a grade. Let them know that you welcome feedback that will make you better. Take English classes seriously! Even classes that seem to be a waste of time can be of benefit if you approach them as job preparation.

Law school admission committees may consider your undergraduate studies. Criminal justice degrees are acceptable and applicable, but there are several other relevant degrees, majors, and minors that would also be equally eye-catching on your application. These include history, English, communications, political science, business, psychology, accounting, economics, finance, and philosophy. There are different opinions as to which are the best degrees. It really comes down to what each particular law school considers as worthy studies and what your personal goals are.

An appealing standout for law school applications (and résumés) is community involvement. This has been a noticeable trend in the past decade. It is important for law school admission and important for the job search that follows. It exposes your unselfish character if you are compassionate with others and give of your time and talents for the betterment of society. You can accomplish two things at once: Be a volunteer at an agency that also gives you experience of some relevance. Join a club at your college and participate in the activities. Volunteer to help students with disabilities. Some colleges will pay for note takers or offer a certificate at the end of a semester. If you can come up with three or four entries on your application for volunteer or community activities, you will be a step ahead of your lackadaisical competition.

Work experience tells a story about you, hopefully a good story. It is difficult to work while attending school full time and trying to achieve an impressive GPA. Any official part-time work that spans at least a year can boost you ahead of your idle opponents. It is best to work for a business that has some kind of consistent schedule, with paychecks from which taxes are deducted. Questionable jobs, working with family members, and jobs lacking consistency might not translate into notable entries on your application. Consider 8 hours every Saturday or a couple of 4-hour shifts on weeknights. If you are interning during the day and working school into your schedule, don't change a thing. Interning will make a better impression on the reviewers of your application than unrelated employment. Don't overload yourself and harm your GPA. Remember: good, better, best!

Honors, awards, talents, and leadership experiences can add zest to your personal statement. No matter how insignificant or how far back in time, consider listing everything that adds color to your life story. Did you ever win a spelling bee, a dance competition, or employee of the month? Did you ever make the honor roll or dean's list? Did you ever win an award in a science fair or speech festival or maybe earn the rank of Eagle Scout? Were you ever on the student council, or did you serve as an officer in any type of organization? Did you serve on a church mission on which you learned a foreign language and possibly gained some leadership experience? You are going up against students all around the country who are similar in age and school experience. It is unlikely that other students will have more to put on their personal statements than the types of things listed here.

How will you pay for law school? You might want to sit down for this part. About 88% of law students finance their education (Equal Justice Works, 2012).

Living entirely on a student loan during your 3-year law degree might be your only option. Knowing that they might be over $100,000 in debt upon graduation may deter some students from pursuing a law career, but it is the only viable avenue for most. Some students make payments after graduation and spread out the debt over a 10-year period, while others establish 15- to 20-year plans. Some law jobs include loan forgiveness incentives, but these are rare and shouldn't be counted on.

THE JOB SEARCH

While you are going to law school, you will be advised to start networking. It is a very competitive market. A 2016 research project by Deborah Merritt, a professor at Ohio State University's Moritz College, examined the job outcomes for more than 1,200 people who graduated from law school in 2010. She found that as of December 2015, only 75% of them were working in positions that required a law degree. "That," Merritt writes, "compares poorly with the national class of 2000, which also graduated into a recession thanks to the dot-com bust. By 2003, 85 percent of that group had found its way into a career in which a J.D. was necessary, and 62 percent were employed at law firms" (Merritt, 2016).

Networking amplifies your job potential. It involves meeting people who are doing what you want to do and conducting informational interviews. By doing these interviews, you learn more about the market and at the same time make valuable contacts. Your networking starts by identifying people you can contact. Depending on your relationship, you might mail a letter, send an e-mail, or make a direct phone call. Before your meeting, you will want to do your homework to learn all you can about the contact's practice. This will help you formulate your questions. You will want to be in business dress for the meeting and have with you a pen, a pad of paper, and your résumé. These interviews are a good time to show your résumé and ask for advice on how it can be improved. You can also ask for advice on how you can improve your presentation. One other important thing to ask each contact is for other contacts. You can simply ask "Are there any other people you can recommend that I talk to?" Here are some possible topics you might cover with a contact:

- The contact's position, career path, and background
- The nature of a typical work day
- Positive and negative features of the contact's job, organization, or practice
- The structure of the organization and practice
- The practice of law in the geographical area
- Future prospects and growth
- Obligations this type of job places on life outside the office
- Important factors used in hiring
- Advice on how to be more marketable for hiring
- Suggestions for other people you could speak with

Remember that your objective is to retain an ongoing relationship with each contact. This is accomplished by sending a thank-you letter or e-mail, attempting contact with those who were recommended, and sending a follow-up report about the efforts you made in setting up meetings with the leads your contact gave you. This was nicely demonstrated in the e-mail I received from my former student Alex.

During your final year of law school, you will want to update your résumé. It is to be hoped that you have added some new information from your first 2 years of law school, such as relevant research, accomplishments in law school, summer internships, or new work experiences in some related areas of law. The expectations for a quality résumé from a law graduate are significantly higher than what is submitted to enter law school. Your participation in law school will have enhanced your vocabulary significantly. You will want to replace any weak verbs with stronger language. You will want to use more specific statements. You will want to add a section titled "Relevant Course Work and Professional Organizations." Remove high school information that helped you get into law school and replace it with data that will impress professionals.

By starting your new résumé early in your third year, you can discover any weaknesses and take corrective action. You may decide to connect with a government agency or a nonprofit organization as a part-time employee or volunteer. You may need to take an extra class outside law school to demonstrate more initiative. You may need to improve your writing skills.

In addition to your upgraded résumé, you will want to prepare a dynamic cover letter that can be revised easily to correspond to different targets. You will need to search out job postings and check them regularly. You should keep records of your search activities and follow up after sending in résumés. Your third year is the time to beef up networking activities because most jobs are filled by word of mouth. You want your name to be tossed around at potential firms even before they consider posting job openings. Another recommendation is to take good care of yourself. It is common during school for students to disregard their health and stress management and put on a few extra pounds. To think clearly and stay positive, you will want to exercise often and eat a healthy diet.

There are several resources available to search for private employers (law firms). To begin with, you should consider the *Martindale-Hubbell Law Directory* (http://www.martindale.com), *The West Legal Directory* (http://www.lawschool.westlaw.com), and the National Association for Law Placement's *Directory of Legal Employers* (http://www.nalpdirectory.com). Some secondary resources are Chambers guides (http://www.chambersandpartners.com), Law Periscope (http://www.lawperiscope.com), The Legal 500 (http://www.legal500.com), HG.org (http://www.hg.org), *U.S. News & World Report*'s law firm rankings (http://www.bestlawfirms.usnews.com), the local Yellow Pages, and employers' websites.

There are numerous government opportunities at the federal, state, county, and city levels. Working for the government offers a wide range of practice areas, and for some, it may provide a better work-life balance than is found in the private sector. Some sources include the *Government Honors and Internship Handbook*, the *Public Policy Handbook*, *Federal Careers for Attorneys* (available at http://www.lawschool.westlaw.com), USA Jobs (http://www.usajobs.gov), Avue Central (http://www.avuecentral.com), the PSJD's guide to government careers (http://www.psjd.org/Government_Careers), *LegalTimes* (http://www.law.com/dc), the *Federal Legal*

Employment Opportunities Guide (found at the PSJD's website), *United States Government Policy and Supporting Positions* ("The Plum Book"; http://www.gpo.gov/fdsys/pkg/GPO-PLUMBOOK-2012/content-detail.html), the National District Attorneys Association (http://www.ndaa.org), National Legal Aid and Defender Association (http://www.nlada.org), National Association of Attorneys General (http://www.naag.org/attorneys_general.php), the PSJD's guide to international public service resources (http://www.psjd.org/International_Resources), and job fairs such as the Midwest Public Interest Law Career Conference.

If you want to seek jobs in public interest, such as at nonprofit organizations and in legal service and legal aid offices, you can search resources such as PSJD (http://www.psjd.org), *Public Policy Handbook* (http://www.law.arizona.edu/publicpolicyhandbook), the National Legal Aid & Defender Association (http://www.nlada.org), *Serving the Public: A Job Search Guide, Action Without Borders* (http://www.idealist.org/career/career.html), the Public Interest Law Initiative (http://www.pililaw.org), Symplicity Job Bank, "Capital Defense Internships and Jobs" (http://www.law.berkeley.edu/capitaldefense.htm), and job fairs, as mentioned earlier.

For judicial clerkships, you can search U.S. Courts (http://www.uscourts.gov), the Online System for Clerkship Application and Review (http://www.oscar.dcd.uscourts.gov), the Federal Administrative Law Judges Conference (http://www.falgc.org), the Federal Judicial Center (http://www.fjc.gov), the *Almanac of the Federal Judiciary* (available at http://www.westlaw.com in the "AFJ" database), the *Federal-State Court Directory*, the *Guide to State Judicial Clerkships* (http://www.vermontlaw.edu/resources/judicial_clerkship_and_internship_resources.htm), National Center for State Courts (http://www.ncsconline.org/Information-and-Resources/Browse-by-State/State-Court-Websites.aspx), *Judicial Staff Directory* (http://www.amazon.com/Judicial-Staff-Directory-Winter-Yellow/dp/0872896471), and the *Judicial Yellow Book* (http://www.leadershipdirectories.com/Products/LeadershipPrintDirectories/Legal/JudicialYellowBook.aspx).

LAW CAREERS

There are several directions you can go after graduation. Some lawyers have private practices and work for the government at the same time. We will mainly explore some of the job types within the criminal justice system, but by using the resources listed in this chapter, you will find that there are unlimited possibilities for volunteering, interning, and being hired in the private sector.

Judge

Lawyers can work as arbitrators, mediators, and judges. Some lawyers get the opportunity to serve as *pro tem* (temporary or part-time) judges while in private practice and eventually land full-time positions. Becoming a judge isn't something you should try to achieve right out of law school; most judges have 5 to 10 years of legal practice experience. A judge watches over hearings and trials to make sure they are handled fairly and that the law is followed. Judges preside over hearings involving traffic offenses, civil disagreements, family law, business disputes, and criminal cases. If a judge presides over a jury trial, he or she instructs the jurors on applicable laws, how to deliberate, and how to announce their verdict. Some judges are elected, and some are appointed.

Judges are paid very well, with an average salary of about $125,000. In 2014, there were approximately 30,000 judges employed in the United States, with the majority working for local and state governments. The Bureau of Labor Statistics calculates a steady outlook for judges through 2024. Most judges started out as lawyers, although several states allow nonlawyers to work as judges with limited jurisdiction. Many states require their judges to be licensed with their state's bar (Bureau of Labor Statistics, 2016).

As a *pro tem* judge in Mesa, Arizona, you would preside over misdemeanor and civil traffic cases filed with the Mesa Municipal Court. You would be responsible for applying relevant Supreme Court rules, state statutes, city ordinances, and case law when presiding over trials to the court, trials to a jury, pretrial conferences, arraignments, motions, and other hearings. As *pro tem* judge, you would be responsible for imposing sentences and determining the conditions that, if met, will allow a defendant's release from police custody. You would be expected to preside over cases in any division of the Mesa Municipal Court in any type of court hearing. A *pro tem* judge can't represent clients on cases pending in the Mesa Municipal Court. *Pro tem* judges are appointed by the presiding city magistrate to specified terms.

To qualify for this position, you would need any combination of training, education, and experience equivalent to extensive (5 or more years') experience as a lawyer, judge, or hearing officer in criminal or traffic cases and graduation from an accredited school of law. For this position, an individual receiving a conditional offer of employment from the City of Mesa must pass a background investigation through

GUEST SPEAKER
CHARLES W. ERVIN, SUPERIOR COURT JUDGE

One question I am asked is if I always wanted to become a judge. I had no idea I would become a judicial officer. My path was a little unorthodox, largely the result of being born into a family of attorneys and law enforcement officers.

I started out as an ocean lifeguard for the City of San Diego. That summertime "dream job" became full time as a police officer. After a couple of years of graveyard shifts, I looked for employment conducive to my return to college. I was hired as a deputy marshal, assigned largely to court bailiff duties.

After finishing college, I applied to law school. As a recipient of a scholarship, I finished 4 years later while working full time. I was also married (to a superior court clerk) and had children, so my plate was full. After passing the bar exam, I accepted a job as legal counsel and advisor to the sheriff in San Diego. After 10 years there, I was elected as a superior court judge in January 2001.

I was assigned to a criminal department and currently work in a high-volume criminal settlement court handling a felony caseload.

Probably the most rewarding aspect of the job for me is seeing positive change in the community as a result of my decisions. It is sometimes difficult to grasp the tremendous effect judicial decisions have on people's lives. I keep a desk drawer for correspondence I receive from crime victims and defendants alike. They concern the positive changes in their lives. I am always a little surprised to see the drawer almost full.

the City of Mesa Police Department, the Arizona Department of Public Safety, and the Federal Bureau of Investigation prior to commencing employment. The pay is $70 per hour (City of Mesa, Arizona, 2017).

Although the potential is greater in the private sector to make significant pay, working for the government carries with it great benefits and, in most situations, job security. Working in the criminal justice system can be satisfying. It gives you an opportunity to contribute to the betterment of society in different capacities. Once you are in the government system, it is easier to move around to new and better positions.

Prosecutor

The prosecutor holds the most power in the criminal justice process. Neither the police nor the judge can overrule the prosecutor as regards whom to file charges against and what charges are appropriate. The prosecutor also has a great deal of responsibility to the public and spends many a sleepless night worrying about the ramifications of losing a case at trial. It can also be a thankless job. It is usually the defense attorney and not the prosecutor who attracts the media attention in celebrated cases. Rarely is adequate credit given to the prosecutor who worked so hard to put a case together in order to prove the case beyond a reasonable doubt.

Prosecutors are arguably the hardest working individuals in the court system. Yet in spite of the necessary conveyer belt process of handling the high number of cases, they still care about the individuals and the community they represent. Prosecutors can be impressively professional in the courtroom and then later be in tears in their office because of the emotions resulting from decisions handed down by the judge or jury. It is common for a prosecutor to miss a couple days of work after losing a case that should have been won.

If you are interested in being a prosecutor, it is doable right out of law school after passing the bar exam. It would be easier to get hired if you worked in a court clerkship or similar introductory job for about 12 months during or after law school. You would likely need to make a 2- to 3-year commitment and could find yourself working 70 hours a week with only mediocre pay.

One type of prosecution work is that of a deputy city attorney. To work in this capacity for Vista, California, you would be in a management position, serving at the pleasure of the city attorney (who is also the city prosecutor). You would be responsible primarily for municipal code civil actions and criminal prosecutions. You would prosecute infractions and misdemeanor violations; litigate civil nuisance abatement actions; interview complainants, witnesses, and enforcement officers; perform legal research; prepare pleadings and motions; make determinations on the advisability of prosecuting, compromising, or dismissing cases; present civil actions in court; act as a legal advisor to the code enforcement and other city departments; respond to subpoenas, public records requests, and requests for the release of city records (discovery motions); render oral and/or written opinions on the applicability and interpretation of city, state, and federal laws; draft and review ordinances, resolutions, and contracts; respond to inquiries from citizens regarding city policies, procedures, and practices; attend meetings of boards, committees, and commissions as requested; and perform other related work as required.

The qualifications are any combination of education, training, and experience that demonstrates an ability to perform the duties of the position. A typical qualifying background consists of active membership of the State Bar of California with a minimum of 3 years of experience in prosecutions of municipal code violations and related civil litigation. Additional desired qualities, which would be the same for all attorney jobs, include the following:

- Excellent communication skills, both written and oral
- A good working knowledge of civil and criminal litigation and trial advocacy skills
- An ability to work cooperatively and effectively with elected officials, executives, management, staff, and the public
- A broad understanding of all facets of municipal government law and an abiding commitment to public service
- Strong analytical and administrative capabilities
- Organizational, team, and goal-oriented skills
- The ability to use current computer programs and have good caseload management
- The ability to be proactive, results oriented, confident, and persuasive

To apply for a position such as this in Vista, you would submit a city application form and supplemental questionnaire. You would have to clearly demonstrate through your application materials that you meet the employment standards as outlined. All properly completed applications would be reviewed, and the most appropriately qualified individuals would be invited to continue in the selection process. Examinations for this position would consist of any combination of written, performance, and oral exams to evaluate your skills, training, and experience for the position. You would also have to successfully complete preemployment clearances, which may include a physical exam, drug screening, and fingerprinting. The salary for this position ranges from $112,872 to $137,208 (City of Vista, California, 2017).

Public Defender

An equally important position is that of public defender. The public defender in Spokane, Washington, performs highly responsible and complex administrative, supervisory, and participatory legal work in directing the staff, policy, and operations of the Spokane County Public Defender's Office. If you held this position, you would perform direct trial-level representation of indigent defendants in a diverse range of criminal and civil cases. The duties are described as follows (Spokane County, 2017):

- Direct the administration of the department, including effective personnel, financial, and resource planning and management
- Develop, implement, and continually evaluate related short- and long-term goals and operational plans

- Develop and implement programs, policies, and procedures consistent with statutory and legal requirements in providing quality public defense and legal services
- Manage the department's professional and administrative staff, including selection, training and development, assignment of work, supervision, evaluation, discipline, and termination in accordance with county policy and collective bargaining agreements
- Participate in labor negotiations, applying contractual terms accordingly
- Develop, prepare, justify, and advocate a multimillion-dollar annual budget adequate to meet current standards for indigent defense
- Monitor expenditures and provide required financial reports to grantors and other funding sources
- Research and develop access to competent forensic and psychological expertise for use in investigation and trial
- Provide leadership to the public defense system by advocating the defense perspective to judges, prosecutors, law enforcement, government leaders, and social service agencies in meetings and committees that set policy and procedures
- Represent the public defender's office on relevant local and state committees, professional organizations, and to community groups or agencies, and advocate on behalf of the department and its clients
- Oversee the maintenance of an on-site archive of closed files, including electronically scanned records and protocols for access thereto

The minimum requirements for this position are graduation from a law school accredited by the American Bar Association and 8 years of progressively responsible criminal trial experience, including 3 years in a managerial position performing administrative functions and supervising professional staff. You would need to be permitted to practice law in the state of Washington at the time of application, with a membership in good standing with the Washington State Bar Association, without qualifications or restrictions on the practice of law. It is desired that the person in this position have a certification by the Washington State Supreme Court to be lead counsel in capital cases. The salary for this position is approximately $140,800.

CAREERS THAT DO NOT REQUIRE A LAW DEGREE

Not all positions in the court system require a law degree. For example, you could consider becoming a bailiff, paralegal, or court clerk.

Court Clerk

To be a deputy court clerk in Georgetown, Texas, you would have to be a high school graduate, or its equivalent, and have 3 years of experience as a court clerk in a computerized system with cash handling experience, or any equivalent combination of experience and training that provides the required knowledge, skills, and abilities.

The duties of a court clerk are as follows:

- Responsible for warrant administration by processing complaints, issuing capias and arrest warrants, recalling warrants as necessary, and ensuring that accurate information is sent for the Failure to Appear program or the collection agency
- Responsible for accurate court disposition and fine records by collecting payments, posting correctly to the court system, balancing a cash drawer, and depositing collections daily
- Responsible for accurate data entry and timely file transfer process of traffic, parking, state, and city violations
- Assists the judge and prosecutors in court sessions by ensuring that case files are complete, preparing court documents, and executing and transcribing court docket and records dispositions
- Ensures prompt communications for court customers by sending timely prewarrant notices, notice of past-due requirements, late payments, and court appearances
- Provides quality customer service to municipal court customers by precisely communicating court processes as defined by law, policy, and judicial orders (both oral and written)
- Interprets for Spanish-speaking defendants, if applicable
- Responsible for accurately capturing documents in a document management system to maximize productivity and provide efficient retrieval of information

The salary for this position is $29,869 to $35,152 (City of Georgetown, 2017).

Municipal Court Supervisor

The municipal court supervisor in New Braunfels, Texas, performs the following functions:

- Supervises and coordinates the smooth and effective daily operations of the municipal court through the planning, organizing, and supervision of work activities for court processes
- Continually implements improvements relating to municipal court policies and procedures, operations, work processes, programs, information technology resources, and service efforts that are in compliance with all laws, policies, regulations, and city goals
- Develops and recommends short- and long-range strategic plans for the court to the director of support services

- Directs and coordinates the docket for jury and bench trials, including the setting of the court calendar and ensuring the readiness of court, both physical and clerical, prior to the judge's taking the bench
- Issues juror summonses, drafts complaints, prepares court dockets, and assists the judge and prosecutor during court sessions with paperwork
- Manages the court's records and is responsible for providing accurate reporting of court statistics and fine and fee information on a continual basis
- Reviews financial records of court fines collected, ensures the accuracy of daily postings, tracks charges filed in court cases and the disposition of each charge, and assures proper and timely clearance of warrants
- Responds to requests for information and ensures compliance with the Texas Open Records Act and other public information laws
- Manages administrative activities, including employee scheduling, payroll reporting, training certifications, and activity reports
- Maintains and enforces all aspects of security and confidentiality of records and information

The requirements for this position include a bachelor's degree and 5 years' municipal court clerk experience in a computerized system, with progressively responsible supervisory experience, or an equivalent combination of education and experience. You also would need be a Level II certified municipal court clerk and possess a valid Texas driver's license. The knowledge base for this position includes the following:

- City policies and procedures and applicable state and federal rules, codes, and regulations
- State of Texas court procedures, legal terminology, legal requirements for court operations and case processing, and laws and regulations governing the release of information from court records
- Principles and protocols for the management of legal documents and court records
- Court accounting systems, rules, and standards and principles of record keeping and records management

This position pays $56,573 to $69,245 (Texas Municipal League, 2017).

DIVERSITY IN LAW CAREERS

According to an article in *ABA Journal* (Weiss, 2011), women make up just under half of law associates (47%). Historically, however, minorities have been underrepresented in the legal profession. The law school population and legal professions do not accurately reflect the racial and ethnic population of our society. To promote diversity, law schools actively seek qualified Native American, Asian, African American, and Latino students, as well as other students of color. Law schools increasingly realize that diversity in the classroom enriches the learning process for all students. Law schools do not apply different admission criteria to minorities, but some law schools may take race or ethnicity into account as one of the many factors in the whole-file review process. Applicants may potentially offer something distinctive to a class, and diversity is just one factor among many (Law School Admission Council, 2017).

If you are bilingual (e.g., Spanish and English), it not only makes you more marketable; it also opens doors that are available only to those who speak two (or more) languages. One example of a position such as this is bilingual staff attorney for Bronx domestic violence victims, for the Bronx Family Justice Center in New York City, which employs an attorney to provide legal representation to monolingual Spanish-speaking victims of domestic violence in family law matters in the Bronx, primarily family offense, custody and visitation, and child and spousal support proceedings, as well as some matrimonial matters. Other responsibilities include conducting community outreach and education in the Bronx, screening walk-in clients, and collaborating with other agencies to be an advocate for systemic change. The attorney works out of the Bronx office, located in the Bronx Family Justice Center.

Duties of this position include the following:

- Maintaining a heavy caseload
- Conducting outreach to underserved communities
- Training law students, pro bono attorneys, social service providers, health care professionals, and community-based organizations on domestic violence and the legal needs of victims
- Representing Sanctuary for Families (a nonprofit organization that aids victims of domestic violence) on task forces and other political and advocacy committees outside the agency
- Recruiting, supervising, and providing co-counsel to pro bono attorneys on all aspects of litigation in family law matters
- Supervising and mentoring multiple volunteers and interns on all aspects of client contact, litigation support, case management, and project development and providing supervision and co-counsel to junior staff attorneys as necessary
- Facilitating clients' access to intra-agency and outside resources and administering the provision of direct financial assistance and donations to clients
- Attending and participating in interagency conferences and legal or bar association committee meetings to keep abreast of developments in the areas of pro bono representation, domestic violence, and legal remedies for victims of domestic violence

The qualifications for this position include fluency in Spanish; a J.D. degree; admission to the New York State Bar Association; at least 3 years of relevant experience (preferred); strong legal, advocacy, and leadership skills; and high motivation to provide knowledgeable and empathic legal advocacy to domestic violence victims, while being sensitive to issues of diversity (Sanctuary for Families, 2017). The salaries for positions such as this vary but are competitive with those of most attorney jobs.

SUMMARY

Attending law school is an option upon the completion of a bachelor's degree. Having a law degree and passing the bar exam opens up doors for more than just criminal justice jobs. Getting into a high-ranked law school is highly dependent on how early you choose that path and adequately prepare for it. Two important factors in being accepted at a top law school are GPA and LSAT score.

The first step to take in preparing for law school is to register with the LSAC. The LSAC has everything you need for applying to law school and eases the process. LSAT practice tests can be found at the LSAC's website. Other highly important factors that admission committees will consider are letters of recommendation, personal statements, undergraduate studies, community involvement, and work experience.

Most students finance their degrees using student loans. Once enrolled in law school, students are advised to start networking with law professionals and building contact bases. During the third year of law school, it is a good idea to redo your résumé and create a professional cover letter in preparation for the application process. There are several job search websites you can peruse to find out which firms are seeking new employees.

Law careers in the criminal justice system include judge, arbitrator, mediator, prosecutor, public defender, court supervisor, staff attorney in victim services, court reporter, bailiff, and court clerk. Working for the government can offer job security and options for movement to new and better careers.

Women represent almost half of law associates, but minorities remain underrepresented. Race and ethnicity can be considered for law school admissions if a college desires enhanced diversity for a better classroom experience. Being bilingual makes you more marketable and opens doors that are available only to those who speak two (or more) languages.

DISCUSSION QUESTIONS

1. What are some preparations you can make while pursuing your bachelor's degree to enhance your chances of admission to a top law school?
2. What are some differences between law school classes and other college classes?
3. What are some advantages of signing up with the LSAC?
4. What types of things do admission committees look at in their decision-making processes?

REFERENCES

Best law schools. (2017). *U.S. News & World Report*. Retrieved from https://www.usnews.com/best-graduate-schools/top-law-schools/law-rankings? int=a1d108

Bureau of Labor Statistics. (2016). *Occupational outlook handbook*. Retrieved from https://www.bls.gov/ooh/

City of Georgetown. (2017). *Job opportunities*. Retrieved from https://georgetown.org/jobs/

City of Mesa, Arizona. (2017). *Career opportunities*. Retrieved from https://www.governmentjobs.com/careers/mesaaz/jobs/633440-0/pro-tem-judge-contract-position

City of Vista, California. (2017). *Job opportunities*. Retrieved from http://agency.governmentjobs.com/vista/default.cfm

Equal Justice Works. (2012, February 1). Law school student debt is just tip of the iceberg.

U.S. News & World Report. Retrieved from http://www.usnews.com/education/blogs/student-loan-ranger/2012/02/01/law-school-student-debt-is-just-tip-of-the-iceberg

Law School Admission Council. (2017). *Home page*. Retrieved from http://www.lsac.org

Merritt, J. (2016). What happened to the class of 2010? Empirical evidence of structural change in the legal profession. *Michigan State Law Review, 2015*(3), 1043–1123. doi: http://dx.doi.org/10.2139/ssrn.2577272

Sanctuary for Families. (2017). *Staff attorney, Bronx Family Justice Center*. Retrieved from https://careers-sanctuaryforfamilies.icims.com/jobs/1234/staff-attorney%2c-bronx-family-justice-center/job

Souman, J. (2009). Walking straight into circles. *Current Biology, 19*(18), 1538–1542. doi:10.1016/j.cub.2009.07.053

Spokane County. (2017). *Employment opportunities (non-civil service)*. Retrieved from http://www.spokanecounty.org/hr/employment.aspx

Texas Municipal League. (2017). *TML career center*. Retrieved from http://www.tml.org/careercenter

Weiss, D. C. (2011, November 10). Have women's law school numbers peaked? NAWL report suggests the pipeline may be shrinking. *ABA Journal*. Retrieved from http://www.abajournal.com/news/article/have_womens_law_school_numbers_peaked_nawl_report_suggests_the_pipeline_is_/

7 CORRECTIONS

INTRODUCTION

Corrections involves supervising juveniles and adults who have been arrested for criminal offenses, as well as those convicted or sentenced at later stages. It is more than just being a guard, keeping prisoners safe, and preventing escape. The system as a whole contributes to a safer community, which includes the following services:

- Rehabilitation of prisoners who will inevitably be released
- Supervision of those sentenced to community programs
- Determination and supervision of those who receive parole
- Supervision of those who receive alternative sentences

Covering all of these responsibilities necessitates a variety of positions, such as state correctional officer, county correctional officer, city jail detention officer, probation officer, parole officer, juvenile detention officer, corrections advisor, treatment officer, corrections counselor, juvenile review and release specialist, community corrections officer, and warden. A career in corrections might be a good alternative to law enforcement for those who are not interested in being first responders.

In this chapter, we will explore some of the jobs offered in corrections and look at some of the unique aspects of these positions. We will also cover some of the knowledge, qualifications, and skills that are required, as well as the salary ranges.

STATE CORRECTIONAL OFFICER

Being a correctional officer for a state prison, or a detention officer for a county or city jail, is a law enforcement job with arrest powers and authority for the use of force. A corrections officer is more than a guard. As a corrections officer, your job would be to maintain order at an institution crowded with disorderly guests. You would do more than just watch for problems to occur. Inmates are better off being active, so you would be supervising work activities and other organized affairs. You would find yourself settling disputes and enforcing rules while conducting searches and moving prisoners to their destinations, such as visits, court or parole hearings, and medical appointments.

If you lean toward becoming a correctional officer, you will be more successful if you have the "gift of gab." Just as police officers need to be good actors and deceivers, correctional officers need to be able to work with brilliant deceivers while being genuine, firm, and respectful. Most inmates are willing to conform to the rules and to verbal commands if they feel respected. A correctional officer must display a balance between power and control and must convey respect. If you have any issues with racial bias or a negative attitude toward criminals in general, they will pick up on it.

The Arizona Department of Corrections (ADC) employs approximately 9,500 professionals. To work for ADC, you need to be 21 years old and have a high school diploma or General Educational Development (GED) certificate. You need to be a U.S. citizen, possess a valid Arizona driver's license, and have no felony convictions. The first step in the hiring process is an entrance exam. You would be assessed through written and oral tests in the areas of general knowledge, human relations, reading comprehension, observation, communication skills, and your ability to follow directions. After passing these introductory tests, you would be given a conditional offer, but you would still have a few remaining hurdles. The first is the background check. As with most law enforcement jobs, you would be required to fill out a background questionnaire that covers your personal, criminal, employment, and driving histories. You would also be asked to submit your proof of age, residency, diploma, and possession of a driver's license. The next step is to pass a medical examination covering hearing, vision, laboratory tests, and medical history. The following step in the process is the physical fitness test, on which you would need to meet the minimum standards of aerobic fitness, muscular strength, endurance, and flexibility. To accomplish this, you might do exercises, such as push-ups, sit-ups, lifts of certain amounts of weight, stretch tests, and stair-step tests. The next test would be a psychological assessment to determine if you fit the profile of a successful correctional officer. A psychologist evaluates the results of these tests, and if there are any discrepancies, the psychologist is empowered to retest you. The final step is drug screening. When taking your first exam, you would be asked to sign a consent form for the screening and would later take that test, once you are contacted and asked to appear. You are given 48 hours in which to complete the drug screening test.

Correctional officers attend an academy, which is usually much shorter than police academies. The Arizona Correctional Officer Training Academy (COTA), which is located in the foothills of Tucson, is a 7-week live-in academy, with room and board provided for the recruits. While you attend the academy, you receive a salary and benefits. The training curriculum at COTA is divided into nine basic areas: ethics and professionalism, inmate management, legal issues, communications, officer safety, applied skills, security custody and control, conflict and crisis management, and medical and mental health issues. In the academy you are tested weekly through various assessment exercises. A vital component of the training is physical fitness, participation in which is mandatory. There are standards you must meet for aerobic and muscular fitness as well as flexibility. Firearm and self-defense classes are taught at the academy, with the aim of keeping the public, staff, and inmates safe. To graduate, you must demonstrate efficiency in self-defense. As part of firearm education, you would be trained in chemical agents, the use of force, and target identification and discrimination. A key ingredient of the training at COTA is on-the-job experience. Midway through the 7-week training, you would be assigned to an institution, in which you are shown a glimpse of the duties and responsibilities of a professional correctional officer.

Once out of the academy, with a salary between $32,916 and $39,664, you would be assigned to one of the 10 ADC facilities statewide to begin your career. On a good day at an ADC facility, you might routinely check each cell in your assigned area for contraband or signs of tampering and then log any violations. On a bad day, you might be covered with urine or feces thrown by inmates, verbally attacked, or assaulted with a strike, a kick, or an improvised weapon. Meanwhile, you are armed with little more than a communication device. Like any law enforcement officer, you would be held to a high standard in use-of-force decisions. You would continuously have your patience and temper tested. You would periodically find your name on official documents as the victim of assault. Some inmates have nothing to lose, so an assault charge is hardly a deterrent.

Even if your long-range goal is law enforcement with a city, county, state, or federal agency, correctional work gives you an opportunity for relevant experience. You will acquire valuable practice in communicating with your superiors, peers, and criminals. You will have a lead on most police academy recruits in the areas of officer safety and use-of-force strategies. However, a word of caution: You will also have the potential for annoying entries in your personnel file. When police agencies do their background checks on lateral applicants, they inquire about the candidates' personnel files. The agencies are interested in favorable entries but also in citizen complaints and internal investigations. Even if complaints or accusations are resolved in favor of an officer, the record remains in the file for a significant length of time, usually 3 to 5 years. The everyday work of a correctional officer can result in two or three file entries a year, even for an exemplary officer. It comes with the job. You may have some explaining to do, but the worst-case scenario is that you may never get the chance to explain if you are dropped from the process due to your personnel files.

In the hiring process for law enforcement jobs, you are often given a polygraph test. You are required to report every crime you have ever committed, not just the crimes you were convicted of. To work for the ADC, you are not required to take a polygraph test, and the criminal history requirement is "no felony conviction." Although there is no polygraph test given, the ADC tries its best to find model employees. They perform a thorough background check in the hopes of weeding out the bad apples, but some still slip through. As with the inappropriate conduct that periodically surfaces in police departments, there are correctional officers who commit vile acts, such as smuggling in contraband or physically and sexually abusing inmates. As in the police hiring process, you will be up against some outstanding candidates. There will also be plenty who are not much of a threat to winning your spot (Arizona Department of Corrections, 2017).

COUNTY DETENTION OFFICER

Detention officers work in county jails. People arrested by county officers and those arrested by state or city departments (and not released within 24 hours) are normally housed in county jails while awaiting their case resolutions. County jails also house criminals who have received a sentence of up to 1 year. Usually the most dangerous criminals are sentenced to longer terms, which are completed in prisons. But even the worst of the worst are held in county jails while they await trial and sentencing.

If you worked as a detention officer for the Guilford County Sheriff's Department in Greensboro, North Carolina, you would be assigned to one of its three facilities, monitoring inmates to ensure a safe and secure environment for sheriff's office personnel, civilian staff, and those incarcerated. Your pay range would be $35,661 to $41,061, with some incentives that can boost your salary. You would be paid extra for having a bachelor's degree, being fluent in Spanish, having served in the military, and willingness to work rotating shifts.

The qualifications to work for Guilford County include the following:

- Citizenship of the United States and age at least 21 at the time of employment
- Residency in Guilford County or one of the contiguous counties
- Ability to perform all of the essential job functions of an inexperienced officer (unassisted) at a pace and level of performance consistent with the actual job performance requirements
- Possession of a high school diploma or GED certificate
- Weight that is proportionate to height
- Ability to pass a drug test and a complete medical examination by a licensed physician, including psychological testing and evaluation
- Ability to pass a comprehensive background investigation by the sheriff's office, which includes work history, fingerprints, and polygraph test
- Good moral character and no history of conviction of a felony or a serious misdemeanor by a local, state, federal, or military court
- Good financial status and history (not in bankruptcy, no unpaid past-due accounts or judgments)

The hiring process for the Guilford County Sheriff's Department begins with an application, either online or in writing. The next steps include orientation, a physical fitness test, a written test, an oral interview, a background investigation, a psychological exam, and a medical exam. Guilford County Sheriff's Department does not require a polygraph test for its detention officers or deputies. Within the detention division, there are opportunities to move around and work on the Detention Response Team, as a field training officer, on the Gang Intelligence Unit, on the intake crew, or on the K-9 unit (Guilford County Sheriff's Office, 2017).

CITY JAILER

Police procedures require certain suspects to be handcuffed and transported to the police station for further follow-up. Police departments need the ability to temporarily detain those who are arrested during routine police work. At the station, an officer needs to be able to make phone calls; collect records; run computer queries; interview victims, witnesses, and suspects; eat lunch; and use the restroom. Leaving a suspect unsupervised is usually unauthorized and can be unsafe to the prisoner and coworkers. About half of the police departments in the United States employ fewer than 10 sworn personnel, thus making it unlikely that they have full-time jails. Smaller police departments often get by with lockable interview rooms or holding cells. Officers depend on one another to watch arrestees while they move around the building to accomplish routine tasks. Larger departments that can afford full-time jails are also tasked with the expenditure for a full-time jail staff.

City jailers take on a huge responsibility as they process prisoners, attend to prisoners' needs, and transport them to court or county jail. Not everyone is cut out for this type of work. Jailers face the possibility of assaults from prisoners, just as county detention officers and correctional officers do. City jailers search prisoners (who have already been searched by officers), finding drugs and dangerous weapons hidden under clothing, under hair, and in body cavities. Prisoners sometimes escape from jailers, usually during court transports. Prisoners in city jails have been killed during fights with one another, during fights with officers, and by suicide. Each time an incident such as this happens, city departments face possible payouts in lawsuit settlements.

As a city jailer in Avondale, Arizona, you would provide care, custody, and control of inmates in city jail; transport inmates (adults and juvenile) and their property to proper locations, ensuring that documentation is completed properly; and administer work furlough and inmate work programs at the discretion of the supervisor. You would complete all bookings and processing for newly arrested subjects on misdemeanor or felony offenses. You would maintain proper accountability and use of supplies for staff and inmate population. You would have full responsibility for a clean, safe environment in the jail. You would conduct numerous counts of the inmate population, conduct fire and safety inspections, and ensure that inmates are released appropriately. Your responsibilities would include supervision of visits, notification of victims when inmates are released, warrant pickups, and servicing orders of protection and injunctions against harassment. As a jailer, you would assist in the functions of patrol units to pick up and transport prisoners when required. You would assist the general public with questions regarding the status of housed inmates, direct callers to appropriate agencies, and provide notary service for patrol when juveniles are referred. Your job duties would include maintaining daily logs of shift activities and creating and maintaining arrest files on all prisoners processed through the police department. Processing prisoners would include paperwork, searching for contraband, fingerprinting, interviewing for any medical conditions, packaging prisoner property, and taking photos. You would need to ensure timely court appearances for all prisoners, escort prisoners to city court for appearances, prepare bond receipts, and collect bonds. There would also be times when you would supervise inmate visits by contacting visitors, making sure they are allowed to visit, checking visitors for warrants and contraband, supervising actual visits, tracking the number of visitors per inmate, searching inmates upon returning to jail, and performing interviews as required. Jailers also purchase food and prepare meals for inmates, including shopping for and storing food, preparing food, and dispensing meals on weekends and holidays. Jailers handle inmate work details by classifying inmates (often called trustees) who are allowed to work, instructing them in what is expected of them, and transporting inmates to off-site locations. There may also be times when jailers would need to respond to various locations to assist patrol officers or detectives on the scene by taking custody of prisoners. Last, you might find yourself performing warrant pickups or turnovers, picking up wanted persons at other jails, prisons, or outside agencies at various locations.

Qualifications for most jailer positions include the following:

- A high school diploma or GED certificate, no felony convictions, and no dishonorable discharge from the U.S. Armed Forces
- Any equivalent combination of experience, education, or training that provides the required knowledge, skills, and abilities, including course work, experience, or demonstrated work abilities in the areas of criminal justice, customer service, communication, social work, psychology, or sociology
- Terminal operator certification, cardiopulmonary resuscitation certification, first aid certification, and impact weapons and firearms certification
- Passing results on a physical fitness test, a panel interview, an extensive background investigation, a polygraph examination, a psychological evaluation, a medical exam, and a preemployment drug test
- For candidates with prior experience, a valid diploma from an approved correctional or detention officer academy or proof of comparable tenure and law enforcement experience as a certified peace officer

The physical fitness test for the Avondale jailer position includes a pass/fail 1.5-mile run in 14 minutes 15 seconds, 23 push-ups untimed, and 31 sit-ups in 1 minute. These are the minimum requirements to pass, but the Cooper Age and Gender Base Standards for Law Enforcement are used to determine an overall fitness percentage that will be averaged and combined with the panel interview scoring percentage before you proceed to the next phase. The pay for this position is $18.05 to $26.17 hourly (Avondale, Arizona, 2017).

Some smaller agencies combine different positions in order to accomplish their needs within the scope of the available budget. An example of this is at the Nodaway County Sheriff's Office in Maryville, Missouri, where there is a full-time position for a dispatcher/jailer. The primary duties are to work 50/50 between the communication center and the county jail. If you took this job you would answer 911 calls, dispatching the sheriff, fire department, and EMS on emergency and nonemergency calls for service. You would make various computer entries such as inquiries, warrants, missing persons, and stolen property. Your jailer duties would include processing and booking inmates, releasing inmates, and overseeing the care and safety of the inmates. You would need to be available to work all shifts, weekends, and holidays. You would need to possess a high school diploma or GED and have no criminal history. The salary is $25,657 per year (Nodaway County Missouri Sheriff's Office, 2017).

PAROLE AND PROBATION OFFICERS

Probation officers supervise convicted criminals who were originally sentenced to probation in lieu of jail or prison. Parole officers supervise those who serve time in prison and receive early release. Otherwise, both jobs are much the same. There is a lot of autonomy and empowerment with these positions. Some agencies require their probation and parole officers to carry firearms. The expectations of this work include keeping the public safe from harm, holding offenders accountable, and helping them succeed. As with many government jobs, the pay is mediocre, and the workload is massive.

A typical workday for a probation or parole officer might include home visits, office appointments, court hearings, and stakeouts. There are more cases assigned per officer than can be handled proficiently, so some clients are insufficiently supervised. Probation and parole officers rely on police officers to contact them if one of their clients gets arrested.

Typical duties for a parole/probation officer in the state of Michigan are as follows:

- Preparation of background reports on offenders convicted in Circuit Court, which will be utilized to determine sentences
- Supervision of offenders placed on community supervision through Court-ordered probation or parole from a state correctional facility
- Supervision of sex offenders and offenders placed on a variety of electronic monitoring devices, including Global Positioning System (GPS)
- Gender-specific, mentally ill, Interstate Compact, or other specialized caseloads as designated by the Deputy Director of Field Operations
- Assignment as an embedded agent to a local law enforcement agency, an institutional parole agent, or an Internet crimes against children agent (ICAC)
- Adherence to policy, procedures, director office memorandums (DOM), and guiding principles of the Department of Corrections in order to meet the goals of the department

In this position in Michigan, you would possess law enforcement powers and be required or permitted to carry a firearm while on duty. This is a position in which you would have regular unsupervised access to and direct contact with probationers or parolees, and it is a DART (Drug/Alcohol Test Designated) position, in accordance with civil service rules. If you are assigned as an institutional parole agent, you may have regular unsupervised access to and direct contact with prisoners more than 50% of the time. You would be required to make considerable independent judgments to carry out assignments that have significant impact on services or programs.

The education requirement for this position is a bachelor's degree in criminal justice, correctional administration, criminology, psychology, social work, counseling and guidance, child development, sociology, school social work, social work administration, education psychology, family relations, human services, or theology. The salary is $40,892.80 to $65,041.60 annually (State of Michigan, 2017).

The probation/parole services for juvenile and adult offenders are similar. Both are concerned with the supervision of released offenders; however, the methods and procedures vary slightly. A primary concern for juvenile probation is to help juvenile offenders avoid the circumstances that facilitated their criminal behavior and to channel them toward becoming productive members of their community. This often involves relocation, especially if the juvenile's family is part of the overall problem. It is common for the juvenile's release conditions to include correctional and behavioral skill counseling.

Adult probationers' crimes can range from very serious or violent crimes to relatively minor offenses. The goal of adult probation is to hold criminals accountable while facilitating change. Adult offenders who have been placed on probation are often required to obtain respectable jobs. The onus is on the adult probation department to provide offenders with the necessary means to avoid criminal behavior. The process of reintegration teaches probationers to accept personal responsibility for their actions. Additionally, the adult probation program employs a restorative justice approach to compensate victims and reduce the probability that the probationers will reoffend.

If you worked for the Florida Department of Juvenile Justice as a juvenile probation officer, your job would be to provide social services to assist in rehabilitating juvenile offenders who are in custody or on probation or parole. You would make recommendations for actions involving the rehabilitation plan and treatment of the offender, including employment, education, and conditional release stipulations. The duties for this position include the following:

- Initiating contact with the youth, family, victims, and law enforcement when referrals are received
- Conducting home and school visits as an integral part of the information gathering process
- Initiating contact with the victim to obtain opinions regarding case handling and disposition
- Using motivational interviewing to engage the youth and family to determine the youth's social, developmental, emotional, financial, and/or other needs
- Obtaining and reviewing collateral information such as abuse and neglect history, education, mental health, substance use, gang-related activity, and other pertinent information
- Conducting and documenting screenings, to identify the youth's risk and needs
- Facilitating the completion of comprehensive assessments, and if results indicate needed services, referring the youth and family for services
- Formulating case management strategies based on assessments
- Making service referrals to the appropriate providers and follow-up actions that are required
- Making supervision and treatment recommendations to the state attorney and other judicial partners
- Discussing with the youth and family a safety plan that focuses on averting exposure to situations of risk, harm, or injury to prevent victimization

To be considered for this position, you would need knowledge of case management practices, interviewing and counseling techniques, and computer programs. You would need to have the ability to make recommendations concerning the processing and handling of delinquent youth, develop case plans, communicate effectively, determine work priorities, and establish and maintain an effective working relationship with community and judicial partners. You would need a bachelor's degree from an accredited college and a valid driver's license. The salary for this position is $1,128.63 biweekly (Florida Department of Juvenile Justice, 2017).

JUVENILE REHABILITATION SPECIALIST

You can find a variety of positions related to probation, parole, and community corrections depending on your state of residence. Probation and parole officers are more or less supervisors, whereas juvenile rehabilitation specialists (JRSs) are more like teachers. In Phoenix, Arizona, these life coaches are called transition-to-adulthood specialists. In New York City, they are called retention specialists. The state of Washington has a position of juvenile rehabilitation coordinator (JRC), which is under the umbrella of the Department of Social and Health Services. As a JRC, you would provide comprehensive case management, transition planning, counseling services, sex offender treatment, facility security, and group supervision to an assigned caseload of youth and their families. You would also provide cognitive/behavioral treatment and skills training to youth committed to juvenile rehabilitation (JR) care by the juvenile courts.

To be a juvenile rehabilitation coordinator in Washington, you must have a bachelor's degree and 1 year of professional experience in casework, counseling, probation and parole, social services, planning, directing, and/or facilitating youth group activities or experience in a related field. If you have 1 year of experience as a juvenile rehabilitation counselor assistant, you would not need any other experience for this job. A master's degree in psychology, sociology, social work, social sciences, or an allied field would also substitute for the required experience. This job pays $3,541.00 to $4,644.00 monthly (State of Washington, 2017).

HOME DETENTION OFFICER

The juvenile division of Cuyahoga County Juvenile Court of Common Pleas employs home detention officers who provide intense supervision, monitoring, and reporting of youth awaiting court hearings or placement. If you worked for Cuyahoga County as a home detention officer, you would have the following duties:

- Provide close supervision, contact, and surveillance of youths referred to home detention
- Contact youths at home, school, or in the community and assist the youths in functioning properly and remaining trouble free
- Assess the youths' behavior and determine the appropriate case referrals
- Make referrals to appropriate community agencies, health centers, etc.

- Complete various reports and documentation related to youths' behavior, accountability, and home detention statistics
- Be available to work all shifts as required

To qualify for this position, you would need to demonstrate an ability to communicate effectively both orally and in writing. You would need skills in interviewing, knowledge of juvenile justice and juvenile behavior, and an understanding of adolescent growth and development. You would need a working knowledge of community resources. You would have to possess basic computer skills and have knowledge of Microsoft Office. It is preferred that the person in this position be bilingual and have an ability to communicate using sign language. You would need a bachelor's degree in social science or a related area. You would be required to have 1 year of work experience with juveniles and possess a valid Ohio Driver's License. You need your own motor vehicle and must be available 24/7. The annual salary is $40,762.09 (Cuyahoga County Juvenile Court of Common Pleas, 2017).

PROBATION AIDE

Sacramento, California, employs probation aides. This position is under close supervision. You would learn to apply the principles and techniques of probation work; supervise and counsel individuals detained in, committed to, or sheltered in one of several county juvenile institutions; supervise minors assigned to work projects; and provide close supervision of minors placed on home supervision. In Sacramento, this position is an on-call job, so you would be required to be immediately available when needed.

The required knowledge base for a probation aide includes the following:

- Principles and techniques applicable to the care and rehabilitation of juvenile delinquents
- The growth, development, needs, and problems of minors; symptoms of behavior disorders; and group dynamics
- Codes, standards, and regulations governing the treatment of juveniles in juvenile halls, camps, ranches, or schools
- Principles of investigation and laws governing the search, seizure, and preservation of evidence
- Counseling techniques, basic housekeeping techniques, hygienic standards, motivational techniques, crisis intervention, self-defense, appropriate use of force and security techniques, and rights and liabilities of peace officers

You would also need to have the ability to accomplish the following tasks:

- Securing the respect and confidence of adolescents, coping with hostility and aggressive behavior
- Working well as a member of a team, exercising good judgment and acting calmly in emergency situations, and recognizing subtle changes in behavior

- Reading, writing, and speaking English at a level necessary for satisfactory job performance
- Preparing concise and clear reports
- Communicating with individuals from a variety of socioeconomic backgrounds, establishing and maintaining effective working relationships

These lists of requirements can be of help to those who write your letters of recommendation. When you contact professors or other references, share with them all you can about the job, so that they can tailor their letters to what the employer is looking for. It will be helpful for your references when they are contacted for background checks. It would also benefit you to study what the employer is looking for before your interview.

The minimum qualification for probation aides is the equivalent of an associate of arts degree from an accredited college or university. Up to 1 year of the required education may be substituted with experience in full-time, or equivalent part-time, paid law enforcement or correctional work at a probation agency, parole agency, or correctional institution. You would also need to meet the following requirements:

- Be a citizen of the United States or a permanent resident alien who is eligible for and has applied for citizenship (any permanent resident alien shall be disqualified from holding the position if his or her application for citizenship is denied)
- Be at least 18 years of age

GUEST SPEAKER

JULIE GLOVER, SERGEANT, SAN DIEGO SHERIFF'S DEPARTMENT

As a former marine and a mom, I wanted to pursue a paramilitary-based career that offered a consistent schedule. I joined the San Diego Sheriff's Department as a detention deputy.

Upon graduating from the 11th Corrections Academy, I was assigned to the Las Colinas Detention Facility. I worked as a deputy for about 18 months and became a training officer. After another 2 years, I was selected as the training coordinator at the facility.

Ready for some new endeavors, I applied, tested, and was selected as a classification deputy at the San Diego Central Jail, a male booking facility. I continued to do my job professionally and with great enthusiasm and eventually returned to Las Colinas Detention Facility as a classification deputy.

Three years later, I was promoted to sergeant. I have been a sergeant for almost 15 years. As a sergeant, I have the ability to mentor and develop subordinates, a truly rewarding opportunity.

As a woman, particularly as a mom, I recognize that the challenge is balancing your family life with your career. With a supportive husband behind me, I have managed to enjoy both.

My advice for potential candidates is to get a formal education. Should you have contact with law enforcement (e.g., a speeding ticket), be respectful and polite. Avoid any negative elements (friends partying too much, using narcotics, etc.). Surround yourself with positive people with like goals and ambitions. This will help you remain focused and enhance your ability to obtain a career in law enforcement!

- Be fingerprinted for the purposes of searching local, state, and national fingerprint files to disclose any criminal record; in addition, a classifiable set of fingerprints must be furnished to the U.S. Department of Justice and to the Federal Bureau of Investigation
- Be found to be free of any physical, emotional, or mental condition that might adversely affect the exercise of the powers of a peace officer

A criminal history and background check would also be conducted for this position. Pursuant to Sacramento County civil service rules, candidates found to have been convicted of felonies will be disqualified. You would frequently be expected to perform a wide variety of physical tasks, such as standing, walking, running, stooping, bending, climbing stairs, and lifting individuals, which require strength, coordination, endurance, and agility. In addition, there may be occasional contact with hostile individuals, and you may be subjected to physical and verbal abuse while restraining individuals. The pay for this position is $57,336.48 annually (City of Sacramento, 2017).

PAROLE BOARD HEARING OFFICER

You may have witnessed scenes in the movies of parole board hearings. A parole board has power and authority similar to that of a judge in sentencing defendants to prison time. Just as during the initial sentencing, decisions are based on a variety of criteria, such as the seriousness of the offense, the prior record, probation and parole history, and input from victims. The parole board also looks at the conduct of an individual while in prison and considers the available resources in the community that may increase an inmate's success in reentering society.

As a parole board hearing officer in Tennessee, you would be responsible for conducting parole grant hearings, revocation hearings, rescission hearings, appeal hearings, and probable cause hearings at all county jails and Department of Correction institutions. You would also take confidential testimony, record and summarize the hearings, make recommendations for release or revocation, and submit the files to the parole board for voting.

The education and experience needed for a position like this makes it unlikely a person would be hired right out of college. You would need a bachelor's degree and experience equivalent to 3 years of full-time professional work in either correctional counseling, probation, parole, or criminal justice administration. Graduate hours can be substituted for experience, and qualifying experience can be substituted for educational requirements. Possession of a law degree and experience equivalent to 1 year of full-time professional experience in adjudication, legal representation, correctional counseling, probation, parole, or criminal justice administration would also satisfy the requirements. The salary for hearing officer is $2,908 to $4,652 monthly (State of Tennessee, 2017).

PRIVATE PRISONS

Most states contract with for-profit private prisons. Prisons in the private sector can be male only, female only, co-gendered, unclassified, or juvenile only. There are twice as many juvenile facilities as there are facilities for adults. In order for private prisons to contract with state governments, they must follow the state's rules and regulations, including training, health care, food service, and education. Although the government can stop doing business with private prisons at any time, the outlook is good for their future growth. At least 12 states have contracted with private prisons for a guaranteed number of prisoners to be housed, which increases the likelihood of job security for prison employees.

To work as a corrections officer with Management & Training Corporation (MTC) in Venus, Texas, you would be one of more than 10,000 employees of the third-largest operator of private adult correctional facilities. Officers there are responsible for the control and discipline of all offenders in the facility, in accordance with MTC and Texas Department of Criminal Justice (TDCJ) directives. If you were to be assigned to the transportation department, you would be responsible for transporting offenders to and from the facility in accordance with required procedures. These are a few of the daily functions you would perform:

- Searching for contraband and providing security
- Counting, feeding, and supervising offenders in housing, working, and other areas
- Transporting and transferring offenders on foot or in vehicles
- Restraining and securing assaultive offenders as needed
- Responding to emergencies

To be hired at MTC you must have a high school diploma or equivalent. Your continued employment would be contingent on passing exams and skill tests in the TDCJ Correctional Officer Pre-Service Training Academy. A valid Texas driver's license with an acceptable driving record is required. In this position, you could enjoy excellent benefits and paid time-off programs, free on-site gym access, 401k matching, education assistance, and a salary comparable with government correctional officers (Texas Department of Criminal Justice, 2017).

DIVERSITY IN CORRECTIONS

The entry of women into correctional work parallels their entry into police work. It has taken some time, but currently, women hold positions in all categories of correctional jobs in all 50 states as probation officers, parole officers, detention officers, supervisors, and administrators. Just as in police work, women continue to prove their value and enjoy higher levels of respect and acceptance from their male counterparts. Equally similar is the value women bring to the work through their different way of approaching the job. As in police work, women are considered less likely to need to use force, because of their less threatening approach and polished verbal skills.

Almost a third of correctional employees in the United States are nonwhite, with Mississippi having the highest percentage of minority employees and Utah the least. Many correctional facilities are working to increase their numbers of minority employees. These efforts are in response to socially desirable goals of building a more diverse workforce in efforts to correct past racial discrimination. Initiatives to increase minority recruitment include correctional representatives' attending job fairs; advertising with media that are predominantly minority based; working more closely with community-based organizations such as the NAACP, the Urban League, and La Raza; and soliciting applicants from historically black colleges and universities (DiMarino, 2009).

SUMMARY

Working in corrections involves more than just guarding prisoners. To keep the community safer, as well as its own employees, the correctional system involves rehabilitation, supervision, monitoring prisoners' behavior, and determining early releases or violations. There are many positions in corrections, such as state correctional officer, county correctional officer, city jail detention officer, probation officer, parole officer, juvenile detention officer, correction advisor, treatment officer, corrections counselor, juvenile review and release specialist, community corrections officer, and warden.

Many police officers enter corrections initially as a rung in their climb toward a law enforcement career. All corrections positions require some level of schooling or experience and the passing of a background investigation and criminal history check. Only some agencies require polygraph tests. Those entering this field as a step toward law enforcement need to be careful not to taint their personnel files. The potential is great for physical confrontations with prisoners, which ultimately end up as investigations and reports in employees' files. Too many entries in a personnel file could shed bad light on an employee, even if the employee did nothing wrong.

When asking for a letter of recommendation, you'll help yourself by providing your source with the list of requirements and qualifications to help the letter writer know what characteristics and skills are the most relevant to include. Keeping that list handy would give you something to peruse prior to a job interview to help you formulate your answers.

Diversity issues in corrections mirror those in police work. Historically, correctional work has been performed predominantly by white men. Correctional systems are actively recruiting women and minorities to improve the quality of their staffs as well as relations with their inmate populations.

DISCUSSION QUESTIONS

1. Applicants for correctional jobs rarely undergo polygraph testing. Do you feel that they should? Why or why not? For what other careers would you recommend that polygraph test results be considered when making hiring decisions?
2. In correctional work and police work, a personnel file is kept that stores records of internal investigations, even if the officer being investigated is found innocent of the allegations. Do you feel this is a necessary procedure? Why or why not?
3. What advantages or disadvantages are there in having women working in corrections? What about minorities? Does your opinion vary depending on the position within the correctional system?

REFERENCES

Arizona Department of Corrections. (2017). *Employment opportunities with ADC.* Retrieved from http://www.azcorrections.gov/adc/employment/ADCCareers.aspx

Avondale, Arizona. (2017). *Employment opportunities.* Retrieved from http://www.avondaleaz.gov/government/departments/human-resources/careers

City of Sacramento. (2017). *Sacramento county jobs.* Retrieved from https://www.governmentjobs.com/careers/sacramento

Cuyahoga County Juvenile Court of Common Pleas. (2017). *Home detention officer.* Retrieved from https://juvenilecourt.applicantstack.com/x/detail-internal/a2i492nktt8x

DiMarino, F. (2009). Recruiting minority employees in corrections. *Corrections.com.* Retrieved from http://www.corrections.com/news/article/21076

Florida Department of Juvenile Justice. (2017). Juvenile probation officer. Retrieved from https://jobs.myflorida.com/job

Guilford County Sheriff's Office. (2017). *Detention officer.* Retrieved from http://www.gcsonc.com/detention-officer

Nodaway County Missouri Sheriff's Office. (2017). *Dispatcher/Jailer.* Retrieved from https://www.indeed.com/cmp/Nodaway-County-Missouri-Sheriff's-Office/jobs/Dispatcher-Jailer-f8022913f9e8ebfc? q=jailer

State of Michigan. (2017). *State of Michigan job openings.* Retrieved from https://www.governmentjobs.com/careers/michigan

State of Tennessee. (2017). *Tennessee Department of Human Resources.* Retrieved from http://agency.governmentjobs.com/tennessee/default.cfm? action=viewclassspec&ClassSpecID=102862

State of Washington. (2017). *State of Washington job opportunities.* Retrieved from https://www.governmentjobs.com/careers/washington/jobs/1766632-0/dshs-juvenile-rehabilitation-coordinator

Texas Department of Criminal Justice. (2017). Employment opportunities. Retrieved from http://www.tdcj.state.tx.us/divisions/hr/index.html

8 PRIVATE SECURITY AND INVESTIGATIONS

INTRODUCTION

The terrorist attacks of September 11, 2001, initiated drastic changes in the United States, including enhanced security along our borders and within our cities, counties, and states. The private security business boomed and was at long last recognized as an important appendage to law enforcement. Why weren't private security personnel used to a greater degree prior to 9/11? Why did private security rapidly expand faster than law enforcement (other than border patrol, of course)?

Security officers have been employed for a very long time at hospitals, shopping malls, apartment complexes, and individual businesses after hours; for transporting money and guarding buildings during remodeling or new construction; at the entrances to big events or important government buildings; and during temporary hoarding, such as in Black Friday or Christmas sales at retail stores. Sometimes the presence of security is essential for insurance purposes, and sometimes businesses hire security officers just because the benefits outweigh the costs.

Sometimes businesses choose to hire off-duty police officers as security personnel, even though the cost is greater. They may feel that the advantage of having a sworn peace officer on the premises offsets the additional cost. What are the advantages? It depends on the purpose of the security. When a business is concerned mainly with deterring crime, a security officer's visibility will likely do the job just fine. If a business or government agency foresees a likelihood of arrests and physical confrontations, using a trained, certified, gun-toting peace officer might be the most prudent choice.

There has traditionally been some tension between private security and the public police. Although there have been substantial improvements, many police officers have long looked at security officers as inferior, and thus have not displayed adequate respect. Security officers who might already feel inferior to sworn law enforcement personnel don't appreciate being made to feel that way by the police. Why the lack of respect? Well, it is no secret that being hired as a police officer is difficult, the training is intensive, and the authority and empowerment are inimitable and comprehensive. Being hired at a private security firm sometimes entails mediocre standards (with no polygraph testing), followed by minimal training, and resulting in slightly higher than minimum wages in exchange for undesirable hours. This is not to say that security officers are any less qualified than police officers, but likely those who crave law enforcement careers, and could qualify, would choose to do so over working in private security. Also, those who desire police work but don't feel that they can qualify, or those who leave or retire from police work, can find great satisfaction in security work. One can also find positions in the security arena that are practical careers with good pay, reasonable benefits, and enough challenge and excitement to impel someone out of bed each day for work.

A new trend during the community era, and particularly following 9/11, has been for law enforcement to work more closely with the community, especially all the personnel who may find themselves as first responders to terrorist activities or other catastrophic events. There has been an increase in training for schools, hospitals, and security firms in the area of incident command. Some police agencies have invited security officers to join them in certain training activities. Many police personnel, who have historically had the "us vs. them" attitude, have reconsidered the way they view civilians, including security officers, and respect them as important parts of a larger team. Police officers, as well as the community as a whole, realize the benefits of having full-time, visible security at places such as water treatment plants, power plants, dams, financial centers, oil refineries, and railroad lines. Why did it take a catastrophic event such as 9/11 to connect law enforcement to all these available resources? Why didn't law enforcement involve its community partners more efficiently in crime prevention strategies decades ago? This can be answered with this parable, which has been used throughout the world, called "The Flying Turkeys":

> There once was a group of turkeys. They spent their days doing turkey stuff—gobbling, hanging out, dreading Thanksgiving, and not flying.
>
> Then one day, one of the turkeys announced that they were all invited to a seminar where they would be trained by a flying turkey. They were so stoked, because this flying turkey was going to teach them how to fly! They couldn't believe it. They got their group together and walked to the seminar.
>
> They stood around in their group waiting.
>
> Then all of a sudden, one of the turkeys noticed something in the sky coming toward them. As it got closer, they saw that it was a flying turkey!
>
> He swooped down and landed in the middle of the group. It was incredible!
>
> For the next few hours, the flying turkey taught them all about flying. He showed them how to use their wings and the wind to fly.
>
> Later that day, he brought them to a cliff, and one by one, each turkey jumped off and flew. It was amazing. The turkeys couldn't believe it. They soared through the air. They went above the clouds. They did flips and dive bombs. They did things they never could have imagined.
>
> It was the greatest experience of their lives. They now knew how to fly. They were so excited. They would never have to touch the ground again! They felt amazing. This was so much better and quicker than walking. Why hadn't they learned this before?
>
> The seminar ended, and they all landed back at the main seminar area. The turkeys waved good-bye as their flying instructor took off and flew to another turkey seminar.
>
> The group of turkeys then talked all about their great day as they walked home.

It is a normal tendency for all of us to be somewhat slow to change. We tend to enjoy our comfort zones. For years, police officers would have briefings, drive to and around their beats looking for bad guys and answering calls, and then return to the station to let someone else have a turn. The crime rate continued to rise, more officers were hired to drive around, and the crime rate continued to rise. Then someone came up with the idea of crime analysis, and someone else suggested a repeat-offender program, and yet another innovator realized the value of involving the community in crime prevention and problem solving. Yet even today, not every agency has adopted these programs and strategies to their fullest potential. Although using resources such as private security in conjunction with police isn't necessarily a cutting-edge vision, it's exciting to see these two powerhouses start to come together toward a common goal.

Some of the prominent jobs related to private security include security officer, private investigator, loss prevention officer, and armed security guard. These jobs carry a level of danger, but most do not involve carrying a firearm. Many security jobs are also done independently, without backup close by. In some positions, such as loss prevention, you are rarely empowered to make arrests, even if the law allows you to. When you are in uniform, the public associates you with peace officers and therefore has high expectations of your assistance, regardless of your limited authority and responsibility. Nonetheless, private security work is a necessary entity in our nation and a continuously growing industry. Some positions in the private sector are actually very similar to law enforcement work. An important difference for students is the age requirement. Most security agencies hire applicants at 18 years old. This could be a great way to get work experience on your résumé and make some decent money while going to school. Let's explore some of the possible careers.

SECURITY OFFICER

Allied Universal Security (AUS) was formed by a merger between AlliedBarton Security Services and Universal Services of America. AUS provides trained security personnel to many industries, including commercial real estate, higher education, health care, residential communities, chemical and petrochemical, government, manufacturing and distribution, financial institutions, and shopping centers. At the time of the merger, AlliedBarton had approximately 60,000 employees in 120 offices across the country. Universal Services had approximately 80,000 employees. Today the merged company has more than 140,000 employees, making it the leading security company in the United States. AlliedBarton was originally headquartered in Conshohocken, Pennsylvania, and has been American owned and managed since 1957. Universal Services of America was originally based in Santa Ana, California, and has been American owned and managed since 1965.

AUS offers on-the-job, web-based, and ongoing training programs for all personnel, from security officers through executive-level managers. Their training includes industry-specific programs that are customized for the security challenges in several of the markets they serve. By using employee retention programs and promotions from within, AUS is able to foster a culture of quality security officers and customer satisfaction. As an AUS security officer, you would be responsible for the safety and security of the facility and act as a visible deterrent to crime and client rule infractions. You would be responsible for detecting and reporting suspicious, unsafe, or criminal acts at or near your assigned post, which may be a threat to the property, clients, guests, or employees at the site. Although essential activities may differ based on which facility you are assigned to, below are some of the standard duties:

- Ensure the facility is provided with high-quality security services to protect people and property
- Report safety concerns, security breaches, and unusual circumstances both verbally and in writing
- Build, improve, and maintain effective relationships with both client employees and guests
- Answer questions and assist guests and employees with their needs
- Answer phones or greet guests and employees in a professional manner

AUS requires its security officers to be at least 18 years of age, to have a high school diploma or General Educational Development certificate (GED), to have the ability to communicate effectively both orally and in writing, to be authorized to work in the United States, and to have the ability to perform the essential functions of the position with or without reasonable accommodation. To work for AUS, you must successfully complete a background investigation and a post-offer/pre-employment drug/alcohol test.

For all full-time positions, AUS offers medical, dental, vision, flex spending, 401k, an anniversary bonus, and an on-the-spot recognition program. The company promotes from within. You can start with no security experience (Allied Universal Security, 2017).

Some colleges employ civilian security officers in lieu of (or to supplement) their campus police forces. One such institution is Grand Canyon University in Arizona, which employs full-time campus safety officers to monitor access to campus facilities, patrol the campus, respond to emergencies, document incidents, conduct investigations, enforce parking regulations, and interact with campus communities. Typical responsibilities include guard assignments and patrol assignments but may involve only one area depending on business need. Performing the guard assignment, which is the majority of shift assignments, means you would be assigned to a specific campus/building stationary access point. For your patrol time, you would use a motorized vehicle (golf cart or car) or be on foot or bicycle, to patrol all areas of the campus, including classrooms and the physical plant (buildings, offices, arena, storage, warehouse, parking lots), to observe and report suspicious activity, and to ensure that buildings are safe and secure. You would write citations for parking and moving violations and enforce the student code of conduct. Your specific responsibilities would include the following:

- Providing escort services for visitors, students, staff, and faculty as necessary and providing other public assistance such as lockout services and jump starts
- Watching for, reporting, and responding to reports of irregularities, such as security breaches, facility and safety hazards, and emergency situations

- Maintaining accurate documentation of patrol and guard activities
- Conducting traffic stops and writing citations and booting vehicles, if necessary
- Conducting interviews and preliminary investigations concerning complaints, accidents, violations of student conduct, or calls for assistance
- Providing assistance for emergencies such as medical, bomb threats, and fires
- Giving emergency first aid (which may include CPR and use of an AED) and determining whether an ambulance or other medical assistance is needed
- Modeling and supporting a community-oriented approach to providing safety and security
- Interacting with faculty, staff, students, and community with a positive demeanor and professional manner
- Participating in disaster/emergency drills and recommending improvements
- Cooperating with campus staff and external law enforcement agencies while conducting investigations
- Testifying in court as needed

For this position, you need a high school diploma or GED. It is preferred that you have at least 1 year of experience as a safety officer or similar occupation in protecting and safeguarding life and property. It would be a plus if you had an associate's degree from an accredited college/university and a certification in CPR, first aid, and first responding. You would need to be physically fit enough to handle the daily responsibilities and have the stamina to chase, apprehend, subdue, and restrain individuals if required. You need a driver's license, and you would need to pass a drug test (Grand Canyon University, 2017).

There is a similar position with Laramie County Community College (LCCC) in Cheyenne, Wyoming. Campus safety officers (CSOs) at LCCC work around the clock, 365 days a year on the Cheyenne campus to enforce campus regulations, campus traffic and parking rules, to provide emergency first aid care, to monitor public safety, and to provide limited emergency vehicle assistance. Officers work closely with the Laramie County Sheriff's Department regarding any criminal activity that may occur on campus.

Under the supervision of the director, the CSOs maintain the safety and security of people and property on the college campus by patrolling areas and enforcing rules and regulations. A CSO performs routine security and public safety patrol duties, including checking for fires, vandalism, suspicious activity or persons, and safety hazards. CSOs are first responders to emergency situations and may need to provide off-campus emergency services if required.

The required education for a job with LCCC is an associate's degree in criminal justice or related field or 2 years of law enforcement experience in lieu of education, during which comparable knowledge, skills, and abilities have been achieved. A bachelor's degree is preferred. You would need 2 years of law enforcement or security experience, a valid driver's license, and basic first aid and CPR certifications. The pay for this position is $15.03 per hour (Laramie County Community College, 2017).

Security officers are also utilized at airports. They are the men and women who examine your passport and boarding pass, check them again at another point, and stand at the scanners looking over your shoes, purse, computer, and carry-on bags. You could be one of them! As a transportation security officer at Klamath Falls Airport in Oregon, you could earn anywhere from $29,131 to $43,697 per year, depending on your experience and expertise.

As a transportation security officer at Wendover Municipal Airport in Utah, you would provide security and protection for air travelers, airports, and aircraft in a courteous and professional manner. This includes the following duties:

- Operating various screening equipment and technology to identify dangerous objects in baggage, cargo, and on passengers and preventing those objects from being transported onto aircraft
- Performing searches and screening
- Controlling terminal entry and exit points
- Interacting with the public, giving directions, and responding to inquiries
- Maintaining focus and awareness while working in a noisy and stressful environment
- Engaging in continual development of critical thinking skills necessary to mitigate actual and potential security threats by identifying, evaluating, and applying appropriate situational options and approaches
- Retaining and implementing knowledge of all applicable standard operating procedures

To work in this capacity, you would be an employee of the Transportation Security Administration (TSA). That agency requires employees to have a high school diploma or a GED. You would need at least one year of full-time work experience in the security industry, aviation screening, or as an X-ray technician. You must also be proficient in the English language. This position is considered part time and pays $19.21 to $25.80 per hour (Transportation Security Administration, 2017).

GUEST SPEAKER
TIMOTHY W. NEWTON, PRIVATE SECURITY SUPERVISOR

In 2008, I enrolled at Everest College–Phoenix to obtain my criminal justice degree. I began working in private security to support my family while attending school, as well as to acquire valuable experience in the criminal justice field.

My first day out of training and orientation, I was teamed with a security supervisor. We were dispatched to several calls that day, including a couple of shoplifting incidents from stores in the mall, rendering first aid to an injured mall patron, and a vehicle break-in in the mall parking lot.

I quickly learned that this was much different from any other job I had been at before; in fact, I looked forward to going to work every day. I liked the challenge of adapting to different scenarios and helping people. I became determined to learn this job from my supervisors and from the police officers I interfaced with on a regular basis. Eventually, I was hired to a position as an armed patrol sergeant-supervisor.

If you enter into a private security career, be prepared to write clear, concise incident reports and patrol logs. You may be subpoenaed to testify in court, as I have a few times. Take classes in report writing, criminal justice management, and policing. At the management level, a minimum of an associate's degree in criminal justice is a normal job prerequisite. The modern security officer also needs to possess better than average communication skills. Your verbal communication is your first line of defense and can defuse many a tense situation.

PRIVATE INVESTIGATOR

Private investigation may be an enjoyable profession for some. Investigators are often hired by large businesses, attorneys' offices, and insurance companies. An example of an investigator position exists in the California Department of Insurance. In this position, you would conduct felony criminal investigations of insurance fraud and related penal statutes, both state and federal. You would make arrests, interrogate suspects, interview witnesses, work with informants, prepare comprehensive written reports, and use sophisticated surveillance and electronic evidence-gathering equipment. Investigators are expected to work undercover and to testify as expert witnesses for prosecutors in state and federal courts. Investigators must work unusual hours on short notice and also travel throughout the state. As an investigator, you would have to carry a weapon and successfully qualify at quarterly weapon qualifications and meet all California Commission on Peace Officer Standards and Training requirements. In this position, you would perform a full range of peace officer duties and responsibilities in the accomplishment of your assignments. Because this position is designated as a peace officer, a background check, fingerprinting, and a psychological screening and medical examination are required. Applicants with prior fraud investigation experience are preferred.

To be eligible for a position such as this, you would need to possess a degree from a 4-year college with a major in criminal justice, law enforcement, criminology, administration of justice, or police science or a minor in law enforcement, criminology, administration of justice, or police science, with evidence that the following courses or their equivalents have been completed:

- Introduction to criminal justice
- Introduction to criminal law
- Basic investigation
- Evidence
- Criminal procedure
- Philosophy of law

The California Department of Insurance also accepts a minimum of 2 years of peace officer experience in a criminal investigative assignment at a government agency and 2 years of college or recent experience in state service as a peace officer investigating automobile, workers' compensation, or property and casualty insurance fraud. The department also desires that an investigator have the ability to be a laision with other law enforcement and prosecuting agencies in the region, be a graduate of the Regular Basic Course or the Specialized Investigators Basic Course, and have verbal and written fluency in Spanish, Vietnamese, Tagalog, Russian, Korean, Chinese, or another foreign language. The monthly salary for this position ranges from $4,412 to $7,103 (State of California, 2017).

Another type of investigator is a health care fraud investigator. Medicare hires investigators all over the country. Their mission is to detect and deter fraud and abuse in Medicare. This position requires the use of a variety of tools to initiate referrals, identify subjects, develop investigations for law enforcement, and assist in education and overpayment recovery. The investigator works with internal resources and external agencies to develop investigations and take corrective actions as well as respond to requests for data and support.

As a health care fraud investigator with NCI Information Systems in Detroit, Michigan, you would perform in-depth evaluation and analysis of potential fraud cases and requests for information using claims information and other sources of data. You would support the development of complex cases that involve high dollar amounts, sensitive issues, or that otherwise meet criteria for referral to law enforcement, recoupment of overpayment, or administrative action based on reactive and proactive data analysis. The responsibilities in this position include the following:

- Conducting independent investigations resulting from the discovery of situations that are suspected to involve fraud, waste, or abuse
- Completing written referrals to law enforcement and taking steps to initiate recoupment of overpaid monies
- Referring suspected instances of apparent unethical or improper practices or unprofessional conduct to the appropriate entity
- Responding to requests for information from law enforcement
- Maintaining cases that were referred to law enforcement
- Participating in on-site audits in conjunction with investigation development
- Providing support of cases at hearing/appeal and ALJ level
- Maintaining the chain of custody on all documents while following all confidentiality and security guidelines

You would be required to have at least 1 year of experience in program integrity, investigation/detection, or a related field that demonstrates expertise in reviewing, analyzing/developing information, and making appropriate decisions. You need a high school diploma, but it is preferred that you have a college degree in a related field such as criminal justice, statistics, or data analysis. Preference is given to those with experience in fraud detection. The annual salary is $43,000 to $57,000 (NCI Information Systems, 2017).

Insight Service Group (ISG) is a national investigative and medical management services firm specializing in cost containment and antifraud-related services. They hire individuals for part-time surveillance and field investigative positions. The ideal candidate must have a strong work ethic, be self-motivated, have good problem-solving skills, and be team oriented. To be employed with ISG you must be able to work independently, have strong time management skills, flexibility to travel, and strong communication skills. You would need to be willing to work flexible hours. ISG prefers that you have a criminal justice degree, but it is not required. Candidates must have the following:

Private investigator license

A reliable vehicle

A cell phone, in order to be in contact with a case manager while on surveillance

A digital video camera with date and time stamp software and the ability to upload video

Proficiency using Word and ability to write detailed reports

- Ability and willingness to travel as necessary within a multistate location (Insight Service Group, 2017)

Attorneys need individuals to do their investigative work. Private firms pay their investigators very well, but only very large firms have full-time positions. Full-time investigator positions can often be found in government departments. One such job is an investigator with the Public Advocacy Division of the Office of the Attorney General for the District of Columbia in Washington, DC. The Public Advocacy Division investigates and litigates civil cases aimed at protecting the public interest.

One of the areas you would work with is the Housing and Community Justice Section, which works with community groups, tenant organizations, and district government agencies to address nuisance properties, litigate cases essential to protecting affordable housing and tenants' rights, and litigates cases to protect residents from other abuses such as wage theft. You would also work with the Public Integrity Unit, which brings enforcement cases against companies and individuals that engage in unlawful commercial activity causing harm to the public or harm to the district government itself, including cases seeking damages or injunctive relief for violations of the antitrust, consumer protection, environmental, antifraud, nonprofit, and charities laws. In your capacity as an investigator, you would plan and conduct complex civil investigations to prosecute violations of the District of Columbia's False Claims Act, particularly alleged nonresident tuition fraud and wage theft, as well as other areas of law handled by the Division.

Responsibilities for the investigator include interviewing potential witnesses; reviewing documents; gathering facts; gathering and preserving evidence electronically; drafting requests for documentation and information; drafting memoranda and/or reports of investigations; serving summonses, subpoenas, and court orders; organizing documents for trial; and generally providing investigative support for cases being investigated and/or litigated by the Division. You would work closely with attorneys in performing investigative activities and effectively liaise with the appropriate personnel in various DC government agencies such as the Office of the State Superintendent of Education and Department of Employment Services.

To qualify as an investigator you need experience performing a wide variety of investigations. Your experience would need to demonstrate the following:

- Initiative, ingenuity, resourcefulness, and judgment required to collect, assemble, and develop facts and other pertinent data
- Ability to think logically and objectively, to analyze and evaluate facts, evidence, and related information and arrive at sound conclusions
- Skill in written and oral reports and presentations of investigative findings in a clear, concise, and impartial manner
- Tact, discretion, and capability to obtain the cooperation and confidence of others
- Familiarity with electronic document reviews

The salary for an investigator with the Public Advocacy Division is $61,491 to $76,082 annually (Office of the Attorney General for the District of Columbia, 2017).

LOSS PREVENTION

Large retail chains hire security personnel to control shoplifting and internal thefts. Positions in loss prevention can be hazardous enough for thrill seekers, a ladder rung for college students pursuing law enforcement, and an alternative to law enforcement for those who fear the dreaded polygraph test. The position of loss prevention officer doesn't usually pay well enough to support a prosperous family life, but it is ideal for part-time work, and it can also be a gateway to innumerable administrative and supervisory positions in the security and investigative arena, with career potential.

An example of a loss prevention job is a store detective for The TJX Companies, Inc., at HomeGoods in Mishawaka, Indiana. HomeGoods is a store that offers a selection of home merchandise, including giftware, home basics, accent furniture, lamps, rugs, accessories, and seasonal merchandise. TJX is one of the largest off-price apparel and home fashion retailers in the United States and worldwide.

Store detectives take an active role in identifying all forms of loss within retail outlets. In this position, you would be responsible for heightening loss prevention awareness, conducting physical security checks, making recommendations for ways to prevent loss, conducting safety inspections and communicating hazards to store management, participating in the orientation and training of new hires, and conducting surveillance to detect and apprehend shoplifters.

The basic requirements for a store detective are a strong desire for a career in retail loss prevention, the ability to work independently, excellent written and verbal communication skills, experience in retail loss prevention and store operations, or a criminal justice background. This job, like most loss prevention jobs, pays by the hour. As with many hiring processes, TJX prefers a résumé, so have one ready (The TJX Companies, 2017).

In Cedar City, Texas, the JC Penney store employs a loss prevention specialist, whose role is to keep the store safe and profitable at all times by investigating any suspicious customer activities or behavior in the store, taking action when needed, and executing company programs. This includes conducting surveillance, for which you would need to blend in well with other shoppers. You would observe customers and contractors in the store and look for any activities or behaviors that may be associated with theft, fraud, or impending violence. Some loss prevention specialists who monitor shoplifters with camera equipment associate this type of job with the omnipresence of God. They watch everyone in the store, without anyone knowing that they are being observed. These employees describe the experience as very exciting. They also make contacts with police officers during shoplifting investigations.

As a loss prevention specialist, you could find yourself interviewing suspects and writing reports. To accomplish this, you would benefit by being skilled at using words in lieu of force when it comes to difficult situations. It would require you to listen effectively and probe for further details when conducting interviews with shoplifters. You would need to be an accurate and descriptive writer who can communicate exactly what happened during a situation to any audience. You would be expected to support shrinkage and safety awareness programs. This would be facilitated by letting team members know what's going on and what they need to do to create the right store experience. Your job would also include maintaining records. You would be in charge of a great deal of detail. The company and law enforcement agencies would be depending on you to have complete and accurate reports to assist any investigation that may need to occur in the store.

In addition to the above jobs, you would participate in court hearings. You would need to become an expert when it comes to the witness stand. You would need to know the facts and deliver them like a seasoned pro. Your job would also include supporting workplace safety by walking the floor to identify and address potential hazards to customers and the staff. You would sometimes be called upon to support internal investigations. As the talent who handles loss prevention issues, there may be times when your assistance will be needed to investigate your peers, who may be acting inappropriately within the store. Your observation skills, loss prevention knowledge, and ability to remain objective with your teammates will greatly assist you with this sensitive undertaking.

JC Penney hires those who have a passion for loss prevention. The company wants someone who is a sponge for learning new loss prevention techniques and is driven to stop crime. It hires those who have a balanced temperament with "a level head," who can handle difficult situations with discretion. It favors detail-oriented personnel who never leave their T's uncrossed or their I's undotted, individuals who check and double-check to ensure that the final product is right. JC Penney likes a person of influence: not a pushy person, but someone who knows how to maneuver in a conversation to get someone to act differently. It wants decisive employees who can make good decisions quickly, even when they may not have all the information available. Lastly, it looks for accountability: very responsible employees who can take ownership of their mistakes as well as their triumphs (JC Penney, 2017).

ARMED SECURITY GUARD

Some security positions require you to carry a firearm. An example of this is G4S, a security provider for the United States government, Fortune 500 companies, nuclear power plants, oil and gas companies, airports, ports, banks, hospitals, factories, warehouses, commercial facilities, residential communities, and more. The company offers entry-level careers, management careers, sales careers, and executive careers across the United States and internationally. The main responsibilities of an armed security officer are as follows:

- Perform security patrols of designated areas on foot or in vehicle
- Watch for irregular or unusual conditions that may create security concerns or safety hazards
- Sound alarms or call police or fire department in case of fire or presence of unauthorized persons
- Warn violators of rule infractions, such as loitering, smoking, or carrying forbidden articles
- Permit authorized persons to enter property and monitor entrances and exits
- Observe departing personnel to protect against theft of company property and ensure that authorized removal of property is conducted within appropriate client requirements
- Investigate and prepare reports on accidents, incidents, and suspicious activities
- Provide assistance to customers, employees, and visitors in a courteous and professional manner

The ideal candidate must possess a high school diploma or equivalent, must complete any state-required training or other qualifications for licensing, must successfully complete a state licensing test if driving a company-owned or client-provided vehicle, and must have at least one of the following:

- Service experience in a military occupational specialty related to law enforcement, security, or any support role in a combat zone
- Graduation from a certified public safety academy (military or civilian) in law enforcement, adult corrections, or firefighting
- Bachelor's degree in law enforcement or criminal justice–related studies
- A minimum of 8 or more years of active service in any military branch
- Associate's degree (or 60 credits) or higher in law enforcement or criminal justice, with current or prior active military service
- If previously employed, meaningful and verifiable work history
- Ability to operate radio or telephone equipment and/or console monitors

You must be at least 21 years old and have access to reliable transportation. You must submit to a preemployment drug test and an extensive background check, including criminal history, personal references, employment and education verifications, Department of Motor Vehicle check, and credit checks. Upon acceptance of a job offer, you would have to successfully complete a psychological and physical exam. The pay for this position is $16.00 per hour (G4S, 2017).

Another common armed position is with the courts. The Bernalillo County Government employs an armed security guard who performs assignments involving the protection of individuals and property associated with the district courts and adjacent facilities. The duties and responsibilities are as follows:

- Providing protective services for judges, court personnel, and other individuals attending the district county legal proceedings
- Directing and advising the general public and court personnel about security procedures established for the courts and promote the understanding and compliance with safety standards developed to ensure the welfare of the people
- Escorting prisoners during court proceedings using approved security methods and ensuring that proper behavior is maintained
- Conducting searches for weapons, materials, equipment, etc., that may jeopardize the safety of the general public
- Maintaining continuous surveillance of individuals within the courts and adjacent facilities
- Assisting corrections officers, police officers, and sheriff's deputies with various activities associated with security

As an armed security guard for Bernalillo County, you may occasionally be assigned to transport prisoners to local detention facilities, hospitals, mental health facilities, or medical laboratories. You would assist court administrators in emergency crisis planning and security matters. You would conduct preliminary and follow-up investigations of criminal acts and prepare and maintain accurate reports and records.

To be considered for this Bernalillo County position, you must be a currently certified or recertifiable law enforcement officer or a retired out-of-state or federal law enforcement officer who is certified or recertifiable by the New Mexico Department of Public Safety (NMDPS). To be offered this position, you would be required to be in compliance with the following:

- Must successfully complete the post-offer employment medical examination
- Must pass an eye and audio examination, with vision equal to or better than 20/60–20/100, both correctable to 20/30
- Must have a valid New Mexico driver's license by employment date
- Must pass a written and oral psychological examination
- Must pass a background investigation authorized and performed by the BCSD

- Must pass a polygraph examination
- Must pass a sheriff's review process
- Must pass the prescribed physical agility test, meeting the 40th percentile as defined by the Cooper Institute
- Must qualify quarterly with issued sidearm

The salary for armed security guard with the Bernalillo County Government is $40,560.00 annually (Bernalillo County Government, 2017).

On a final note, you can be self-employed in the private security/investigations arena. Some places will contract with individuals to handle their security, stakeouts, or investigations. The possibilities are endless but not likely to be steady. You could work for apartment complexes, stores, bars, special events, sports teams, or even wealthy individuals who just want a driver. Usually you would need to create the jobs yourself by approaching businesses or individuals with your offer. You may even need to advertise and hope to be hired by someone who needs what you offer. It might be best to get some experience before branching off and starting your own company, but having a small company with employees and clients is very doable.

DIVERSITY ISSUES IN PRIVATE SECURITY

Minorities, women, and physically challenged individuals have become valuable resources for organizations in need of security specialists. Today's security professionals are part of a multicultural workforce representing a variety of racial, ethnic, religious, and gender backgrounds. Despite the workplace diversity in the security sector, men still represent the majority of employees. More and more women are entering the field because of the wide range of opportunities that are available.

SUMMARY

Since the terrorist attacks of September 11, 2001, the security industry has grown enormously. Working in private security or investigations doesn't always pay well, but it can represent a step on the ladder toward police work, or it can be a gateway job for a career in an advanced or supervisory position. This type of work is also popular for retired law enforcement personnel.

Police have historically looked at private security as inferior. Since 9/11, police agencies around the United States have made great steps in including private security in trainings to enhance defenses against catastrophic events, including terrorism.

The prominent jobs in private security include security officer, private investigator, loss prevention officer, and armed security guard. There are various levels of danger in these positions but often less authority than police officers have, and very few security jobs involve backup or carrying a weapon. Some jobs can be exciting and rewarding.

Most employers in private security and investigations require applicants to be at least 18 years of age and prefer degrees and/or related work experience. Rarely does a job in the private sector require a prospective employee to undergo a polygraph test, but almost always the hiring processes include background checks. There are opportunities for individuals to be self-employed in the security field, but it is difficult to find steady work. Women, minorities, and those with physical handicaps are continually entering the private security sector.

DISCUSSION QUESTIONS

1. What might be some reasons a person would enter security work as opposed to law enforcement?
2. Should security officers all undergo polygraph tests, be trained equally as thoroughly as police, and receive better pay? Explain.
3. How can law enforcement work with private security in crime prevention and responding to threats or incidents of terrorism?

REFERENCES

Allied Universal Security. (2017). *Allied Universal Security careers*. Retrieved from https://securitycareers-aus.icims.com/

Bernalillo County Government. (2017). *Current county job postings*. Retrieved from https://www.governmentjobs.com/careers/bernco/jobs/1778548/court-security-officer

G4S. (2017). *Armed municipal courts security officer*. Retrieved from http://careers.g4s.com

Grand Canyon University. (2017). *Campus safety officer*. Retrieved from https://gcu.wd1.myworkdayjobs.com/en-US/GCU/job/AZ-Phoenix/Campus-Safety-Officer_R00009099-1? source=Indeed

Insight Service Group. (2017). *ISG*. Retrieved at http://job-openings.monster.com/Private-Investigator-Dover-DE-US-ISG-Insight-Service-Group/11/184551980? MESCOID=3300593001001&jobPosition=1

J. C. Penney. (2017). *JCPenney careers*. Retrieved from http://jobs.jcp.com/jobs/6770992-security-loss-prevention

Laramie County Community College. (2017). *Campus safety officer*. Retrieved from https://careers-lccc.icims.com/jobs/2130/campus-safety-officer/job

NCI Information Systems. (2017). *NCI careers*. Retrieved from http://www.ncicareers.com/job_detail.asp? JobID=5467076&emid=3640

Office of the Attorney General for the District of Columbia. (2017). Office of the Attorney General. Retrieved from https://oag.dc.gov/release/investigator-2-public-advocacy-division-36-2017-closing-063017

State of California. (2017). *Cal careers*. Retrieved from https://jobs.ca.gov/CalHrPublic/Jobs/JobPosting.aspx

The TJX Companies. (2017). *Careers*. Retrieved from http://www.tjx.com/careers/

Transportation Security Administration. (2017). *Careers*. Retrieved from http://www.tsa.gov/careers/

SECTION 3

PREPARING

9 VOLUNTEERING AND INTERNSHIPS

INTRODUCTION

Almost every job advertisement has the word *experience* in the requirements section. Hiring someone with experience can benefit a company in three ways. Money can be saved that might normally be spent to train a new employee. The company can get the needed work done quicker by not having to wait for an employee to get trained. Lastly, the company can take advantage of the opportunity to check with a prior employer during a background check. Herein lies a dilemma. How does one get experience if employers only hire people with experience?

The idea of volunteering while going to school is not appealing to college students who already feel overwhelmed. It is especially far reaching for students who are also working part time. Nevertheless, volunteering or interning is an essential step in the climb toward a career. Students who have an internship listed on their résumé have a far better chance at being hired upon graduation. Sometimes students seek internships but can't find one available in their chosen careers. Sometimes it is easier to find volunteer positions than it is to find relevant internships. What is the difference between volunteering and interning? Which is better?

The word *volunteer* implies that you donate some time for the benefit of others with no expectation of payment or reward. Although this is true, you can still reap huge benefits by including volunteer experiences on your résumé, revealing your aggressiveness in your approach to job preparation. Volunteer work is great for the résumé and doesn't necessarily have to be job related to catch the eye of the employer. Because of unexpected hiccups in the economy and subsequent budget cuts, many agencies have made available more opportunities for volunteer positions. Volunteer work is normally not too taxing on your time. A typical program might require 8 to 12 hours a month. Upon completion, your supervisor will usually agree to write a letter of recommendation or provide some type of certificate of appreciation.

Internships differ from volunteer positions because you expect something in return. You expect to get experience and not just be used for tasks nobody else wants to do. Internships are harder to find than volunteer positions because they require more responsibility from a supervisor. Supervisors generally feel an obligation to create useful experiences for you, whereas in a volunteer position, you are there for the company and will do whatever it needs you to do. If you volunteer for a law firm, you may spend much of your time filing papers. If you intern for a law firm, you may find yourself in the courtroom taking notes for an attorney and, after court, making follow-up phone calls to clients. Some internships are paid positions, but this is rare and should not be too high a priority. Don't pass up great opportunities being penny wise and pound foolish.

Popular volunteer or intern positions in law enforcement involve victim services, crime scene work, police aide, detective aids, pawn detail, evidence managing, auto theft and impound lot assistance, and data entry for records. There are also volunteer and intern positions at courts, law firms, victim service agencies, and a variety of other criminal justice units. Most agencies will post volunteer and intern information on their websites.

Whether you apply for a volunteer position or an internship, you may have to undergo some type of testing process, which likely includes a background check and could possibly include a polygraph test. The testing experience will be valuable. If you intern at an agency you hope to work for someday, your foot is far in the door. Most agencies won't pick up interns they wouldn't consider hiring. In this chapter, we will explore some internships that are related to criminal justice careers in law enforcement, courts, and corrections.

LAW ENFORCEMENT

Other than the small departments, most local, county, state, and federal law enforcement agencies have programs in place for interns or volunteers (or both). They also have websites on which one can find out the basic information about these programs. When navigating a website, you will usually find internships under links such as "Careers," "Employment," or "Jobs." Sometimes there will be a link just for students. Not all agencies advertise openings for internships, so it is best not to depend solely on job search websites. You should check the websites of agencies you are interested in. If they aren't accepting applications, they will sometimes accept your contact information so you can be notified when there is an opening.

If you were to check the career section on the website for the Minneapolis Police Department, you would find volunteer opportunities under the "Get Involved" link. There are links for five different volunteer positions:

- Block Club Leaders
- Police Reserve
- Police Band
- Police Chaplain Corps
- Police Athletic League (PAL)
- Police Precinct Advisory Councils

A police band is unique, but this demonstrates just how limitless volunteer possibilities are. Police athletic leagues are common, and police reserve programs are even more widespread. Minneapolis doesn't list any internships (Minneapolis Police Department, 2017).

The Phoenix Police Department has a student internship program through the Citizens Offering Police Support (COPS) unit. To qualify as an intern with the Phoenix Police Department COPS program, you should be either a first- or second-semester senior and meet your college or university requirements for a credited internship. You must have no felony convictions and meet the drug standards. You must have fewer than eight driving violation points, fewer than two chargeable accidents, no convictions for DUI, and no loss of license as a result of a moving violation, within the previous 36 months.

The Employment Services Bureau oversees the internship program. It is offered for the fall, spring, and summer semesters. The Phoenix Police Department accepts internship applications from in-state and out-of-state college and university students. A letter of introduction and approval must be obtained from the school attended by the applicant. The letter should specify the following:

- Curriculum (student's major course of study)
- Student status (applicants should be a first- or second-semester senior at a major university or second-semester sophomore if in junior college)
- Anticipated graduation date (month and year)
- Number of credit hours being sought through the internship (3, 6, 9, 12, or 15 credit hours)

An employment services background investigator processes the applicants. Student interns are processed as follows:

- Prescreening interview (by telephone for out-of-county and out-of-state applicants)
- Completion of background questionnaire by the applicant and subsequent interview with the employment services background investigator to review questionnaire for completeness and accuracy
- Fingerprinting
- Customary records check and background check
- Polygraph examination
- Controlled substance screening
- File approval by recruiting unit sergeant
- Placement if file is approved (students are notified if application is denied)

Once a student is successfully processed, the volunteer coordinator finds a suitable assignment for the intern. Any bureau or precinct within the department may request an intern. The bureau or precinct with the greatest need at the time of placement will be a determining factor as to where the intern is placed. Interns will be used in the most beneficial way possible to supplement their academic assignment with police functions, such as patrol ride-alongs, a shift in the communications bureau, and other temporary assignments that would round out their internship. Interns may operate police department vehicles to run errands.

The number of hours you would intern depends significantly on your school and its curriculum requirements. The typical COPS intern spends 20 hours per week in his or her assignment. In extremely rare cases, select students can intern 40 hours per week, but that is difficult to facilitate. The majority of the students who intern develop close networking relationships with several members of the sworn and civilian force in their assignment. Those same interns typically convert to volunteers after their internships conclude, and they continue to contribute to the program and the department.

One of the other internships at Phoenix PD for college students is with the Planning and Research Bureau. The intern reviews the current Phoenix Police Department policies and operations procedures, checking for redundancy and conflicting statements. Naturally, the applicant for this position needs good reading comprehension and writing abilities.

Other internships with Phoenix PD include the block watch program and the property management bureau. The block watch intern assists department personnel in monitoring the distribution of block watch grants throughout the community. This entails acquiring knowledge of grant administration and researching funding sources. Interns with the property management bureau assist the clerical section by providing administrative support, researching property invoices, and purging cleared invoices. These tasks will require interns to have the patience to search old handwritten records and the ability to complete a review of computer-generated records. Interns may be required to process documents notifying owners of the availability for release of impounded property or issue legal notices prior to public auction. Additionally, interns may be required to file invoices and cards, both numerically and alphabetically. Phoenix PD also has internship programs in community relations, resource bureaus, administration, drug enforcement bureau, patrol division, and the violent crimes bureau (Phoenix Police Department, 2017).

The Middle District of North Carolina has an internship opportunity with the U.S. Marshals Service for qualified juniors and seniors. This unpaid internship is designed to provide a wide range of actual work experience to enable interns to become familiar with the performance of both administrative and U.S. Marshal functions. Interns are used in general operations, investigations, seized assets, judicial security, and management. They bring on interns who are interested in a sworn law enforcement career, with priority given to those who desire to work as a Deputy U.S. Marshal. Applicants must be in good academic standing and enrolled at an accredited college or university as a full-time student in their junior or senior year, with an overall GPA of 3.0.

Interns with the Middle District of North Carolina are required to work a minimum of 24 hours per week in the Greensboro, North Carolina, area. Recommended fields of study are the social sciences (criminal justice, psychology, sociology, and political science). Desired applicants are those who are strongly motivated, physically fit, have strong communication skills, and possess an ability to work in a professional environment with a large number of personnel (U.S. Marshals, 2017).

The FBI offers internships and entry-level positions in a wide range of disciplines to students of all backgrounds. Their unique opportunities offer students from all walks of life a great head start on their career. Interns can gain unparalleled experience with their honors internship and visiting scientist programs. Students can also begin a career directly after graduation with FBI's collegiate hiring initiative.

The honors internship program is a 10-week, paid internship for college undergraduate and graduate students. Students work side-by-side with FBI employees at the Washington, D.C., area headquarters or in field offices around the country. This program is open to a wide range of academic areas and offers experiences students may not be able to find anywhere else. The applicants for the honors internship program are required to meet the following requirements:

- U.S. citizenship
- Currently attending a college or university full time as an undergraduate, graduate, or postdoctorate student
- Have and maintain a 2.95 cumulative GPA or better at the time of application, throughout the application process, and for the duration of the internship program
- Pass all of the FBI employment background investigation requirements and be able to receive a "top secret" security clearance

The FBI is interested in applicants with a wide range of educational backgrounds: accounting, business, STEM (science, technology, engineering, and mathematics), English, film, finance, foreign languages, human resources, information technology, journalism, law, marketing, public relations, and visual arts. They look for those who have strong analytical abilities, are flexible, take initiative, work well with others, and have excellent written and oral communication skills.

The intern assignments are based on the skills currently needed in the FBI. As part of the application, candidates are asked to pick their top three desired field offices or headquarters locations, and these are taken into account during the selection process. Possible assignments include the FBI's headquarters in Washington, D.C.; Quantico, Virginia; Clarksburg, West Virginia; Huntsville, Alabama; and Winchester, Virginia. Quantico opportunities include the training, operational technology, or laboratory divisions. Clarksburg offers opportunities in criminal justice information services, Winchester offers opportunities in the records management division, and Huntsville offers opportunities in the Terrorist Explosive Device Analytical Center (TEDAC).

The FBI's collegiate hiring initiative recruits graduating seniors or individuals who have graduated with an undergraduate, graduate, or PhD degree. Recent graduates are needed to support a huge part of the FBI's mission, from supporting squads and operations to analyzing business processes and ensuring security. The collegiate hiring initiative also gives recent graduates the chance to explore and transition into the many exceptional career paths the FBI has to offer, as well as into other opportunities within the federal government and private sectors. The requirements are the same as those for the honors internship program.

The FBI's visiting scientist program gives applicants the chance to work in the FBI laboratory, one of the largest and most comprehensive crime labs in the world. Applicants work with state-of-the-art equipment to conduct laboratory and/or computer research and participate in forensic science research initiatives for 1 to 5 years. Only individuals possessing strong academic credentials, outstanding character, and a high degree of motivation will be selected for the visiting scientist program. In order to be considered, applicants must meet all of the following qualifications at the time that they apply:

- Students must be attending a college or university that is accredited by one of the regional or national institutional associations recognized by the United States Secretary of Education
- Student applicants must have a minimum cumulative GPA of 2.5 or above on a 4.0 scale and be in good standing with their undergraduate or graduate degree program
- Postgraduate applicants still pursuing their degree must be on track to complete their degree prior to the starting date; postgraduate applicants with degrees must have received their degree within 5 years of the desired starting date
- Faculty applicants must be full-time permanent faculty members at an accredited U.S. college or university
- All candidates must be citizens of the United States
- Candidates must meet all FBI eligibility requirements, be able to pass an FBI background investigation, and receive a "secret" security clearance

The paid interns are selected based on academic records, recommendations, applied research interests, and compatibility of background with applied research programs and projects at the Counterterrorism and Forensic Science Research Unit. Selection is also dependent upon availability of funds, staff programs, and equipment. The initial offer to participate in the visiting scientist program is conditional because candidates selected must undergo an extensive FBI background investigation and receive an FBI security clearance in order to be eligible to participate in the program. The program is open to U.S. citizens without regard to race, sex, religion, color, age, physical disability, national origin, or veteran status (Federal Bureau of Investigation, 2017).

There is an internship with the U.S. Drug Enforcement Administration (DEA) that introduces participants to the field of controlled substance chemical analysis. Participants will learn how the laboratory receives seized drug evidence, how the lab stores it, and the chain of custody procedures that are involved. Interns will also learn how different analytical techniques are used during the analysis of seized drugs. In the process, participants will also gain understanding of the pharmacology of drugs and the U.S. laws involved in the enforcement of controlled substances. Interns will also learn about the analysis of latent prints on evidence items.

Candidates for an internship with the DEA should have good communication skills and a strong interest in chemistry and its application to forensic science. The minimum requirements include courses in general, analytical, and organic chemistry and a minimum GPA of 3.0. Interns must make a minimum commitment of 10 hours per week. This can be arranged in either 2 half days or 2 full days per week. Each applicant under consideration has to undergo a background investigation prior to acceptance, which takes up to 6 months (Drug Enforcement Administration, 2017).

There is a new federal internship program called Pathways offered by the United States Office of Personnel Management (OPM). The Pathways program offers federal internship and employment opportunities for current students, recent graduates, and those who have advanced degrees. There are three different paths available:

- Internship program
- Recent Graduates program
- Presidential Management Fellows program (PMF)

The internship program replaces the Student Career Experience Program (SCEP) and Student Temporary Employment Program (STEP). This program is designed to provide students enrolled in a wide variety of educational institutions, from high school to graduate level, with opportunities to work in agencies and explore federal government careers while still in school and while getting paid for the work performed. Students who successfully complete the program may be eligible for conversion to a permanent job in the civil service. Here are some key provisions and features of the internship program:

- The internship program is primarily administered by each hiring agency
- Agencies may hire interns on a temporary basis for up to 1 year, or for an indefinite period, until the intern completes his or her education
- Interns may work either part or full time
- Each agency must sign a participant agreement with the intern that sets forth the expectations for the internship
- The intern's job will be related to the intern's academic or career goals
- Agencies have to provide information regarding their internship opportunities and post the information publicly on USAJobs.gov
- Internships have a flexible schedule of work assignments
- Students may be employed year round
- Open to all students enrolled at least half time in an educational institution that has been accredited by an accrediting body recognized by the U.S. Department of Education in pursuit of any of the following educational programs:
    - High school or general equivalency diploma (GED)
    - Vocational/technical certificate
    - Associate degree
    - Baccalaureate degree
    - Graduate degree
    - Professional degree

To be eligible for a Pathways internship, candidates must meet the following criteria:

- A student throughout the duration of the appointment
- At least 16 years old

- Enrolled or accepted for enrollment as a degree-seeking student (diploma, certificate, etc.)
- In good academic standing and maintain at least a 2.5 overall scholastic average on a 4.0 scale or equivalent, with no grade below a "C" during the internship
- Taking at least half-time academic or vocational and technical course load in an accredited high school or technical or vocational school
- In a post-secondary certificate program in a qualifying educational institution, equivalent to at least one academic year of full-time study that is part of an accredited college-level, technical, trade, vocational, or business school curriculum
- A U.S. citizen

The Recent Graduates program is intended to promote possible careers in civil service to individuals who have recently graduated from qualifying educational institutions or programs. To be eligible, applicants must apply within 2 years of completing a degree or certificate. Successful applicants are placed in a developmental program that has the potential to lead to a civil service career in the federal government. The program lasts for 1 year.

To be eligible for the Recent Graduates program, applicants must have recently obtained a qualifying associate's, bachelor's, master's, professional, doctorate, vocational, or technical degree or certificate from a qualifying educational institution. A recent graduate may apply for a position in the program if the application is received not later than 2 years after completion of all requirements of an academic course of study. Participating agencies will ensure, within 90 days of appointment, that each recent graduate is assigned a mentor who is an employee outside the recent graduate's chain of command. The agencies will ensure, within 45 days of appointment, that each recent graduate has an individual development plan (IDP) that is approved by his or her supervisor.

The Presidential Management Fellows program (PMF) is centrally administered by the PMF program office within the OPM. Bearing the presidential moniker, the program is an entry-level flagship leadership development program for advanced degree candidates. The program is designed to attract and select the best possible candidates with the goal of developing a cadre of potential government leaders. It provides resources and assistance to program participants during their first years of employment and encourages individuals to become effective leaders. The program creates a lasting bond, as well as a spirit of public service, ultimately encouraging and leading to a career in the government (Immigration and Customs Enforcement, 2017).

OPM announces the opportunity to apply for the PMF program (usually in the late summer or early fall). Applicants go through a rigorous assessment process to determine finalists. They select finalists based on an evaluation of each candidate's experience and accomplishments, according to his or her application and results of the assessments. OPM publishes and provides agencies with the list of finalists. Agencies provide OPM with information about their PMF opportunities and can post PMF appointment opportunities for those who are finalists on the PMF website year round. In addition, a job fair is typically held for finalists each year.

Those who obtain an appointment as a PMF serve in a 2-year excepted service position. The PMF program office provides newly hired PMFs an opportunity to participate in its orientation and training program. Interns receive at least 80 hours of formal, interactive training each year of the program, for a total of 160 hours. PMFs are placed on a performance plan and must obtain a successful rating each year (United States Office of Personnel Management, 2017).

Immigration and Customs Enforcement (ICE) internships are basically the same as those listed in the Pathway program. The internship program targets students enrolled in a wide variety of educational institutions, from high school to graduate school. Benefits include providing students with short- or long-term internship opportunities, which allow for the exploration of a federal career while being paid for the work performed. Within 120 days of successful completion, some participants may be noncompetitively converted to a permanent position or a term position lasting 1 to 4 years.

For the Recent Graduates program, eligibility is limited to applicants who are within 2 years of degree or certificate completion. Veterans who are unable to apply within 2 years of receiving their degree due to military service obligations can apply up to 6 years after completing their degree. Successful applicants are placed in a dynamic 1-year career development program. After successful completion of program requirements, participants may be noncompetitively converted to a permanent position or a term appointment lasting 1 to 4 years.

U.S. Customs and Border Protection (CBP) has a Pathways program with the same three internships. They also have a student volunteer program, which offers unpaid training opportunities to high school and college students. These opportunities provide work experience related to the students' academic goals and provides them an opportunity to explore career options, develop their personal and professional skills, and earn school academic credit for their internship.

In keeping with CBP's commitment to a partnership between law enforcement and America's youth, they created a Boy Scouts of America Explorer program. It offers opportunities in character building, good citizenship, and fitness for young men and women ages 14 through 21. Some Explorer units offer training in specific areas, like nautical training and law enforcement. Law enforcement Explorer posts offer programs in law enforcement and criminal justice, which provide Explorers with practical training and hands-on experience in those areas. The program provides opportunities for Explorers to participate in federal enforcement–related activities within the CBP (U.S. Customs and Border Protection, 2017).

COURTS

Courts have positions for volunteers and interns in victim services. Coconino County in Arizona has a victim/witness internship program. Interns assist with crisis response, criminal justice court advocacy, systems work, event planning, agency marketing, community presentations, vicarious trauma prevention, and in-office support. Crisis response interns provide crisis services, emotional support, and assistance to victims of crime shortly after the commission of a crime or sudden death. To be eligible to become a crisis response intern, you must meet the following criteria:

GUEST SPEAKER

JENNIFER D. GRIFFIN, DIRECTOR OF TRAINING AND THE ADMINISTRATOR FOR THE COUNCIL ON POLICE TRAINING

Currently, I am the Delaware State Police (DSP) director of training and the administrator for the Council on Police Training (COPT) for the state of Delaware at the rank of captain.

I am also a part-time adjunct instructor at the University of Delaware Criminal Justice & Sociology Department; I teach the following three courses: Introduction to the Criminal Justice System, Criminal Justice Ethics, and Problems in Law Enforcement. I have my doctorate from the University of Delaware in sociology, with specializations in deviance and gender.

"Typical" would most likely not describe my current assignment. As the director of training at the DSP's training academy, I have the pleasure to interact with new recruits who are in training to accomplish their dream of becoming a Delaware state trooper or municipal/town police officer. The DSP training academy trains troopers and police officers from municipal law enforcement agencies in the state of Delaware. As the director, my job is to ensure that the training environment and curriculum are such that future officers are prepared mentally, physically, and emotionally to provide exceptional and professional police services in the state of Delaware. I also oversee the ongoing training of troopers and officers throughout the state, to ensure that they receive continual training on the most up-to-date tactics and topics.

As part of my duties, I also oversee the DSP canine unit and the firearms training unit. Both units are critical to the training of new and current police officers in the state. Our canine unit trains and deploys canine units throughout the entire state of Delaware. These units also support multi-agencies to ensure all police agencies, regardless of size or resources, have canine support. The DSP firearms training unit organizes and runs a year-round, multi-million-dollar indoor training facility that trains federal, state, and local police officers in the most advanced firearms and tactics.

As the COPT administrator, I am responsible for administering the mandatory training and education for police officers, with responsibility and authority to obtain professional assistance from other police and professional organizations to accomplish the purposes and objectives of the COPT program.

To be the director of training for the DSP, one must first be a trooper with DSP and then progress through the ranks to earn the captain rank. This position is selected by the superintendent and executive staff of the DSP. Throughout my 19 years of service with the DSP, I have held numerous positions and ranks to prepare myself for this rank and position. Being responsible for the training and supervision of the training academy, canine unit, and firearms training unit requires one to understand and implement best practices for training, as well as laws, rules, regulations, and policies and procedures.

As the administrator of the COPT, one must understand the state law pertaining to this position and have solid communication skills to work with all of the law enforcement agencies in the state. This position is also responsible to administer the certification and the decertification of police officers for the entire state, regardless of agency.

To get hired by DSP, an applicant must complete and pass a written examination that measures cognitive abilities, a work styles inventory, and a life experience survey. If the written exam is passed, a candidate continues to the physical fitness test, which includes strength (as many push-ups as possible in 1 minute), endurance (as many sit-ups as possible in 1 minute), and aerobic capacity (1.5-mile run). If a candidate passes this test, he or she proceeds to the oral board interview, which measures the ability to communicate information or ideas to other people in the areas of comprehension and reasoning, oral expression, interpersonal interactions, decision making, and initiating action. Next step is the polygraph interview, which focuses on the areas of criminal activity, drug usage, employment history, financial decision making, and driving history. And last is the background investigation, which includes another in-depth interview with the candidate as well as multiple interviews with the candidate's family, friends, neighbors, supervisors, co-workers, acquaintances, and so on. The investigator will also verify the candidate's education, employment, military, financial, criminal, and traffic history.

Once all of the above steps are completed, a recruit will attend the DSP training academy, a residential full-time (with weekends off) 22-week program of intensive and comprehensive police training. Studies involve a wide variety of topics including tactics, laws of arrest, criminal procedures, search and seizure, emergency vehicle operations, first aid, verbal judo, computer science, firearms proficiency, cultural diversity, and crisis intervention. Recruits must be willing and able to receive oleoresin capsicum spray (pepper spray), as well as incapacitation from an electronic control device (Taser).

Upon successful completion of the live-in academy, the recruit trooper is assigned to one or more troop locations for an additional 12 weeks of field training with veteran officers. Applicants must obtain Delaware residency and a Delaware driver's license prior to their field training assignment. (For more information, see http://www.dsp.delaware.gov/dsp_recruiting_selection_process.shtml).

I offer my students and those interested in law enforcement the same advice: Always do the right thing, even if no one is looking. Decisions that seem insignificant in the moment can have long-lasting and dream-ending consequences. Police officers should be beyond reproach, so living to the highest standards is a must. Follow your dreams and make sure that everything you do supports that goal. You have to be physically, emotionally, and mentally fit to perform as a police officer every day because your fellow officers and the community are counting on it. Don't let yourself or them down.

- Be enrolled in a college or university pursuing a master's or bachelor's degree and approved internship as part of the degree program
- Be 21 years of age or older and possess a valid driver's license and proof of auto insurance
- Be available by cell phone and able to respond to locations using your own transportation
- Successfully complete crisis response training and bimonthly training
- Commit to four crisis response on-call shifts per week
- Commit to intern for a minimum of one semester and the required number of hours to complete the college or university internship requirements
- Commit to one weekly meeting with the staff supervisor
- Commit to assisting in the development of curriculum based on your experience, with guidance from staff supervisor
- Agree to a criminal background check and not have a felony conviction in the past 10 years (discretion may be given depending on the criminal offense), a criminal misdemeanor in the past 3 years, or a serious driving offense in the past 3 years

Court advocate interns provide assistance to victims of crime as they participate in the criminal justice system, working in tandem with a victim/witness advocate. In addition, court advocate interns act as crisis response volunteers. To be eligible to become a court advocate intern, you must meet these criteria:

- Be enrolled in a college or university pursuing a master's or bachelor's degree and approved internship as part of the degree program
- Successfully complete the crisis response training
- Participate on the crisis response team at least once per week
- Be 21 years of age or older and possess a valid driver's license
- Be available by cell phone and able to respond to locations using your own transportation
- Commit to intern for a minimum of one semester and the required number of hours to complete the college or university internship requirements
- Agree to a criminal background check and not have a felony conviction in the past 10 years (discretion may be given depending on the criminal offense), a criminal misdemeanor in the past 3 years, or a serious driving offense in the past 3 years

Management interns provide assistance in finance and business, agency marketing, fundraising, office support, vicarious trauma prevention, research and data management, evidence-informed practices, community education and prevention, community collaboration, policy and systems improvement, and general office support. Management interns are encouraged to successfully complete the crisis response training and commit to three crisis response shifts per month. To be eligible you must meet these criteria:

- Be 18 years of age or older
- Commit to intern for a minimum of 3 months and be available to intern during the work week and/or special events
- Have a solid understanding of office systems including Microsoft Office products
- Agree to a criminal background check and not have a felony conviction in the past 10 years (discretion may be given depending on the criminal offense), a criminal misdemeanor in the past 3 years, or a serious driving offense in the past 3 years (Victim Witness Services Coconino County, 2017)

The Santa Clara County Attorney's Office in San Jose, California, has a Victim Services Unit (VSU) that offers student internships. The VSU provides services to victims of violent crime. Victim/witness advocates provide crisis intervention, resource and referral assistance, emergency assistance, criminal justice education, and court accompaniment. Victim/witness claim specialists assist victims with applications to the California Victim Compensation Board, which provides financial reimbursement for crime-related expenses.

The student internship program requires a 6-month commitment. Potential interns must be students currently in the field of psychology, sociology, criminal justice, social work, or a related field. Interns have the opportunity to learn about victimology, victim rights, the criminal justice process, and the impact of violent crime.

Interns assist with public outreach presentations, development of training materials, research, written correspondence, and data entry. In order to qualify, a student must meet these criteria:

- Be a U.S. citizen, lawful permanent resident alien, or a noncitizen with proof of eligibility to work in the United States
- Be 18 years or older (individuals under 18 will require a work permit)
- Be enrolled in an accredited institution or a school licensed by a state agency or have graduated from such an institution or school within the last 6 months
- Have an overall GPA of at least 2.5 on a four-point scale
- Submit a completed county job application for employment
- Pass a physical examination if instructed to (Santa Clara County Attorney's Office, 2017)

CORRECTIONS

Volunteering or interning in corrections can provide a look at the day-to-day realities of corrections work and help students determine whether a correctional position is an appealing or viable career choice.

Internships generally last for a specific period of time (often a school semester), and the duties are usually well defined by the agency. Most colleges and universities have internship programs and coordinators who will help students find and secure positions. Correctional internships may be full time or may require as little as a few hours a week. They may be paid or unpaid and sometimes count for class credit. The focus is on learning, gaining experience, and developing job-related skills.

Florida Department of Corrections' (DOC) interns are placed under the supervision of a correctional professional who works with them to develop a meaningful internship opportunity focused on utilizing the intern's academic knowledge and skills in a professional work setting. If you were to be placed at the central office in Tallahassee, you would locate, notify, and assist victims of crimes committed by inmates and offenders under Florida DOC supervision. You would work closely with bureau staff in providing information and interacting with local, state, and federal law enforcement agencies in an effort to clear pending warrants for offenders on community supervision. You would also provide management and oversight of the electronic monitoring program and provide statewide emergency operations management for the Office of Community Corrections (OCC). You may have the opportunity to travel to local facilities, supervision offices, and courts to assist professional community corrections staff in duties relating to offender supervision. You would need to be proficient in Microsoft Office, possess a valid driver's license, and provide your own vehicle.

Florida DOC also has an internship for a public information assistant. The position of public information officer is important in corrections. Public information officers have the responsibility of facilitating communication between government organizations, the general public, and the news media. You can find public information officers in all levels of government. They are often assigned in the upper levels of organizations. It is common for large and medium government organizations, including police and fire departments, to have a public information officer.

As a public information assistant with Florida DOC, you would be a team member in the Office of Communications. You would work closely with offices and institutions statewide, as well as the department's web and video production teams, to create educational tools and promote department initiatives. You need to have strong writing skills; be creative; have the ability to multi-task, troubleshoot, and problem solve; and be able to network and foster relationships both internally and externally. The internship requires a minimum of one academic semester for 20 to 30 hours per week, Monday through Friday.

Another internship with Florida DOC is in community corrections. The intern in this position assists the community corrections staff by performing offender supervision, maintaining records, and handling other duties that support offender services. The intern establishes a positive working relationship with other community corrections staff, offenders, and collateral agencies. The community corrections intern participates in all required orientation and ongoing training sessions as recommended. The person selected for this position needs to understand case management functions and supervision planning and become familiar with collateral treatment agencies and with collateral criminal justice agencies. If you had this position, you would need to observe and understand the function and procedures of the agency's decision-making bodies.

The person chosen as the community corrections intern should be proficient in the use of Microsoft Word. This intern works closely with probation officers and supervisors in the assigned probation office, observes probation officers conducting interviews and making referrals to community resources and services with supervised offenders, assists with employment verifications and investigations, observes criminal court proceedings, assists with data entry, and assists in other assigned activities within community corrections (Florida Department of Corrections, 2017).

Idaho Department of Corrections has internship positions for drug and alcohol rehabilitation, probation and parole assistant, presentence investigator, human resource assistant, religious activity assistant, information technology, case management, and research analyst assistant. For any of the internships, the candidate must be at least 18 years of age and be enrolled in a post–high school academic program. The candidate must successfully pass a background investigation and may be required to be POST (peace officer standards and training) certified, depending on position. The person seeking this position could be disqualified due to any prior felonies, misdemeanors, drug use, probation, or adverse driving convictions. These internships are all unpaid (Idaho Department of Corrections, 2017).

The Tennessee Department of Correction (TDOC) internship program provides Tennessee college students with an opportunity to work and learn in a hands-on, public safety environment. Internships are available in the state prisons, community supervision offices, and at the headquarters. With this internship, you would have the opportunity to apply classroom knowledge in the field, gain valuable work experience, develop new skills, and gain prized networking contacts. This internship is open to juniors, seniors, and graduate students studying criminal justice, sociology, psychology, and other related fields. Selection is based upon applications, recommendation letters, résumés, and interviews. Before a selected candidate can begin an internship with TDOC, a drug test and background check must be completed and passed. All interns must be enrolled in a college class to participate in the program. Internships with TDOC are available for academic credit only. The amount of academic credit granted to each student differs. Applicants need to submit an application, résumé, and recommendation letters and will also undergo an interview (Tennessee Department of Correction, 2017).

DIVERSITY IN VOLUNTEERING AND INTERNSHIPS

The same issues with diversity in the workplace exist with internships and volunteer opportunities. The organizations that make efforts to improve diversity in the workplace are also striving toward equilibrium in their student recruitment programs. A good example of this is The Washington Center for Internships and Academic Seminars (TWC), a nonprofit, independent organization that serves hundreds of colleges and universities in the United States and other countries by offering selected students challenging opportunities to work and learn in Washington, D.C. for academic credit. TWC is the largest program of its kind, with 90 full-time staff and more than 50,000 alumni, many of whom are in leadership positions in the private, public, and nonprofit sectors (The Washington Center, 2017).

TWC promotes a federal diversity internship initiative (FDII) to help students from a wide variety of backgrounds access opportunities with selected government agencies. This initiative is designed to assist the federal government with hiring and training the next generation of leaders. It supports federal agencies so they can meet the priorities of promoting diversity in the federal workforce, increasing the number of veterans hired by the government, and increasing the representation of people with disabilities.

The FDII is available for all qualified candidates without regard to their race, religion, gender, color, national origin, sexual orientation, age, physical or mental disability, veteran status, or any other characteristic that is prohibited by state or local law (The Washington Center, 2017).

More and more, we see organizations following diversity best practices. It is more common to see websites that include a diversity statement from the management. Employers are more innovative in tackling diversity issues by retitling key jobs in order to demonstrate their commitment to equality. The need for diversity in organizations has become more apparent and more efforts are being made in recruiting. A strong resolute stance is the new norm. Gone are the days of corporations simply "promoting a tolerant environment" or just "valuing differences."

SUMMARY

Almost every decent job requires experience. Herein lies a dilemma. How does one get experience if employers prefer or require experience? Volunteering time while going to school is overwhelming for college students. It is especially difficult for students who are also working. Nevertheless, volunteering or interning is an essential step in the climb toward a career. Students who have an internship listed on their résumé have a far better chance at being hired upon graduation.

Volunteering is donating time for the benefit of others with no expectation of payment or reward. Although this is true, you can still reap huge benefits by including volunteer experiences on your résumé, revealing your aggressiveness in your approach to job preparation. Internships differ from volunteer positions because you expect something in return. It is more of a work contract. You expect to get experience and not just be used for tasks nobody else wants to do. Internships are harder to find than volunteer positions because they require more responsibility from a supervisor. Supervisors generally feel an obligation to create useful experiences for you, whereas in a volunteer position, you are there for the company and will do whatever people need you to do.

Whether you are applying for a volunteer position or an internship, you may undergo some type of testing process, which likely includes a background check and could possibly include a polygraph test. The testing experience will be valuable. If you intern at an agency you hope to work for someday, your foot is far in the door. Most agencies won't pick up interns they wouldn't consider hiring. In this chapter we explored some internships that are related to criminal justice careers in law enforcement, courts, and corrections.

The same issues with diversity in the workplace exist with internships and volunteer opportunities. More and more we see organizations making efforts to improve diversity in the workplace and strive toward equilibrium in their student programs. Gone are the days of corporations simply promoting a tolerant environment or just valuing differences.

DISCUSSION QUESTIONS

1. Do you think it is essential that students volunteer or intern?
2. Do you feel organizations should be more lax in their requirements for interns and volunteers? Explain.
3. What are some pros and cons of participating in volunteer or internship programs?
4. What types of things do organizations look for in volunteers or interns?

REFERENCES

Drug Enforcement Administration. (2017). *DEA internship opportunities*. Retrieved from http://www-chem.ucsd.edu/undergraduate/research/dea-intern.html

Federal Bureau of Investigation. (2017). *FBI jobs*. Retrieved from https://www.fbijobs.gov/students/undergrad

Florida Department of Corrections. (2017). *Internships*. Retrieved from http://fldocjobs.com/intern/index.html

Idaho Department of Corrections. (2017). *Internship opportunities*. Retrieved from https://www.idoc.idaho.gov/content/careers/internship_opportunities

Immigration and Customs Enforcement. (2017). *Internship program*. Retrieved from https://www.ice.gov/careers/internships

Minneapolis Police Department. (2017). *Get involved*. Retrieved from http://www.ci.minneapolis.mn.us/police/outreach/index.htm

Phoenix Police Department. (2017). *Student internships with COPS*. Retrieved from https://www.phoenix.gov/police/neighborhood-resources/volunteer/student-internships

Santa Clara County Attorney's Office. (2017). *Victim services unit internships*. Retrieved from https://www.sccgov.org/sites/da/Pages/VSUInternship.aspx

Tennessee Department of Correction. (2017). *Internship program*. Retrieved from https://www.tn.gov/correction/topic/tdoc-internship-program

United States Office of Personnel Management. (2017). *Hiring information: Students and recent graduates*. Retrieved from https://www.opm.gov/policy-data-oversight/hiring-information/students-recent-graduates/

U.S. Customs and Border Protection. (2017). *Student programs*. Retrieved from https://www.cbp.gov/careers/outreach-programs/youth/students-recent-grads

U.S. Marshals. (2017). *Middle District of North Carolina—Internship information*. Retrieved from https://www.usmarshals.gov/district/nc-m/general/internship.htm

Victim Witness Services Coconino County. (2017). *Internships*. Retrieved from http://www.vwscoconino.org/get-involved/internships/

The Washington Center. (2017). *Federal diversity internship initiative: U.S. government internships*. Retrieved from http://www.twc.edu/internships/additional-programs/federal-diversity-internship-initiative

GETTING A FOOT IN THE DOOR

INTRODUCTION

The goal is the job, the objective is the interview, the catalyst is an impressive résumé, and the means is a comprehensive portfolio. If you don't get called in for an interview, you weren't impressive enough on paper. In this chapter, we will look at effective preparation for the application, the interview, and the job itself. Review this chapter and start doing all the preparation pragmatic to your present circumstances. You can be sure your competitors are!

PORTFOLIOS

The current trend in job applications is the electronic submission. This method has numerous advantages. All of your documents can be scanned and compiled into one file, ready for posting. You can easily add to your portfolio and update the files periodically. You can have it ready for those tight deadlines when you happen across job postings. It can be at an employer's computer in minutes if need be. What types of items are appropriate for your portfolio?

Your portfolio contains all the useful documents you can collect, including your résumé and curriculum vitae (CV). Useful documents may include recommendation letters, certificates, thank-you letters, school transcripts, and sample reports or school research papers. You will scan everything electronically, but you will also keep everything together as hard copies, ready to take with you to interviews. Keep your portfolio organized, and update it electronically after every semester. At a minimum, you should have recommendation letters from your professors and a list of completed classes.

Letters of Recommendation

Employers routinely require letters of recommendation. These can take considerable time to collect. Once you determine the best people to ask, you need to discreetly relay the information you want covered, request that the letters be provided quickly, and meet with the letter writers to pick up their recommendations. A practical option is to collect generic letters early on, each time you encounter a person who would be favorable for your background check. These can be nonspecific and all-inclusive letters that recommend you for employment, graduate school, internships, and volunteer programs.

You can scan the letters into your computer and include them in your portfolio. If your source keeps your recommendation letter saved on his or her computer, you could easily go back and ask for an updated version with the current date and a more specific objective. An adjusted letter would take little effort once the original letter has been created. You may need four or five modified letters before you finally land a job. If your professor is willing to send you letters electronically, you can simply e-mail your request for any changes, and a new letter could be on your computer relatively quickly. Consider obtaining letters right away from friends, family, and acquaintances in respectable positions in the community, such as church members, lawyers, police officers, council members, and prominent business owners. These are important because some applications stipulate that your references have known you personally for a particular period of time. Often the duration of acquaintance is merely requested information, with no other specified criteria.

Some professors are willing to write letters for students provided they get to know the students well enough. Approach your professor at the beginning of the semester and find out if he or she would be willing to write you a letter if you prove worthy of it. Bringing attention to yourself early on is key. Some professors can have a student base of 400 to 500 per semester. Participate often in class, sit near the front, talk to the professor periodically, have great attendance and punctuality, get at least an A–, and then ask for a letter near the end of the semester. Consider college as assertiveness practice and job preparation, not just an annoying stumbling block of life.

The types of compliments you want to see included in your letters involve attendance, punctuality, communication skills (both oral and written), critical thinking skills, interaction skills with individuals and groups, integrity, work ethic, organization, stress and anxiety control, work quality, and overall attitude and demeanor. These are some common traits that are explored during background checks. Professors may not be able to witness all of these, but make sure they witness as many as possible.

Certificates

Certificates are impressive and can nudge you ahead of others who haven't collected any. Certificates demonstrate recognition for accomplishments. They generally accompany awards and trainings. People start receiving certificates early on in life for things such as Eagle Scout, honor roll, student of the month, student council service, spelling bees, and so on. You might take these certificates for granted when you are younger, but they are still pieces of your life story. Each time you find an opportunity to obtain a certificate for an accomplishment, put a higher priority on it. If there is a free seminar offered at school or anywhere else, ask if certificates or training records will be provided. Scan certificates and add the files to your electronic portfolio.

There are certificates you can earn for free online. A good resource for a quantity of certificates with a variety of choices is the Federal Emergency Management Agency (FEMA) Independent Study Program (Federal Emergency Management Agency, 2017). At this website, you will find several trainings; some even offer college credits at participating colleges. A valuable training to have for criminal justice jobs is the National Incident Management System (NIMS). NIMS (also known as the Incident Command System) is a standardized approach to the preparation for, response to, and management of catastrophic events. NIMS was developed in 2004 by the U.S. Department of Homeland Security. It establishes a standard set of procedures used by emergency responders at all levels of government to conduct large-scale response operations. NIMS enables responders at all levels to work together more efficiently to handle domestic incidents, no matter the cause, size, or complexity, including catastrophic acts of terrorism and disasters. NIMS is also functional for small-scale and routine incidents, such as traffic accidents, fires, and even parades.

FEMA desires that everyone learn the NIMS and thus furnishes the independent study website as a resource for training. These independent study exams now require a FEMA Student Identification (SID) Number. You can register for one at https://cdp.dhs.gov/femasid. After completing the interactive training, you should be knowledgeable enough to pass the quiz. After passing the quiz, a link for the certificate will be e-mailed to you (usually within 24 hours). Exhibit 10.1 is a sample FEMA certificate.

It is not pertinent that the training you choose is related to the job you are seeking. All certificates add pizzazz to your portfolio and show accomplishments. A reviewer of your résumé may not even examine what your certificates are for, but 5 to 10 certificates mentioned on your résumé will surely be noticed.

You can also obtain online training from the National Institute of Justice. After completing an easy registration, you can select free online courses in different areas

Exhibit 10.1 ■ FEMA Certificate of Achievement

Emergency Management Institute

This Certificate of Achievement is to acknowledge that

COY H JOHNSTON JR.

has reaffirmed a dedication to serve in times of crisis through continued professional development and completion of the independent study course:

IS-00100.a
Introduction to the Incident Command System,
ICS-100

Issued this 20th Day of October, 2008

AUTHORIZED IACET PROVIDER

Cortez Lawrence, PhD
Superintendent
Emergency Management Institute

0.3 IACET CEU

of criminal justice. A certificate can be printed out immediately. This site has an assortment of courses ranging from forensics and criminal investigations to corrections and courts (National Institute of Justice, 2017). Here is a list of their online courses:

- Firearms Examiner Training
- What Every First Responding Officer Should Know About DNA Evidence
- What Every Investigator and Evidence Technician Should Know About DNA Evidence
- Collecting DNA Evidence at Property Crime Scenes
- Español for Law Enforcement
- Forensic DNA Education for Law Enforcement Decisionmakers
- Principles of Forensic DNA for Officers of the Court
- DNA—A Prosecutor's Practice Notebook
- Law 101: Legal Guide for the Forensic Expert
- Crime Scene and DNA Basics for Forensic Analysts
- Laboratory Orientation and Testing of Body Fluids and Tissues
- Laboratory Safety Programs
- DNA Extraction and Quantitation
- DNA Amplification
- Amplified DNA Product Separation
- STR Data Analysis and Interpretation
- Population Genetics and Statistics
- Communication Skills, Report Writing, and Courtroom Testimony
- Non-STR DNA Markers: SNPs, Y-STRs, LCN and mtDNA
- Advanced and Emerging DNA Techniques and Technologies

Another option is to create your own certificate opportunities. As specialized training comes along in which you can obtain some level of expertise, ask the providers if you can create your own certificate for them to sign. Some trainers will be happy to accommodate you. You can purchase certificate-making software for a reasonable price online and start creating your own. An example might be a club or volunteer program you participate in at school, in church, or in the community. Not all agencies take the time to hand out some form of acknowledgment. Sometimes you will get a thank-you letter, which is also valuable for your portfolio, but why not ask for a signed certificate as well? You can design it yourself and, although unnecessary, you can ask for logos electronically to really spice up the aesthetics of your masterpiece.

Education Documentation

Although you are rarely asked to submit your transcripts initially with your résumé, it does sometimes happen. Eventually you will have to provide your transcripts to your employer, so why not get those ready to go? If you have an associate's or a bachelor's degree, get four or five sealed and certified transcripts added to your hard-copy portfolio packet. If you have not yet completed your degree, you can obtain transcripts early on that verify what credits you have already earned. If you are just a semester or two away from a minimum educational requirement, you may receive an exception and get an interview. If an employer is looking for a woman with a bachelor's degree who speaks Spanish, she might choose to hire a fluent Spanish-speaking female student close to finishing her degree over another candidate with a completed degree who speaks only basic Spanish.

CV and Résumé

A CV is less than a portfolio but more than a résumé. In terms of length, a résumé is best kept to a one-page, one-sided document listing your skills, relevant experiences, education, and awards. A CV is a longer, more detailed synopsis than a résumé and could be anywhere from two to five pages in length. A CV is more commonly used for academic jobs, but it could be beneficial to have one prepared and ready to use if an opportunity arises allowing you to submit more than what is on your résumé. Your CV provides an overview of your accomplishments throughout your life. There is no standard format, but you should always make sure the most relevant information comes first. Your goal should be to keep it short but inclusive of everything remarkable. One helpful trick is the use of incomplete sentences. Instead of saying "I received 40 hours of grant-writing training," you could shorten it to "40 hours' grant training." You will use bullet points more on a résumé than on a CV. When it is appropriate to add bullet points to your CV, use them modestly.

The résumé will be the document most frequently attached to your job applications. For some jobs, your résumé is the application, but for some criminal justice jobs, you could find yourself filling out 25- to 30-page applications. For most volunteer opportunities, internships, and employment (other than positions requiring polygraph testing), the résumé and letters of recommendation will influence whether you are called for an interview. At minimum, your résumé should include the following:

Name:	Should stand out at the top of the résumé
Contact information:	Include address, phone number, and e-mail address
Objective:	What job are you seeking?
Education:	This area can include trainings
Experience:	List any work experience that is relevant
Skills:	For example, word processing speed, Spanish language skills, grant writing
Awards/Activities:	Mention certificates, memberships, volunteer programs such as Boy Scouts, church choir, campaign volunteer, dean's list, honors

In deciding how much information to include on your résumé, look at the aesthetics from the critical viewpoint of the employer. A résumé needs a balance of white space and a blend of bullet points, boldface, italics, and underlining. If your résumé has too much white space, go ahead and include a few of the things you left off for the more important items. If it appears too full, work with the formatting or remove some less relevant minutiae, but keep it at a 12-point font. It is best to single-space your résumé, with spaces between different sections. Make sure to include a heading for each section. Remember the rule "KISS": keep it simple, stupid. See Exhibit 10.2 for a sample résumé.

Exhibit 10.2 ■ Sample Résumé

Arturo Meeks
2620 N Circle West, Beverly Hills, CA 90210
Cell: (310) 555-9880
Arturo.Meeks@gmail.com

Objective: Security Officer

Profile: *Motivated and assertive individual with a mild-mannered personality; accustomed to multitasking and being diplomatic and tactful with professionals and nonprofessionals at all levels.*

Relevant Skills

- Report writing
- Grant writing
- Computer savvy
- Emergency procedures
- Project management
- Bilingual (Spanish and English)
- Organization and scheduling
- Communications

Relevant Experience

- Volunteer with California Fish and Game as Ranger Aide (2015 to present)
- Grant writing certified (2017)
- Participated in 22 police or ranger ride-alongs (2015–2018)
- Organized two state-wide explorer conferences (2015–2016)
- Preparation of police reports as a police explorer with Beverly Hills PD (2014–2016)

Employment History

- Criminal Justice Tutor at Beverly Hills Community College (2016–2017)
- Night Manager at Walmart – Beverly Hills, CA (2015–2016)
- Manager at In-N-Out Burger – Beverly Hills, CA (2012–2014)

Education History

- Bachelor's degree in Criminal Justice from UCLA (2018)

Awards and Certificates

- Distinguished Service Award—Explorer Division – Beverly Hills PD (2016)
- Five certificates from FEMA for emergency procedure training (2017)
- Dean's list at UCLA for four straight years (2015–2018)

Should a résumé be colorful? Great question! You want readability, which is why you spread out the white space and include a variety of bullet points, boldface, italics, and underlining. Another supportive feature for a readable document is contrast. Not knowing how your electronic document will look after an employer prints it out, you are always safer with black ink on white background. If you will be submitting your résumé as a hard copy, you may choose to risk adding some boldface, strong colors, such as red or blue, on some expensive paper, but be aware that yours would stand out. That may be good, but maybe not.

A key phrase to have on your résumé is "grant writing." Government agencies and supportive agencies depend on grants for some of their key programs. By hiring grant writers, an agency increases its potential to secure available government money and

GUEST SPEAKER

COLTON JOHNSTON, ATTORNEY AND LAW CLERK

I currently work with the Denver District Court as a law clerk to a civil court judge. In this capacity, I am involved in every stage of the trial process, from the filing of a complaint to the post-trial motions deadline. I keep track of all ripening motions, I draft a large portion of the court's orders, I serve as the bailiff during jury trials, and I am the judge's right-hand man for all research questions. A typical day involves reading legal briefs (motion, response, and reply) to prepare orders, answering civil procedure questions from our court judicial assistant, and attending hearings to maintain a record for trial.

A clerkship is a very typical post-graduation job for a lawyer. Clerkships vary from 1 to 2 years, depending on the jurisdiction. My current clerkship is for 1 year. As for necessary qualifications, graduating at the top of your class from an ABA-accredited law school is only the first step. A successful law clerk must have a firm grasp of the legal research platforms (i.e., Westlaw and Lexis), strong writing and citation abilities, and a deep understanding of civil procedure.

I gained this experience through various jobs during law school. I was a judicial intern for a civil/criminal docket, I was a student attorney in the DU Civil Litigation Clinic, I was a legal intern at Robinson & Henry's family and civil litigation departments and was subsequently hired as a law clerk in the firm's Denver office, and I was a research assistant throughout law school. Finally, I served as the articles editor for the *Denver Law Review*, which was critical to my current writing ability.

After my first summer working as an intern to a judicial law clerk, I was awarded the outstanding student award in the externship program. The experience was so rewarding that I knew I wanted to serve as a clerk before moving on to practice law. During my third year of law school, I struggled with the decision to take a clerkship in downtown Denver (not exactly the six-figure job one expects with a law degree) or go after several other interested firms. Taking the clerkship has been critical to becoming the lawyer I am today.

As a clerk, you have the opportunity to witness hundreds of attorneys in trial, listen to the judge's critique of each lawyer's practice on paper or in court, and have a judge critique your own writing on various court orders. There is nothing to compare. Because of this opportunity, I was recently hired by JacksonWhite PC, a firm for which I have dreamed of working since before I started law school. I will be joining the firm's elder law division this year as a new associate.

Any student wishing to be an attorney should remember that it is not for everyone. Law is all about research and writing, and it's not quite the same as hanging out with Harvey Specter in Pearson Hardman's tower or calling Saul. However, for those interested in helping the oppressed by gaining a voice that can effect change for others: maintain a strong GPA, take practice LSAT exams each Saturday (especially logic games), and most important, go meet with attorneys to see whether their work fits your goals.

improves the likelihood of retaining current grants. Grant-writing training is offered all over the country, with costs ranging from $100 to $200. Training is available online or in person and can be done in 2 days or in weekly classes for a longer period. At the conclusion of the training, you receive documentation of your certification. This could be the best $100 you spend for job preparation.

Another eye-catcher to have on a résumé is "Spanish speaking." Even if your level of expertise is only basic or conversational, the opportunity to list it among your skills can push you ahead of monolingual candidates. Taking Spanish classes at college is sufficient and can be credited toward your bachelor's degree. The more proficient you become in Spanish, the more value you will have in the job force. Even if you list on a résumé that you are currently enrolled in a Spanish class and a grant-writing class, it could effectively push you ahead of others who haven't matched your efforts.

Naturally, your educational level will be significant on job applications, even if a degree is not required. The word *degree* is another strategic one to use. If you have just started college, state on your résumé that you are currently enrolled in a particular degree program, as opposed to just "attending college." If you are attending a community college, you might not currently be enrolled in an actual bachelor's degree program, but you can mention "associate's degree" with an added note of your intention to transfer to a bachelor's degree program. If you haven't actually completed any degree, being enrolled in college (with a plan for a degree) will be better than not listing the key words at all.

INTERVIEW PREPARATION

What have you done to prepare yourself for this job? Plan on encountering a question such as this in the interview. Better yet, hope for such a question. You will want the opportunity to sell yourself. Too many applicants take the hiring process for granted or don't really want the job badly enough. They don't commit themselves adequately to the preparation phase and lose the job to someone not so indolent. There are some activities you can participate in that will exhibit your seriousness about the job and will help prepare you for the interview, such as ride-alongs, court observations, attorney interviews, and of course, hard work.

Police Ride-Along

Many agencies allow citizens to participate in citizen ride-along programs. A ride-along can be anything from a 4-hour stint to the full 10-hour shift. Some agencies require that you live in their cities in order to ride with their officers. Exceptions to this rule might be for school projects or to investigate an agency for possible employment. Most students have at least four different agencies they qualify to ride with, including campus police, city police, county sheriffs, and their state police agencies. Agencies that don't regularly allow citizens to ride along will usually permit their officers to provide such opportunities for family members or friends.

The protocol for a ride-along ordinarily involves a short request form to be filled out to allow a background check to be done. You will also be asked to select what days and times you are available for the ride-along. The agency will call you back within 2 to 7 days with your scheduled time. You will be asked to be at the police station at a certain time, where the officer will meet you. Some students are able to attend the briefing at the start of the shift, which can be very enlightening. In the briefing, you get to meet the other officers you will be seeing again and again at the various calls for service throughout your ride-along. You start picking up bits and pieces of clearer understanding right from the start as the officers train, share information, and get mentally ready for their tour of duty.

A ride-along is an opportunity for a potential police applicant to see and feel things that could not be experienced any other way than being right there in the action. It is easier to answer scenario-based interview questions when you have been in the unique situations officers encounter. One-on-one time with an officer is a great time to ask questions. Ask her why she touched the trunk of the car as she approached the driver. Ask why she called in a traffic stop before she turned on her overhead lights. Ask why she made a particular driver get out of his car, but not other drivers. Ask for some advice on the oral board questions. Obtain her e-mail address so that you can ask more questions in the future.

Most agencies won't allow more than one ride-along within 6 months. However, it would be beneficial to ride with a variety of agencies and officers, so sign up for more than one department at a time. Try not to key only on the organization you hope to work for.

Dress like a detective! Your opportunity for exposure to the most exciting parts of police work correlates with your appearance. If you look like a student riding along, you will be treated like one and will likely spend a lot of time in the car. If you look professional and could pass for a detective, the officer can reasonably allow you to be closer to more scenes without distracting the citizens he or she is gleaning information from. Although it would be beneficial to be in jeans and tennis shoes for a foot chase, your potential for a better experience is increased in slacks and a buttoned shirt with professional shoes. Polo shirts are also acceptable, but a buttoned shirt is even more prudent. Women should apply the same strategy. Female detectives generally wear nice slacks, a buttoned top, and classy shoes, with their hair back. Dressing the way you would for an interview would be impressive and could get you more exposure to the routine calls and possibly to some daunting crime scenes.

Court and Attorney Observations

Most students have not been in a courtroom other than for a traffic ticket or a minor criminal offense. When you are asked what you have done to prepare yourself for an internship or a volunteer position at a law firm or government agency, what do you have on your list so far? How would it sound if you were able to say, "I have attended various court proceedings, including misdemeanor and felony trials, in both state and federal court. I have also shadowed two different attorneys for a day; I accompanied them to court and assisted in their everyday workloads, including court preparation and follow up"?

Like police, many attorneys will allow students to meet with them and follow them around for a day. Often a student can participate in some of the work, including case preparation, court note taking, and client follow-up. What you actually learn from the experience is secondary to the value of demonstrating your assertiveness and motivation to enter a law career. If you don't find an opportunity to shadow an attorney, you should at least visit some courtrooms and observe the proceedings.

Other than some civil and family cases, all trials are open to the public. You can walk into any courtroom at the city, county, or federal level and observe the hearings that are taking place at that time, as long as seats are available. No appointment is necessary, but you could call and find out if anything interesting is happening, when the proceedings will occur, and in what courtroom they will be held. Most court personnel are familiar with student projects and are happy to assist you with advice. Once you are in the court building, you will walk through the security scanners at the entrance, which are usually much less intrusive than those at airports. If you prefer help, you can contact the information desk for advice on what types of cases are in the works. You could also just walk around the court and read the dockets, which are usually posted outside each courtroom, to see if anything sounds interesting.

A variety of hearings take place at the courthouse. Observing 1 day of a 2-week felony murder trial would certainly be interesting, but even the misdemeanor courts have some eye-opening and rewarding activities to witness. If you are pursuing a law career with an emphasis on the criminal justice system, it would be advantageous to witness what goes on during the initial appearances. It will give you a genuine understanding of the heavy workload a new attorney will be expected to endure. Spending 2 hours watching initial appearances will leave no doubt in your mind that our court system has all the work it can possibly manage.

Practice

Prayer is a common practice prior to an interview. The candidates who are competing against you may be saying prayers as well. If someone gets a job or wins a big game or wins a state lottery, it is normal and proper to thank God. Religious leaders encourage us to pray for help in all of our endeavors, such as teaching or attending classes, writing papers, facilitating or attending meetings, or having important conversations with people. However, it is not purported that God chooses who wins and who loses. For example, religious leaders do not believe that God intervenes to make a poor person rich in a random drawing of lottery numbers. What would any of us learn from that? God wants us to work for what we get and to learn through our trials and struggles.

It's not enough to just say, "I've worked my whole life for this." It is true that our life's experiences have molded us into who we are, but that does not equate to being prepared for interviews. Being a great shortstop does not make a person a great hitter or a great pitcher. We need to specifically practice being interviewed. We need to search for all the possible questions and go over potential answers until we are very good at it. If we get the opportunity to participate in an interview, we need to learn from it. We should ask the interviewers how we did and what we can improve on. We need to do our best, and ask God to help with the rest. Not the other way around.

FIREARMS

Firearms are an aspect of police work, like driving, report writing, handcuffing, and fighting, in which you will need to become proficient. You will have the opportunity to learn and/or improve on all these skills in the academy. Often, range masters need to help recruits change their bad habits from years of shooting the wrong way. For this reason, shooting experience isn't always a positive thing, but firearms training (with instruction) can be. You are not likely to be asked in an interview if you are a good shooter, and you should likewise avoid sounding as though you put too much importance on your shooting ability. However, adding this to the list of what you have done to prepare for police work could be beneficial if it comes across properly: just one small part of a larger picture. If the topic doesn't come up in the interview and is thus of no avail to your hiring, prior firearms training will still pay off during the academy, especially for women. In general, women struggle more than men with firearms proficiency in the academy.

Chances are there is a firearms range within an hour of where you live. Our nation is heavily dotted with gun ranges of all types. Look for an indoor range in your area with trainers on site. Most ranges rent guns, eye protection, and ear protection and allow you to buy ammunition if you are at least 21 years of age. If you are under 21, you will need to bring someone with you who is of age. Trainers are usually on duty and normally do not cost you any extra. They will teach you the proper stance, proper gun handling, proper target acquisition, tactical loading, and jam-clearing techniques.

The price can range anywhere from $40 to $75 for a 50-round session. You normally don't need an appointment, but all ranges differ in their everyday operations. Again, this type of experience and training is relevant to police work but is rarely usable in an interview. If you are male and choose to refer to your firearms experience in an interview, it should be downplayed as just one of many things you have done to prepare yourself. Women, however, can get away with giving firearms training more emphasis. If a female job applicant were to say that she went on her own to learn firearms skills because she knew that women struggle with firearms proficiency in the academy, it would come across as a positive.

PHYSICAL FITNESS

For law enforcement and corrections, physical fitness plays an important role in the job. Even if you aren't the biggest and the strongest, you need to be able to chase, fight, and overpower people for the safety of yourself and others. The hiring process doesn't normally involve any fighting or arrest tactics, but assessing basic physical fitness is almost always a part of the procedure. The physical fitness test differs among agencies but can include things such as an obstacle course; a distance run; some push-ups; some sit-ups; jumping; stretching; a wall climb; and a body drag using a heavy, full-size dummy. Getting physically fit will not only help you ace the physical fitness test but will help you create a better first impression in the interview that follows. If you are overweight, make sure you are a member of a gym and have an exercise plan in place when you walk into your interview. You could resolve concerns an employer might have cultivated from the first impression. If you have already dropped some significant weight, let interviewers know so that they won't assume you are sedentary.

Some women seeking law enforcement jobs need to practice climbing a 6-foot block wall. This requires upper body strength as well as some technique. The 6-foot wall is often part of an obstacle course, so climbing the wall quickly is important. There are several sources online, including YouTube videos, that you can learn from before you actually attempt this task. Some women may have problems with push-ups if they are not properly prepared. Even if a woman outruns every applicant and doubles everyone in sit-ups, she will be disqualified if she fails even one part of the test.

A battle for men is the stretch and reach component. You may be asked to perform a stretch test in which you sit with your legs straight in front of you and reach forward as far as you can. This is usually a pass-fail test with a standard number of inches you have to reach from a certain designated point. Athletic women can sometimes touch their noses to their knees, so the stretch test isn't as much of an issue for them. Male applicants often struggle with this.

Most agencies will alter the requirements for different ages, such as a longer time allowance for the 1.5-mile run for those over 30 years old. However, it is rare for an agency to make any exceptions for gender. Not only would it be unfair to men if women had a shorter fence to climb, it would also be insulting to capable women who want to earn the job on their own merits.

EDUCATION AND GRADES

Strive for good grades, especially if you want a law career. If you want to be accepted to a top-40 law school, you will need good grades and a good score on your Law School Admission Test (LSAT). Some law schools offer full-ride scholarships, which are contingent largely on grades and LSAT scores. To improve on your grades, research the professors and choose those who will award an A+. Look at what others are saying about the professors on RateMyProfessors.com. Try to find professors who would be a good fit for your learning style. If possible, find out which professors have reputations for writing recommendation letters.

Not all jobs require a bachelor's degree. It is common to require a bachelor's degree for law school and federal law enforcement. It might surprise you, though, what types of degrees are relevant. You might think the obvious degree for any law enforcement job would be in criminal justice. However, the FBI, for example, also looks for applicants with accounting, psychology, biology, and chemistry degrees. The FBI generally requires either law enforcement or military experience as well. You are generally better off working for a municipal agency for 4 or 5 years before applying to the FBI. Municipal agencies often offer tuition reimbursement as well. You can finish your degree after graduating from the police academy.

THE LSAT

The LSAT is administered four times a year at various testing stations throughout the United States. It generally takes 4 hours to complete. You should plan to take the test prior to December if you want to enroll in a law school for the fall. You are allowed to take the LSAT more than once if you want to try to improve your score, but law firms can gain access to all of your scores. The LSAT consists of multiple-choice questions in the areas of logical reasoning, analytical reasoning, and reading comprehension.

You can start practicing for the LSAT as early as you like. There are free and paid websites with practice tests. Once you choose an available practice test, try to simulate the real circumstances of the LSAT. Stay within the time allotted (35 minutes per section) and work under the pressure of the clock. For better practice taking the real test, make sure to answer every question. There is no penalty for a wrong answer, so after the process of elimination, take your best guess from the choices left and move on. Get in the habit of moving right into the next section without a long break. On the real LSAT, you will be given 5 to 10 minutes between tests. There is also a 35-minute writing test during the LSAT, but it isn't actually scored. Law firms use it to assess your writing skills, so it would behoove you to write it well. A superb practice program would be to take the test every week for the entire year leading up to your actual test. In reality, 10 to 15 practices would probably suffice, but as with chocolate, more is better.

THE APPLICATION FORM

There is so much competition for positions that some applicants are weeded out before they get an opportunity to participate in any part of the testing process. It isn't always because of a drug history or a criminal record; sometimes, it is for very minor mistakes on the application or seemingly incomplete information. An application for a law enforcement job can be 25 or more pages in length. You may start doubting how much you want the job by the time you complete the application. Most applications ask for similar information, so each time you fill one out, it should get easier, especially if you prepare a good portfolio to work from.

You want to stay consistent on all of your applications, so make a copy of your first one and use it as a reference for subsequent agencies. If you declare that you used marijuana 15 times on one application, stay with that number on all applications. Also, stay consistent with dates for your jobs and degrees. You can use the same references, so keep their addresses and phone numbers together.

Here are some basic tips to help with filling out applications:

1. Do not make any spelling errors. Unlike professors who might dock a point or two on an essay, employers will just throw your application out and move on the to the next candidate.
2. Don't leave any blanks. If there are questions that do not apply to you, respond with "n/a," which means the question is not applicable. If something seems redundant, do not write something like "see réswumé." Just answer it again in a complete sentence.
3. Direct your answers toward the job you are seeking. You are trying to show why you are more qualified than other applicants for the specific position, so keep it focused.
4. Avoid providing negative information. Your goal is to get an interview. If possible, hold all negative information until after they get a chance to like you.
5. Be totally honest.
6. Don't request a specific salary if asked on the application. It is best to say something like "open" or "negotiable."
7. Provide a list of references (who are not relatives) who have witnessed your positive qualities.

8. Keep your application and résumé consistent.

9. Do not use slang. Use professional language and then make sure to practice professionalism in case you get called in for an interview.

10. Proofread your application before you submit it.

WRITTEN TESTS

Law enforcement agencies' (and some correctional agencies') hiring process includes a written test. The written test isn't something you can prepare for, but here are some samples of what you can expect to come across:

Read the notes from this call for police service. Pick the answer that most completely and correctly represents the information.

1. Responded to domestic at 100 Main Street. Spoke with victim Jane Jones. Observed visible injury laceration on Jane Jones' right forearm. Jones refused to cooperate.

   a. I responded to a domestic. Upon my arrival, I spoke with the victim, Jane Jones.

   b. I observed a visible injury laceration on her right forearm. Ms. Jones refused to cooperate with my investigation.

   c. I responded to 100 Main Street in reference to a domestic. Upon my arrival, I spoke with the victim, Jane Jones. I observed a visible injury laceration on her right forearm. Ms. Jones refused to cooperate with my investigation.

   d. I spoke with the victim, Jane Jones. I observed a visible injury laceration on her right forearm. Ms. Jones refused to cooperate with my investigation.

   e. I responded to a domestic. Upon my arrival, I spoke with the victim, Jane Jones. I observed a visible injury laceration on her right forearm.

   Answer: c.

2. Officer Harper responded to a residential burglary. The victim stated that, while he was on vacation between 7/2/18 at 4:00 pm and 7/8/18 at 11:00 am, person or persons unknown did unlawfully enter his residence and take his property.

   When did the victim discover the burglary to his residence?

   a. 7/2/18 at 4:00 pm

   b. 7/2/18 at 11:00 am

   c. 7/8/18 at 4:00 pm

   d. 7/8/18 at 11:00 am

   Answer: d.

3. Deputy Williams responded to an armed robbery in progress. Upon his arrival, he was advised that the suspect fled in a late model blue Honda Accord sedan.

   The vehicle was described as a

   a. 2008 blue Honda Accord

   b. late model dark blue Honda Accord

   c. late model blue Honda Accord sedan

   d. late model blue Honda Accord

   Answer: c.

4. Referring to the last scenario, Deputy Williams responded to

   a. A robbery in progress

   b. An armed robbery in progress

   c. A burglary in progress

   d. An armed robbery that happened in the past

   Answer: b.

5. Gang Unit Investigator Smith fills out a field interview (FI) card on a suspected gang member. The gang member's street name is "Killer G" and he is a documented member of the Eastside Boys. "Killer G" has numerous tattoos that help to verify his gang status, including a tear tattoo on his face, an "EB" tattoo on his left chest over his heart, and a tattoo of a compass with a large "E" on his right forearm.

   "Killer G" has how many tattoos?

   a. 1

   b. 2

   c. 3

   d. 4

   Answer: c.

6. "Killer G" had an "EB" tattoo on his

   a. right forearm

   b. right chest

   c. face

   d. left chest

   Answer: d.

7. Departmental policy requires that all officers who use force must complete a written use of force report. The report must include the circumstances leading up to the officer's decision to use force, the level of force used, the justification for the force used, and the outcome of the officer's use of force.

   The departmental policy requires

   a. That officers explain to suspects why they are using force before such force is utilized

   b. That officers explain verbally the circumstances leading up to the decision to use force, the level of force used, the justification for the force used, and the outcome of the use of force

   c. That officers explain in a use of force report the circumstances leading up the officer's decision to use force, the level of force used, the justification for the force used, and the outcome of the officer's use of force

   d. That no use of force report be filled out if no injury resulted from said use of force

   Answer: c.

8. You are a city police officer on patrol and observe a car driving left of center and not stopping for a stop sign. You stop the car and, upon speaking with the driver, you believe that the driver is DUI. You also note that the driver is a member of your employing municipality's city council. You should

   a. Give the city council member a ride home

   b. Allow the city council member to go on his way in his car

   c. Continue as you would normally with your investigation and notify your supervisor

   c. Write a citation for the two traffic violations and release the driver

   Answer: c.

9. You are on patrol with your Field Training Officer (FTO) and respond to a commercial burglar alarm at a grocery store. Upon responding, you and your FTO find an open door with no sign of forced entry. After successfully clearing the store, your FTO grabs a case of water and says no one will miss it. You should

   a. Ask for your share of the water

   b. Tell him to put the water back

   c. Ignore the situation since you are new to the department

   d. Report the situation to your FTO's supervisor

   Answer: d.

10. Your department has a written policy that forbids officers from taking any bribes, gratuities, or gifts. You stop at a local diner and find that the waitress wants to give you, the police officer, a 50% discount. Of these four options, you should

    a. Leave money on the table equal to the full amount of the menu price and normal tip you would have left, avoiding a scene

    b. Argue with the waitress and manager, insisting on paying the full bill

    c. Walk out without paying anything

    d. Pay the bill as indicated, with the 50% discount

    Answer: a. (Even if you might narrate a different answer in an interview, you would need to select the best choice from what you are offered. The key word is *argue*. If the wording were different and instead said "politely discuss," B would be a valid choice. An argument could create more of a problem than giving the impression that you accepted a gratuity.)

11. *Miranda v. Arizona* was a very important U.S. Supreme Court case from 1966 that affected law enforcement officers. Among other things, the rape case involving migrant farm worker Ernesto Miranda dictated that a warning must be given to suspects who are not free to leave if they are questioned as to specifics of the case. What this says is

    a. Miranda warnings must be given any time a suspect is placed in handcuffs

    b. Miranda warnings must be given if the suspect is questioned as to the specifics of the crime and he or she is not free to leave

    c. Miranda warnings must be given in rape cases

    d. Miranda warnings must be given to all people interviewed by law enforcement officers

    Answer: b.

12. *Carroll v. United States* was a 1925 U.S. Supreme Court case that clarified a law enforcement exception to the search warrant requirement of the Fourth Amendment. Under the Carroll doctrine, as it is now known, law enforcement officers may search automobiles without a search warrant as long as they have probable cause to do so and the automobile is movable. In other words,

    a. Officers may search an automobile only with the written voluntary consent of the driver

    b. Officers may search an automobile because the car is movable

    c. Officers may search an automobile without a search warrant as long as they have probable cause to do so and the automobile is movable

    d. Officers may not search an automobile

    Answer: c.

13. *New York v. Belton*, a 1981 U.S. Supreme Court case, clarified that law enforcement officers, upon making an arrest, may search the immediate "lunge area" within the reach of the arrestee, including any open or closed containers. Such a search may be conducted at the same time as the arrest. Therefore,

    a. Officers may search the vicinity of the arrestee, including any open or closed containers

    b. Officers must have consent to search the area around the arrestee

    c. Officers may search beyond the reach or "lunge area" of the arrestee

    d. Officers may not search any further than the person they have arrested

    Answer: a.

14. Which sentence below is grammatically correct?

    a. I am an educated person who wants to be a police officer

    b. I am an educated person whom wants to be a police officer

    c. I am an educated people who wanted to be a police officer

    d. I was an educated person who wants to be police officers

    Answer: a.

15. While conducting traffic enforcement in an area with a posted speed limit of 45, the reading on your radar for a passing car is 73. How many miles over the speed limit is the vehicle driving?

    a. 23

    b. 26

    c. 28

    d. 32

    Answer: c.

Some agencies will use pictures as part of their written exams. You are asked to view a picture for a couple of minutes, and then, when the picture is taken away, you answer some questions based on what you can remember. These written tests are usually pass-fail, requiring a score of at least 70%. Although it is a pass-fail test, scores are sometimes used to help recruiters with hiring decisions at the completion of all assessments.

Often, a written exercise accompanies the test. It is usually just a one-page essay on a topic that is not too difficult to write about, such as a personal experience. The papers are graded by an English expert of the department's choice. These are usually pass-fail, so you should brush up on your grammar and punctuation.

Although the written test isn't something you can study for, you can certainly perform better by getting plenty of sleep the night before. You can also try to take care of the little things that are on your mind so that you can concentrate on the test.

Additionally, you can take care of yourself through good nutrition and exercise, in order to be alert and prepared on test day.

PSYCHOLOGICAL TESTS

Another step in the law enforcement hiring process is a psychological test. This is generally a 2- to 4-hour exam consisting of 200 to 400 questions. The test is normally multiple choice, which facilitates quick grading. You won't be asked to choose the correct answer; instead, you are asked to "agree" or "disagree," or something similar. The questions often seem alike, even though they are slightly different. The mistake some people make is to answer the questions the way they think they are supposed to instead of just being truthful. If the question changes, it is okay for the answer to change. It is best to not overthink it and to answer all of the questions fairly quickly. An example of similar but different questions is as follows:

I like socializing in big groups.	Agree	Disagree
I enjoy large groups more than small groups.	Agree	Disagree
Being in groups makes me uncomfortable.	Agree	Disagree
I prefer settings with just a few friends.	Agree	Disagree
I prefer large groups over being by myself.	Agree	Disagree
Large groups cause me to have some anxiety.	Agree	Disagree

You would likely respond to these statements differently because they are asked differently. You don't want to go back and worry that you are being inconsistent. Just answer each question according to how you interpret it. If you like socializing in big groups, it doesn't mean you prefer large groups over small groups. You also use your own frame of reference. If you interpret "large group" as referring to the audience at a concert or a professional sporting event, you might answer differently than if you were visualizing a family reunion. Just stay consistent with your interpretations, and you should be fine.

SUMMARY

Having a wide-ranging portfolio is the means to an exceptional résumé, which is key to getting the opportunity for an interview. Building your portfolio and preparing for the testing starts now. Your portfolio is a packet containing all the documents you have collected throughout your life, including awards, certificates, recommendation letters, transcripts, and thank-you letters. You can double or triple the material in your portfolio by collecting letters from your professors and by completing some online training that provides certificates. Two helpful key phrases for your résumé are "Spanish speaking" and "grant writing."

Your one-page résumé is sometimes all you are asked to submit as a job application. Therefore, it is important to build a dazzling one. A CV is two or more pages long, containing much more information than a résumé. It is more common for academic jobs, but if you are allowed to submit more data, it would be best to have a CV ready to go. Applications for law enforcement jobs are lengthy, and failure to fill them out completely can disqualify an applicant. Once you fill out your first application, copy it and use it to fill out other applications. This will save you time and help keep all applications consistent.

To prepare for tests and interviews, go on a police ride-along, visit court proceedings, get some firearms training, get physically fit, volunteer wherever feasible, and apply for internships. To prepare for the LSAT, start a program of taking free online tests weekly. Although written tests for law enforcement aren't something you can study for, you can prepare more effectively by getting plenty of sleep and by taking care of any responsibilities that might be on your mind and taking away your full focus. Psychological tests are the norm for law enforcement and can be long and tedious. The key is to stay consistent and answer quickly without overthinking. Grades don't play a big part in law enforcement, but they do for law school. Search out professors at RateMyProfessors.com and find those who are a good fit for you. Find a professor who will award an A+ and will also write a recommendation letter. Grades and LSAT scores make a big difference in being accepted to top-rated law schools.

DISCUSSION QUESTIONS

1. What types of items are appropriate for your portfolio?
2. What traits are common for an employer to check into during a background check?
3. What are some sources for certificates?
4. What are some typical components of a résumé?
5. How can you prepare for the LSAT?
6. What can you do to prepare for a law enforcement written test?

REFERENCES

Federal Emergency Management Agency. (2017). *ISP courses*. Retrieved from https://training.fema.gov/is/crslist.aspx

National Institute of Justice. (2017). *NIJ hosted online training courses*. Retrieved from https://www.nij.gov/training/courses/Pages/welcome.aspx

THE INTERVIEW

INTRODUCTION

Not many jobs require written tests in the hiring process. Rarely does the process include a physical test or a polygraph exam. But almost every job in the United States involves a hiring interview in the selection process. Would you do the same thing if you owned your own business? What would you hope to accomplish in your interviews with applicants? What would you be looking for? Is it safe to say that you would want to know as much as possible about the applicants, so that you could choose the best one possible for your open position? What types of things can you reasonably expect to learn about a person in a 20- to 30-minute interview?

In the case of police officers, the various types of written tests and psychological tests can weed out those who don't have the necessary intelligence. The background investigation and polygraph test can weed out those who are an integrity risk. Anything else that is important must be determined in the short dialogue of the interview. Therefore, the interview can (and does) weed out applicants for a variety of reasons. It also serves as the best opportunity to move ahead of other candidates who may be less prepared or just aren't right for a position.

In a perfect world, the most qualified person would be hired for an open position, but the truth is, it's the best interviewees who are getting the callbacks. You may be the ideal person for the position you seek, but it is unlikely that you could just walk into an interview, tell that to the interviewer, and ask when you start. Part of being that ideal person is to know how to perform well in an interview. Knowing the answers to interview questions is significant, but there are additional factors to consider if you want to have the edge over other candidates. In this chapter, we will explore some generic and specific interview hints, followed by common questions and appropriate answers. Some of the upcoming information is relevant solely to police work or corrections. As in many areas in life, there are a good, a better, and a best. Let's get you there!

PUNCTUALITY

Your goal should be to show up at the office lobby about 10 minutes early. It is a good idea to be even earlier to the building and use the extra time to get focused, pray or meditate, and review this chapter and any other helpful items you brought with you. About 20 to 30 minutes of reflection and review could be beneficial after your drive. If you are driving from a long distance, you should factor in some of the predictable holdups, such as rush-hour traffic, accidents, or a long line at your habitual coffee stop. If you haven't already seen the building you are driving to, you should plan some

GUEST SPEAKER
MICHAEL NORZAGARAY, FORMER JUVENILE PROBATION OFFICER

My lifelong goal was to become an attorney. After receiving my bachelor's degree, I attended the Whit tier College School of Law. When I realized in my final semester that I was a father and husband first and foremost, law school had to take a back seat. The dream didn't die there!

After working as a project manager for a development company and the marketing director of a construction and landscaping company, I pursued a position with the Maricopa County Juvenile Court Center. After being a bailiff for the Juvenile Court Center for about a year, I applied and became a Level I juvenile probation officer.

As a probation officer, I was responsible for supervising juveniles who had been placed on standard probation for such offenses as shoplifting, incorrigibility, burglary, sex offenses, involuntary manslaughter, and so on. Acting as the eyes and ears of the judge, I ensured that probationers remained in compliance with the terms and conditions of their probation.

In my 15 years as a juvenile probation officer, I held positions of intensive probation officer, dentition officer, intake screening officer, diversion officer, and standard probation officer. My opportunities to help youths refocus their talents and strengths in prosocial behaviors and avoid further involvement with the court system brought a great sense of satisfaction.

Applicants for juvenile probation need a passion for helping incorrigible and/or delinquent youths redirect their strengths and talents in a more positive manner. In this field, you need excellent oral and written communication skills and good analytical, interpersonal, organizational, and team-player skills. A bachelor's degree in either the social or behavioral sciences is preferable. Consider working with youth sports or volunteering with boys' and girls' clubs, the YMCA, church youth groups, and the like. The more youth experience, the better.

time to find the location and a parking spot. You also should plan a restroom break. These are just the things you can plan for. Now add another 10 minutes as a cushion for unpredictable obstacles. It is best to spend your drive focused on your interview rather than on the long lights, heavy traffic, and those drivers who do not belong in the fast lane. You will likely feel some anxiety about the interview, so why add to it by having to rush past bad drivers to get there? It could be difficult to calm down after feeling so much anger toward those who choose to drive the speed limit for whatever reason. If nothing goes wrong, you may have 45 to 60 minutes to sit in your car and prepare. Is that so bad?

APPEARANCE

As mentioned earlier, there are a good, a better, and a best for almost everything. This is true with the routes we choose to take, the products we buy, the careers we choose, how we cut our hair, and the clothes we wear. One thing you can't avoid is making a first impression. You are stuck with that! This is especially critical for interviews. Why not shoot for the best you can?

Men need a suit in a dark color. Black, dark blue, and dark gray are power colors. These colors are always best if you want to influence others. A white shirt with a tie is best. Wear a conservative tie of either a plain color or a symmetrical design, such as stripes. The color of the tie can make a difference in how you are perceived. Consider a blue, burgundy, green, or yellow tie. You can also get away with wearing a red tie, but it can come across as too emotionally strong. Wear your hair short. If it is extremely long and you are interviewing for a job in which long hair is okay, wear it back in a ponytail. It is best to be clean shaven, but you might be able to get away with neatly trimmed facial hair for some jobs. Cover as many of your tattoos as possible. Remove your earrings, nose rings, lip rings, tongue studs, and any other face metal.

Women need a dark-colored dress, a dark skirt, or dark pants. It is best to wear a white top and possibly a dark, matching jacket over the top. The dress or skirt should be no shorter than just above the knee. In general, your apparel should not be overly revealing; at the same time, you shouldn't come across as too conservative. It is best to wear black, closed-toe heels that are no higher than two inches; you might be able to get away with stylish, open-toe shoes. When it comes to makeup, keep yourself looking as natural as possible. Avoid anything that would bring too much attention and cause distractions. The eyes are the most important because that is where you want the interviewer to focus. Wearing your hair up or back is the safest approach. It needs to look as if you put a lot of time into it, even if you didn't. Having your hair up or back will look professional and keep you from absently playing with it, revealing nervousness, during the interview. Wear nice earrings or studs, but nothing that catches the attention of the interviewer too much.

As discussed in Chapter 2, attractiveness is one of the most important factors in influencing others. Attractiveness goes beyond your facial features. Attractiveness includes the totality of your look and your aura. You want to exude confidence. That is easier done if you know that you look good. It also helps to know some tricks of body language.

BODY LANGUAGE

Imagine a boss who tells her recruiters something like this: "We are looking for people who think they are all that, and then some. Try to find us someone who has the 'I'm too cool' look on her face. We want someone who doesn't smile, someone who acts like he has nothing left to learn. We're looking for someone blasé, with a negative point of view and an uncaring demeanor."

Is there any job out there for which you would prefer someone who is unfriendly or unapproachable? If you are thinking of correctional officers or probation officers, you are misinformed. In these jobs, you want your employees to be firm and careful of the boundaries they set, but you also want someone who is part of the solution, not the problem.

If you are not a natural smiler, start practicing. It needs to be part of the new you. Smile at every person you pass. Smiling makes you likable. When you are being interviewed, your body language needs to coincide with your assertions. Smiling is the easiest and most effective body language you can use. If you are a friendly person, show it. If you are not, maybe you could be a custodian or a warehouse worker, with minimal interaction with others.

At a job interview, the first impression you make includes the person working the front desk. Sometimes the person who greets you and asks you to have a seat will make comments to the interviewer before or after your interview. It may be something sarcastic before the interview, such as "You guys are going to love this one." It could also be something after the interview, such as "Did that blonde girl with the nice dress suit do well? I really liked her!" If the receptionist doesn't like you, he or she is not going to push for you if the opportunity arises. You should smile at everyone but especially the receptionist.

Make eye contact with everyone involved in the interview as evenly as possible. Be careful not to stare too deeply or too long. Keep the eye contact to short intervals so that the other person doesn't feel uncomfortable or get distracted. If someone gets left out of your conversation, he won't feel enough connection to you. Looking at every person will make them feel that you respect them individually.

INTRODUCTIONS

Let the interviewers dictate your behavior. In most cases, someone will come to get you and walk you to the interview room. When that person approaches you, stand and listen carefully to everything said. In almost any other circumstance, it would be an appropriate gesture to offer a handshake. For job interviews, it is usually best not to offer your hand unless an interviewer offers hers first. People have different comfort spaces. The safest way to learn another's comfort space is by letting him dictate how close you get. Sometimes handshakes are not practical because of a room's layout.

The eye-contact rule is especially important in the introduction phase. Look at each individual as you are introduced, and at least nod your head in acknowledgment. Let the interviewers dictate your behaviors. If they haven't yet asked you to sit, remain standing during the introductions. Again, do not walk around the table and reach your hand out to shake hands unless the interviewers invite it. Hugs are out! Just a smile, a nod of your head, and a response to whatever they say. If they say something such as "Thanks for coming," just respond succinctly with something such as "Thanks for this opportunity." If they say something along the lines of "Nice to meet you," it is best to either say "Likewise" or "Nice to meet you too." Your eye contact lets them know you are acknowledging them individually. Clichés are fine. It's best not to try to say something clever or witty at this time. The interviewers' job is to study you and learn as much as they can about you. Let them ease into it at their pace. You will have 20 to 30 minutes to present your personality.

When you are seated at the table and ready to go, what do you do with your hands? If you naturally use your hands to articulate, set them on the table and clasp your hands so that you don't fidget. After each answer, clasp them back in place. If you don't need them to articulate, set them in your lap. That way you can fidget with them out of sight if need be to hide your nervousness. Women also need to moderate jewelry on their wrists and fingers, making sure any bracelets and rings are not distracting. Sit as calmly and comfortably as possible. The interviewers will be looking at you and will notice nervous movements. You want them to be paying attention to what you are saying.

Although it is important to be comfortable, you will want to sit up and lean in slightly toward the interviewers. This body language makes you appear interested. Folding your arms or sitting back could make you look uninterested, defensive, and/or less welcoming. Look at the person talking and try to stay focused on the entire question. While answering, share eye contact with everyone.

A more advanced body language trick (used with one-on-one interviews) is called mirroring. The idea is to subtly behave or speak in the same way as the person you are visiting with. Subconsciously, this sends a message to the person that you are on the same level. This can help build rapport faster. However, mirroring is not something you want to do in an interview until you get good at it. When you are in a conversation with someone with whom you want to connect, try practicing this technique. If the other person crosses his legs, wait just a moment and then cross your legs. If the other person leans on the palm of her hand, do the same thing a moment or two later. If the other person talks quietly, keep your own voice at a lower level. Skilled law enforcement interviewers use this technique on suspects and victims to break through defenses and build rapport as quickly as possible. As a side note for you future interviewers, mirroring works well when interviewing children.

In a hiring interview, it is best to use the words *sir* and *ma'am* sparingly. Do use them because it is an easy way to say "I respect you," but overdoing it can have an adverse effect. These words are often used too much in response to closed-ended, yes-or-no questions. It is perfectly fine to just say "yes" or "no."

SAMPLE ORAL BOARD QUESTIONS

Can you answer these three questions with unmistakable articulation?

- What word describes the asexual reproduction of a genetic carbon copy of a plant or an animal?
- Which Kurdish chemical element has the shortest name?
- What three impugnations in the 18th century best refute Einstein's theory of relativity?

If you're not prepared for your hiring interview, it will feel as if you're answering questions such as these. Reading through this chapter will be valuable before an interview, but also consider visiting with at least one person in the agency you are applying to, or at least someone in the same field of work. Ask every question you can think of and take notes. Do this type of preparation within a couple of days of the interview, each time you interview.

Interviews for law enforcement jobs generally consist of two types of questions. You will normally start out with generic questions about yourself and about your goals or intentions. The interviewer will then transition into scenario-based questions to assess your knowledge and thinking process. Scenario-based questions generally cover topics of ethics, teamwork, and the use of force. In this section, we will look at questions that have actually been used or are similar to questions actually used in oral board interviews. You are also provided here with comments and reasonable answers that might be helpful.

1. What have you done to prepare yourself for this position, and what goals have you established for your professional life?

It is to be hoped that you have a list of examples to offer for the first part of this question, such as college classes, ride-alongs, interviews with others in the field, tours of relevant facilities, court observations, volunteer or internship opportunities, and any extra trainings or studies. Each of these should already be listed in your portfolio for easy review. Some agencies will ask for a portfolio or curriculum vitae prior to or during your interview, but even if they don't, it is best to bring it, review it in the car, and then carry it into the interview.

You can be somewhat relaxed with questions about your goals or what you want to accomplish. Answers to these types of questions aren't meant to make or break you. It is fine to be predictable and ordinary. Interviewers hear the same things over and over. It is better to stay on the safe side and not try to be too creative. Let them hear the same things again. There really isn't a lot of variety you can add to your answers to questions such as these. One piece of advice for this question, and throughout the entire interview, is to focus on what sounds good for the agency and not too much on what is best for you. Obviously, you should avoid answers such as "I plan to be your boss someday" or "I hope to ride motorcycles." Use this opportunity to articulate well because this is a predictable question to which you should have a well-rehearsed answer. Consider an answer such as this:

> My goals are to become a well-rounded and well-trained police officer. I've reviewed the department's mission and vision statements, and I understand that the chief expects her officers to be well rounded, dividing their time between responding to calls for service, investigating crimes, conducting high-visibility patrols in residential, commercial, and retail areas, making positive contacts with citizens, using person and vehicle stops to detect and deter criminal activity, addressing neighborhood traffic concerns, and making crime prevention contacts with citizens and business owners. My goal is to become proficient in as many facets as possible to best represent my department.

This answer can be modified to fit other criminal justice jobs. Impress interviewers by letting them know that you did your homework.

2. What attributes do you feel are important for a law enforcement officer to possess, and how would you apply these attributes to your performance as a police officer?

Just as with the first question, there are generic answers to this question, and it is best to not go off on tangents. Include things such as honor, integrity, courage, and professionalism, but avoid attributes such as being a good shooter, a good pursuit driver, proficient in martial arts, or physically strong. With good articulation in the early, predictable questions, interviewers will be hopeful for you before you even get to the scenarios. For a question such as this, it would be best to name just the main attributes and then spend a little time relating each one to your performance. Spending too much time coming up with attributes will only make the second part of the question more difficult. Stick with three or four, and give an example of each one in order. Use acronyms or phonetics to help you remember what you plan to say and to help you remember the order. For example, the attributes listed above could be remembered using the word *hiccup*, for HICP. Then, when you start to give examples of how you would apply these attributes, you would be well organized. An example could be something like this:

> I know that as a police officer, I represent the city, the chief, and all other brothers and sisters in blue. I would conduct myself ethically at all times in a way that would bring honor to my profession. I would use the empowerment and trust given me with honesty and integrity by adhering to all federal, state, city, and department guidelines. I know that part of my job is to protect citizens and their property. I would face those who challenge the safety of our citizens with courage and steadfastness. I would perform professionally in all my encounters with citizens, attorneys, judges, supervisors, and fellow officers. I would keep myself physically fit and neatly groomed and wear the uniform with pride.

Questions such as this might be used in interviews for courts and corrections as well. If you have a planned answer, it can be easily adjusted to fit the way the question is asked. Again, why not prepare for these predictable questions? Write down answers for questions you expect, and then go over these answers in your mind while you drive, between classes, in the shower, and on the treadmill.

3. What can you tell us about our agency, and what factors influenced you to apply here?

The U.S. Marshals Service is one agency that assigns a lot of weight to how well an applicant researched the organization. Many other agencies use this type of question as well. Try to memorize some important facts about the department or firm, including size, leadership, mission statement, and job description. The more the better! This is a make-or-break question. Always, always research the agency and be prepared for a question of this nature.

When asked why you chose a particular agency, honesty is really the best way to go. The criminal justice field is very competitive, and students are always advised to apply for all openings that come along. If you apply only at the agency you prefer, you may miss several other opportunities and never get the job you are waiting for. The truth is, you want to be in law enforcement or law or corrections. Where you do the job is secondary. You might prefer another agency just because it is a shorter drive, but be honest with the interviewer. The person doing the interview already knows the truth and will be more impressed if you tell it like it is. After listing several facts about the agency, you could answer the second part of the question like this:

> I have set my goal to become a police officer. I have enjoyed ride-alongs at four different police departments, and although they are different geographically, the work is similar. I know this field is very competitive and that I am competing with hundreds of other candidates. I also realize that departments are not always hiring. I have prepared myself the best I can and hope that I am hired here and can start my career. However, if

I am not hired here, I plan to continue applying to other agencies until I succeed. I am prepared to move to another city or state if necessary to work in law enforcement. I am loyal, and whoever hires me will get my best effort. If I am not hired here, I will follow up by asking what I need to improve on, and I will use that information to continue my self-improvement. I have a lot to offer the agency that gives me the chance, and I hope it is this one.

4. Being a police officer can be a stressful job. Please identify some of the aspects of this job you believe would be stressful and explain how you would cope with the stress of the job.

This kind of question is relevant for any type of work. There has been more emphasis on stress in recent decades. Officers have high suicide and divorce rates. Stress affects health both physically and mentally. Attorneys and correctional officers face similar stresses, with internal politics, heavy workloads, and deadlines. Law enforcement personnel, court personnel, and correctional officers are constantly performing their duties in situations that trigger anxiety. Mandatory stress management trainings have been instituted at many agencies. You answer could be similar to this:

Putting aside personal feelings and dealing with criminals and their victims can be challenging. Many police officers see examples of human indecency and pain on a day-to-day basis. Seeing people, particularly the elderly and children, who are the victims of murder, beatings, robberies, rapes, and other violent acts can be causes of stress. Police officers also work different shifts. Having to appear in court may interfere with an officer's sleep, personal time, and current work assignments. Changes in work hours can cause the body stress. In addition to working with the public, a lot goes on inside a police department. Dealing with administrative issues, paperwork, and internal investigations can all cause stress.

Police work is also a dangerous job. Officers never know when they show up for work if they'll return home that evening. An officer's day may fluctuate from slow boredom to a sudden dangerous situation. Dangerous encounters can trigger the fight-or-flight response when presented with a threat. It is important to recognize this condition and to know how to respond to it. The fight-or-flight response has a lot to do with perception. Regular training can help officers manage perceived threats. I deal with stress in a variety of ways.

Exercise has been proven to have a beneficial effect on a person's mental and physical states. For me, exercise is an extremely effective stress buster.

I eat plenty of fruit and vegetables, and I make sure I have a healthy and balanced diet.

I make sure to set aside some time each day just for me. I use that time to organize my life, relax, and pursue my own interests.

An effective breathing technique slows down my system and helps me relax.

I talk to my family, friends, and work colleagues. I try to always express my thoughts and concerns.

There are other stress management tricks you can use that might be substituted or added. Writing your "to-do" list before retiring to bed can help you sleep better at night. Curbing your caffeine intake can help with sleep. Procrastination can be a stress enhancer. Getting assignments done early and leaving early for appointments can help relieve stress. Doing service for others can help get your mind off your own problems. You can keep a better perspective by having enjoyable events to look forward to, such as vacations or special date nights. Getting sunshine can increase serotonin and improve mood. Self-talk can be helpful. This technique is used by counselors as an intervention to help people change self-destructive thought processes.

5. Officers must complete accurate and detailed reports yet still be available to respond to calls for service or perform proactive patrol activities such as monitoring the flow of traffic. Please provide a specific example that demonstrates your ability to multitask.

Questions that ask you to give examples are difficult. You will start to think back and try to come up with the best example possible, and you will feel rushed. You know you have several, but your interview is short, and the interviewer is waiting to hear your answer. Here are some similar questions:

- Tell us about a time when you had difficulty with a coworker or group member and how you handled it
- Tell us about a time when you had to perform under pressure and how you handled it
- Tell us about a time when you had to work with a partner or a team and what you did to help the project succeed
- Tell us about a time when you had to be in charge of a project and what you did to make sure you experienced success
- Tell us about a time when something went wrong on a project you were involved with and how you handled the turn of events

These types of questions can be somewhat predictable if you understand how interview questions are created. First, the interview team is presented with the goals of the interview. In other words, it is determined first what an interview is intended to reveal about an applicant. Someone or some group decides what they want to find out, and then they create the questions accordingly. If you look at the examples above, these are all important aspects to explore. If you think as they do, you will be able to have tentative answers prepared. A possible answer could be something like this:

> I have had many opportunities to demonstrate my ability to multitask. I can honestly say that I am good at it and have provided you with three recommendation letters from professionals who have witnessed me handling multiple tasks and mastering my responsibilities. My approach to handling several responsibilities is to write everything down. I prioritize the tasks right away and make a time map of any important time-sensitive details. Writing everything down has improved my quality and timing. Once it is on my "to-do" list, I know I will be able to stay on task when

> something new or unexpected comes up. I have also been on three ride-alongs and observed how officers handle all their multitasking. One example that comes to mind is. . . .

Make sure to have an example for each of the sample questions above. When you are faced with adversity, handle it well, and then use it to your advantage in future interviews. If you currently do not get along with a coworker, make the steps to correct the problem and use the experience as an example in your interview. If you are in a group in a college course, and one of the members is the worst person ever to walk on our planet, change your purpose, and it will change the outcome. Look at it as an opportunity instead of your awful luck of the draw.

6. Dealing with difficult and noncompliant people is an inherent part of an officer's job. Police officers must deal with people during emotional events and must take people into custody who verbally and physically resist arrest. Describe what actions you will take to deal with these types of situations.

This is the area that can make or break you. Learn the general use-of-force guidelines of the agency you are applying for. Justifications for the use of force are generally just a couple of clicks away on your computer. You can look up your state's statutes and find the section on justifications for force. You need to know what you have the authority to do. If you also understand the atmosphere of the discretionary powers at the agency, the scenarios will be easier to answer. The nice thing about this question is that you are not asked to determine if you would make an arrest or not. Instead, you are being assessed for your thought process on problem-solving skills, human relational skills, safety concerns, mental control, and several other possible traits. The best advice is to answer the way the chief would want to hear it. Remember that the purpose of all questions is to assess certain traits about you, so you can usually hear a question and figure out what they want to assess. These types of questions weed out the candidates who didn't go on ride-alongs or at least get prepped by an officer or a professor. Scenario-based questions are also used in correctional job interviews. You can prepare for scenario questions by practicing with the officer you do your ride-along with. Have the officer ask you questions and critique your responses.

In Chapter 2, you were provided with a brief lesson on the use of force. It is important to understand the use-of-force continuum and the Fourth Amendment connection to this topic. One side of the continuum consists of a scale of different levels of force an officer can use to accomplish the necessary enforcement. The other side of the continuum is different behaviors of the perpetrator that justify an officer's equal or slightly higher level of force. An example would be a suspect who has no weapons and sits on the ground, telling an officer that he is not going to jail. The officer has the authority to use verbal judo or certain pain compliance holds to encourage the suspect's cooperation, but pointing a gun would be unreasonable in this situation. The Fourth Amendment guarantees citizens that they will be treated reasonably. It also restricts the government from going beyond what is necessary. These are good key words for your answers: *continuum*, *reasonable*, and *necessary*.

Going back to Question 6, you can see that it is somewhat vague. The question leaves a lot to a person's interpretation. The question insinuates a plethora of possible answers because it uses words and phrases such as *people* (children, adults, gang members, known criminals), *emotional events* (car accidents, shootings, stabbings, sexual assaults), and *physically resist arrest* (guns, knives, broken bottles, fists). The best way to answer a question such as this is to cover as many possibilities as you can. It will show that you aren't closed minded and can see that there are many optional routes. It will also let you show off how much you know. You may not get another chance to demonstrate your knowledge of the use of force. One possible answer could be as follows:

> The level of force is dictated by the situation. Officers should use verbal commands in combination with command presence. Whether you instruct a person to "Stop!" "Don't move!" "Be quiet!" "Listen to me!" "Let me see your ID!" or "You're under arrest!" voice commands in conjunction with your mere presence can prevent many situations from escalating. The right combination of words and command presence can de-escalate tense situations and prevent the need for a physical altercation. When someone is noncompliant or resisting arrest, soft, empty-hand techniques might be necessary, involving the use of bare hands to guide, hold, and restrain; applying pressure points; and take-down techniques that have a minimal chance of injury. When a suspect is actively resisting, less physical measures might be insufficient. Pepper spray or a Taser might be a better option, depending on department policy guidelines. Less lethal weapons can be used in accordance with policy when other alternatives are impractical and when lethal force is not justified. Hard, empty-hand techniques, such as kicks, punches, or other striking techniques, such as the use of a baton, could be justified if a suspect is actively attacking an officer. Of course, deadly force should be used only when a peace officer has probable cause to believe that a suspect poses a significant threat of death or serious bodily injury to the officer or others. The main thing is to understand department policy and procedure in terms of use-of-force guidelines and to maintain proficiency with training.
>
> My personal philosophy will always be to use the amount of force only that is necessary and reasonable. I believe I have the ability to communicate with hostile or difficult citizens because of my 2 years of experience working as an intern for the U.S. Marshals Service and 1 year working in corrections as a detention officer. I assisted in over 50 verbal confrontations with hostile suspects or prisoners, which resulted in only 1 physical fight. I was exonerated for that fight and given a commendation for my self-restraint and overall behavior. My portfolio contains three letters of recommendation from my past supervisors, which all mention my ability to communicate well with combative subjects.

7. You are driving in your marked police car along a canal bank at midnight, and on the other side of the canal, in an open field, you see a man holding an axe standing over another man on the ground. The man with the axe has lifted it over his head, ready to swing down and hit the other man, who is not resisting in any way. What course of action would you take?

Scenario-based questions pertaining to the use of force often deal with lethal force. Interviewers may want to know if you are willing to take a life. They also want to know if you recognize the reality of the situation. You would not want to try to swim across the canal to save the man. The axe is ready to come down. You would not drive around the canal to the other side; you would be too late. You would not drive your car toward the canal and attempt to jump over because you don't have time and it might not work anyway. You do not want to try to shoot the axe out of the hands of the assailant. You might miss such a small target. The victim might be killed, and the stray bullet might hit someone else on the other side of the field. The sad truth is that a police officer may have to shoot someone during his or her career. You never shoot to kill; you shoot to stop. Your target is the center of mass. The biggest area of mass is the torso. The center of mass is in the area of the lungs and heart, which officers call the 10 ring because in firearms training, 10 points are awarded for hitting the small circular target over the chest area. Although a shot to this area could be fatal, an officer's job is to stop the threat, not to kill the assailant. Hitting the area of the vital organs will stop an axe-wielding killer quicker than a leg shot. Officers don't shoot to wound, and they don't fire warning shots. The only shot allowed at a human is to stop a threat. A possible answer might come across like this:

> I know that taking someone's life is one of the hardest things I might have to do as part of my job. Deadly force should only be used when necessary to protect myself or a third party against serious physical harm or death. In this scenario, I realize that every second counts. I will be yelling commands to the assailant from the moment I step out of my car and also pulling my weapon out as quickly as possible. I will point my weapon at the person wielding the axe and aim at the center of mass. If he does not discontinue immediately, I will fire on the suspect until he is no longer a threat. I realize that I could miss my target, or that he could be under the influence of a drug such as PCP and not be affected immediately by my first shot. I will shoot as many times as necessary to stop the threat. I will be cognizant the entire time of the background so that I can best position myself in a way that avoids hurting anyone who might be in the line of fire.

The interviewers may have follow-up prompts for a question such as this. You may be asked if you would hesitate. You will need to be careful not to ruin the great answer you already gave. The good thing is that interviewers are generally held to strict standards of fairness. So whatever they ask you, they have already asked it of everyone else before you. Make sure to confirm what you have already said, unless the scenario is changed in any way. Come back with the surety that you would shoot the suspect as quickly and as often as necessary to stop the threat.

8. You pull a driver over for speeding and find that it is your mother, who borrowed a friend's car. What is your course of action?

Do not write your mother a ticket! Knowing when to exercise discretion can be difficult with more serious infractions, but normal everyday traffic violations are much easier. It may seem more complicated if the scenario includes a fellow officer or maybe the mayor or a chief of police from another agency. If the traffic stop is for a routine traffic violation, don't cite any of these people. Make your answer come across as an easy decision. Here is a reasonable answer:

> I know an officer has great discretionary powers. Every situation is different and should be judged on its own merits. Not every person who violates the law gets a ticket or goes to jail. There isn't enough room in the jails or time in the courtrooms to process every violator. I realize that a common goal of the criminal justice system is to deter crime. I would handle a traffic violator differently who disobeyed the law blatantly than someone who may have accidentally breached a traffic law. I plan to use my discretionary power as fairly as possible and for the right reasons. Sometimes a person changes behavior just from the fear that was experienced in the traffic stop. I feel that if I would give a break to someone I don't even know, I would surely give a break to the person who raised me, fed me, and drove me to soccer practice.

In the situation in which the question involves a fellow officer, stay with the same way of thinking, but you can also add that you know that an officer will be treated more harshly in court than a regular citizen would be. Judges must be careful with the appearance of favoritism, as must officers. They have less discretion and would need to be harsher in sentencing than they would for a normal citizen. This is just an additional reason why you might give a warning to an officer who should already know better than to speed.

Be careful not to refer to an authority figure as a hypocrite for violating a traffic law. Everyone violates traffic laws, whether it is intentional or accidental. In reality, every time an officer writes a ticket for speeding, it could be considered hypocritical. Stay focused on the concept that you will write tickets if you feel it is for the better good of society as a whole. If you feel that a violator needs a ticket to help deter future behavior, you should write the ticket. If you feel that a warning would produce the desired result, just issue a pleasant warning and leave that violator with a positive feeling about the police.

Officers will sometimes write tickets out of anger at the way violators talk to them. Although this type of ticket seems unfair, officers are only human and might feel that violators need a "behavior adjustment." If you are asked a question that includes a belligerent violator who lacks respect for the law and for people, remember the purpose of the ticket. If you feel that the ticket will help society as a whole, you should write it. If you feel that the ticket would make things worse, you might go a different route and use the stop as a way to change the violator's opinion of police through kindness. You have that kind of power out on the street. These decisions are totally up to you. Just make sure you don't write a ticket out of anger. Just as in raising children, discipline for the good of the child, not to make yourself feel better.

9. As an officer, you must be able to communicate and obtain useful information from people. Assume you are an officer dispatched to contact a suspicious person. You locate the subject, who is elderly and apparently disoriented. How would you handle this situation?

Much of police work consists of difficult situations, but not all are criminal. You could be assigned to handle almost anything. Luckily, there are other agencies out there to assist the police in cases that can be handled by other experts. Police are sometimes dispatched for "other agency assists" because the level of danger isn't known initially. Police officers have guns, handcuffs, radios, training, and authority.

Thus, any situation in which danger is a possibility will involve police. This is one possible answer:

> Police often rely on the instincts and perceptions of citizens to detect activity that is out of the ordinary. Police have a duty and responsibility to follow up on reports of suspicious persons. Upon arriving on scene at such a call, it would be important to ask questions and determine what type of situation I am dealing with. In such a situation, an elderly, disoriented person could have Alzheimer's disease or some other related dementia. It is important to identify and understand the signs of Alzheimer's disease and related dementias and how to communicate with people who have these conditions. This helps better serve both people with these conditions and the community as a whole. I would communicate to my supervisor what I was dealing with, and determine what services the police department could offer, if needed.

It is sometimes crucial to say that you would contact your supervisor, but never use that as an easy out on your answers. The interviewers might not let you off that easily. It is common for an interviewer to follow your answer by saying that your supervisor is busy at a helicopter crash. If this happens, the interviewer wants to assess your knowledge of the particular situation. Give general answers; do not be too specific. It is best to let an interviewer know what you would do under a variety of scenarios. For example, you could call the man's family, friends, or doctor. You could contact a crisis intervention team if your city has one. You could call an ambulance if the man needs to be assessed for dehydration or other common problems with disorientation. You always want to do something. It is okay to admit that you don't know what to do, but follow that with your best guess. It is better to admit that you don't know than to pretend you do and disqualify yourself with an inappropriate answer. If a weak answer knocks you out of the top list of candidates, you will have an advantage by knowing what types of questions to prepare for the next time you have a hiring interview.

10. An officer must accurately report information. Assume you are assisting another officer with an inventory of a prisoner's property by completing the impound form. You see the other officer take a quarter from the prisoner's property, put it in his pocket, and place a different quarter in the property bag. The other officer tells you that he is a coin collector and that that particular quarter is a solid silver quarter. What would you do?

What is the interviewer trying to find out about you with this question? Are you going to be a tattletale? Are you going to be unethical and just turn your back on what your fellow officers do? You are always safe to lean toward what you would say to the chief if he or she were asking the question. Answer this type of question something like this:

> This is an integrity issue. Police are expected by the public to be held to a higher standard than the general public. Police officers' ethics and integrity should be beyond reproach because the public relies on police to respect civil rights. I would confront the officer and remind him that there are department policies in connection with handling prisoners' property. I would also advise the officer that this is an ethical issue. I would document

> exactly what happened in the police report. I would notify the officer that I am required to do so. I would make sure that the immediate supervisor is aware of the police report. It is important to document these things as a matter of record for performance review purposes and for future reference in case of repeated misconduct. Repeated problems or an accumulation of minor infractions of policy or procedure could become a problem. As such, this information must be available to supervisors.

Be careful of questions of this nature that might be assessing if you are too quick to jump to conclusions. Regardless of the scenario, you will normally be expected to take some form of action. Doing nothing is usually the wrong choice.

11. Department policy states that officers are not to accept gratuities, for example, free drinks or meals. You have just finished eating at a restaurant on your patrol beat, but the waitress is adamant in refusing to give you a bill. How would you deal with the situation and why?

With a few exceptions, police officers may not accept gratuities. Local and state police officers are first responders, and accepting a gratuity might make an officer feel obligated to favor the donor at a future time, when the officer should instead be unbiased. It might also make the donor feel that the officer owes him loyalty. You also want to avoid a scene at a restaurant. This is a possible answer, although a little over the top:

> Police departments have rules for a reason. Although the payment of free coffee is perhaps a commonly received gratuity in many jurisdictions, business owners might expect extra services in return for giving gratuities. When law enforcement officers offer additional services to private businesses in exchange for a free cup of coffee, they detract from other citizens within their communities. Police service cannot be perceived as going to the highest bidder; decisions must be based on need. Many argue that the coffee is inexpensive and that owners are showing appreciation by offering a cup and enjoying the fact that officers spend time in their shops. Therefore, what is the harm? On the other hand, what happens in a discretionary issue when an officer stops the owner or an employee for speeding? The officer may base the decision of whether to cite on the fact that he received free coffee. Should the free coffee factor into the officer's decision? Police officers often face the dilemma of accepting gratuities. Some officers view the acceptance of free coffee and free or discounted meals as an entitlement, while others view it as an unethical act. Law enforcement agencies should consider the perceptions of communities, as well as business owners, when accepting gratuities. Where there are departmental policies against accepting gratuities, they should not be accepted. I think the best practice is to be diplomatic with the restaurant server, thank him and explain that one cannot accept a gratuity, and leave payment with the cashier.

Could you just leave the money at the table, plus a tip, and not say anything? This is a solution, but be careful in your answer to this type of question. You want to focus on what the interviewers are trying to find out about you. You want them to know that you understand the real issue. It isn't only about whether you will accept the gift. If you just leave money at the table to cover the food and tip, it might all end up in the server's pocket, and the owner might think you accepted the gratuity. Plus, other citizens who may have witnessed the conversation would assume that you took the gratuity and just left a tip for the waitress. Even though you personally refused to go down that slippery slope, other damage could still be done to the police department as a whole.

12. Police officers work in ethnically diverse communities. Please describe how diversity affects the role of a police officer in the performance of his or her duties.

This may be an easy question for you. Make sure to use proper terms when appropriate. If you are a Caucasian man, you wouldn't want to start out by saying, "I don't have any problems with minorities; I married one." Use terms such as *African American*, *Mexican American*, *Native American*, and so on. Using these terms will demonstrate that you have had some kind of training in the area of diversity. Make sure not to downplay this issue. It is a very important and controversial issue in the criminal justice system. Here is a possible answer:

> Historically, many minority groups have been treated badly by the government—some by officials in the United States and others by governments in the countries from which they came. Harsh treatment can create distrust and fear of the government and authority figures in some minority communities. That distrust may make it difficult for minority groups to trust police or other authority figures in society. When approached by police, a minority member may express alarm or doubt, or be coldly polite. It is important to keep backgrounds and experiences in mind as we reach out to different people. We may need to consider altering how we approach and interact with individuals from diverse communities. However, grouping people into categories such as these also can be misleading. We must be careful to avoid making broad assumptions about people based solely on appearances or ethnic or racial affiliation. Poor relations between community members and police can lead to feelings of distrust, anger, and fear. A situation involving the shooting of a minority citizen by a police officer, for example, could potentially cause heightened racial tensions. Citizens may think the police are prejudiced and have unfair policies. People from diverse backgrounds and experiences need to develop trust, understand one another's experiences, and work together on solutions.

You could also add comments about how important it is to have diversity within the ranks of criminal justice jobs to capitalize on dissimilar viewpoints and ultimately make better decisions for the community as a whole.

DO'S AND DON'TS

Some of the important do's and don'ts of interviewing have been covered, but here are a few more to help you succeed:

Do . . .

- Get plenty of sleep the night before the interview.
- Give a good firm handshake if the interviewer offers a hand.
- Listen to the last names of the interviewers and try to remember them. It would be impressive if you have the opportunity to insert a name or two later in the interview, instead of just saying "sir" or "ma'am." Remember to use "Mister" and "Ms." or "Councilwoman," "Judge," "Doctor," or "Professor" (along with the last name) if you know the proper title.
- Maintain a friendly and humble demeanor in your facial expressions.
- Bring your portfolio to the interview. It might not be required, but having it will be impressive. There may also be opportunities to pass a recommendation letter around or a certificate of relevance.
- Use good vocabulary, and avoid slang and jargon or pause words such as "uh."
- Tell the truth.
- Focus on what you can bring to the agency, not on why the job is important to you.
- Come across as appreciative and respectful without sounding desperate.

Don't . . .

- Chew gum during the interview.
- Have the smell of smoke on your clothes when you walk into the interview.
- Eat too much fiber or gassy foods (beans, broccoli, cabbage, cauliflower, brussels sprouts) within 24 hours of the interview. Your comfort is paramount to your performance.
- Slouch. Sitting up straight (yet comfortably) might take practice, but it is helpful to show confidence through body language.
- Let your cell phone make any noise during the interview. However, if you do forget to shut it off, just apologize and move on. You could even make a joke about it at that moment, such as "Wow, that's a good way to impress my interviewers." Well-timed and tasteful humor is always welcome, even in the most professional settings. You are especially okay if you are laughing at yourself.
- Speak negatively about past employers or coworkers unless it is absolutely necessary to explain a bad report.
- Bring in personal issues and family problems to the interview if it can be avoided. However, you should always be honest if asked.
- Rush to answer a question. It is okay to repeat a question to make sure you understood it. That will buy you more time for your response. A slight pause is fine after each question, so that you can visualize the path you want to

take with your answer. Seasoned criminals use the pause technique during interviews; why shouldn't you?

A PERSONAL NOTE TO MINORITIES, WOMEN, AND LGBTQ INDIVIDUALS

I have had the pleasure of working for, and alongside, minorities, women, gays, and lesbians during a 27-year law enforcement career. The police department was better because of them. We became like family through the years, but these remarkable individuals all had their share of depressing experiences dissimilar to my own, as a straight white man. There will always be some prejudice and bias in the workplace. Cultural and religious issues will be present as well. Caucasians, men, and heterosexuals who don't see it may never see it. Remember the serenity prayer: "God, grant me the serenity to accept the things I can't change, the courage to change the things I can, and the wisdom to know the difference."

Hopefully you will have the courage to aggressively seek the job you want and not be dispirited by the unfortunate past or the imperfect present. There are a good, a better, and a best in many areas of our lives. Be the best you can be at the best job you can earn, and persist in making our world better.

A NOTE TO LAW STUDENTS

This book is intended mainly as a supplement to introductory criminal justice texts. Students who are old enough can start applying for jobs in law enforcement and corrections during their bachelor's degree programs. If they are fortunate enough to get hired early on, they can return to school after the academy and usually get their tuition paid for by their agencies. However, those going into the law field generally won't be faced with internship or hiring interviews until after their bachelor's degrees and at least 1 year of law school. Chapters 6 and 10 have some helpful information about what you can do to plan and prepare at the start of your bachelor's program. There are internships and volunteer programs available to those working on their bachelor's degrees, but not everyone can devote time to them while going to school full time.

In internship and volunteer interviews, you can expect questions similar to law enforcement interview questions:

- Why do you want to work for this law firm and not the millions of others?
- If you had a choice, what field of law would you work in?
- Where do you see yourself professionally in 7 years?
- What do you really want to accomplish in life?
- Are you satisfied with what you have achieved in law school thus far?
- How well do you react to difficult and stressful situations?
- What are your strengths and weaknesses?

If you are shortlisted for the position, you will likely have a second interview, at which you will be asked questions such as these (Common Job Interview Questions and Answers, 2013):

- How would you handle a denied petition?
- As an attorney, what circumstance would make you realize that it's time to settle?
- What do you think of the proposed Social Security Reform Act?
- In what cases should medical records not be released?
- In what cases should workers' compensation records not be released?

Advanced interviews for a position at a firm will likely have case study questions. Case studies involve solving legal issues on various topics, such as criminal cases, civil cases, traffic accident cases, and other types of cases that require critical thinking. Case studies are commonly used when interns are seeking positions at personal injury firms. Excelling at case studies and general interview skills can create the opportunity for you as an intern to undertake significant projects and gain firsthand experience in a legal environment.

A valuable website for postgraduate law students is hosted by the National Conference of Bar Examiners (2017). At this site you can purchase practice case studies and summaries. The average price per case study is $30.00. These case studies can seem foreign for new law students, but they are fairly routine for law graduates. Here is an example of a multistate performance test (MPT) involving a case study in which the examinee is asked to draft a "leave-behind" to persuade the legislature to enact legislation to require payment of royalties when artwork is resold:

Memorandum

To: Examinee
From: Charles Lieb
Date: February 28, 2017
RE: Proposed Resale Royalties Legislation

The Franklin State Assembly is considering legislation that would require royalties—payments for continuing use of artworks—to be paid to artists and their heirs for resales of artworks in the state (Bill no. F.A. 38). Such royalties would benefit artists and their heirs who, under current law, receive nothing from such resales.

Our client, the Franklin Artists Coalition, is strongly in favor of the legislation and has asked for our assistance in its efforts to persuade the legislature to enact the legislation.

I am attaching a letter from our client and materials, which will provide background on the legislation and its subject matter and from which you may discern the arguments being advanced for and against enactment. Please assist me in preparing a document (a so-called leave-behind) that may be given to legislators and their staff members after in-person visits by our client. The purpose of the leave-behind is to persuade legislators to vote in favor of the legislation. (Note that the recipients of the leave-behind will include nonlawyers.)

Your draft of the leave-behind should accomplish two goals: (1) it should make the case for the legislation and respond to the arguments against, and (2) it should persuasively deal with the single legal issue involved. I am attaching a template for the leave-behind for you to use. Draft only the material indicated in brackets, and do not repeat the opening and closing text.

Letter from Client

Dear Charlie:

As we discussed on the phone earlier today, we would like you to assist us in seeking enactment of legislation pending in the Franklin State Assembly that would mandate royalties on resales of works of visual art. I am enclosing the text of the proposed legislation, Franklin Assembly Bill 38 (F.A. 38).

Our neighboring state of Columbia enacted such a statute in 1973. Similar legislation was introduced in our other neighboring state of Olympia in 2006 but, unfortunately, never got out of the Olympia Senate's Committee on the Arts, which voted to table the proposed legislation "for further study." I am enclosing hearing testimony given by the witnesses who appeared for and against the Olympia legislation. F.A. 38 was drafted to address some of the objections to the Olympia bill.

(Continued)

(Continued)

I know that the effort in Olympia raised a purely legal aspect of this issue, which we must address as well and which I will leave in your capable hands.

As I mentioned, we need a leave-behind that we can use to persuade legislators to vote our way, and given your firm's experience with the Franklin legislature, we could really use your help.

Summary

In this performance test, the law firm that represents the Franklin Artists Coalition hypothetically employs the examinee. The coalition supports enactment of legislation that would require a 5% royalty to be paid to artists or their heirs on the resale of their visual artworks. To this end, the coalition has asked the law firm to prepare a document that can be handed out to legislators and that will set forth the need for and benefits of the legislation, especially in light of the fact that similar legislation was introduced but not adopted in the neighboring state of Olympia. The examinee's task is to draft the leave-behind, which is a persuasive document that will convince legislators to vote in favor of the resale royalties legislation. In doing so, examinees must set out the arguments in favor of the legislation, respond to the objections, and address the legal issues.

After graduating from law school, you will search for interview opportunities at corporations, firms, or government agencies. There is no standard protocol for lawyer job interviews as there is in police and corrections. In other words, anything is possible. A large part of the curriculum in law school involves job preparation. You will graduate with more than just new knowledge. You will be attractive to employers with your renewed motivation, confidence, and optimistic perspective.

SUMMARY

You should expect to be interviewed for any job you apply for. In a perfect world, the best candidate would get the job. In our world, the best interviewee often gets the job. Some important hints for success are to be about 10 minutes early, have the proper appearance, use body language tricks to help show yourself off, and make a good first impression in your introduction, which includes a smile.

There are two types of questions in the interview. The first part of the interview involves questions that you might expect, such as what you have done to prepare yourself for the job, why you chose this career, and what you know about the agency or firm. The second part involves situational questions that assess your thinking process. You can prepare for these types of questions by learning about use of force (in police and corrections interviews); knowing the firm's or agency's policies; and having examples in your mind of situations you have been in, such as handling difficult people, crisis situations, and teamwork experiences.

Historically, women and minorities have experienced inequality in the workforce. Women continue to enter jobs that have traditionally been carried out by men. Although there has been significant progress in welcoming women to police and correctional jobs, there is still more ground to cover. Although not many, there is a handful of men in police agencies and correctional facilities who are skeptical about women's abilities to perform all facets of the job.

Women need to be mentally prepared for interviews by men. The vast majority of men have no issues, but there is always a chance that a male interviewer could be skeptical. Men change their views of women in law enforcement as they witness outstanding female employees do the job well. The interview is not the right time to make a statement about women's rights. Women should portray in interviews that they are team players and can work with anyone. Once women are hired, they can prove to any skeptics that they belong there through their performance.

Those seeking law enforcement jobs or careers in corrections can start interviewing right away, before they complete their bachelor's degrees. Seekers of law careers attend 3 more years of law school beyond the bachelor's degree before being eligible for a permanent full-time job. However, law students may find internship or volunteer opportunities during their bachelor's programs and should prepare well for those interviews.

CONCLUDING REMARKS

It is time to start thinking seriously about the future. Knowing exactly where you want to be in 10 years is not crucial right now, but the sooner you can choose a career path, the better. Setting goals can help in your decisions to enroll in the necessary courses, earn good grades, participate in volunteer and internship programs, obtain certificates, get work experience, and build a résumé.

It is important to be realistic about your goals. Desire to do a particular job doesn't necessarily translate into being good at it, and disinterest doesn't mean that you're deficient in the skills needed to do the job. However, people tend to like doing what they are good at, and people excel at things they like to do. Therefore, being or becoming good at what you choose to do for your job correlates with satisfaction in your career. Remember the saying from Laurence J. Peter: "If you don't know where you are going, you'll probably end up somewhere else."

To set realistic goals, you should evaluate the talents and skills you already have as well as those you need for the career you are interested in. You then need to be realistic about your goals. One advantage of getting a degree is improving your knowledge and skills for a career. Improving your abilities often means stepping outside your comfort zone. Consider public speaking, which is a valuable skill for many professions.

Remember! The goal is the job, the objective is the interview, the catalyst is an impressive résumé, and the means is a comprehensive portfolio. If you don't get called in for an interview, you weren't impressive enough on paper. For some jobs, your résumé is the application, but for some criminal justice jobs, you could find yourself filling out 25- to 30-page applications. For most volunteer opportunities, internships, and employment (other than positions requiring polygraph testing), the résumé and letters of recommendation will influence whether you are called for an interview.

Certificates are impressive and can nudge you ahead of others who haven't collected any. Applications routinely require letters of recommendation. These can take considerable time to collect. Once you determine the best people to ask, you need to discreetly relay the information you want covered, request that the letters be provided quickly, and meet with the letter writers to pick up their recommendations.

The current trend in job applications is the electronic submission. This method has numerous advantages. All of your documents can be scanned and compiled into one file, ready for posting. You can easily add to your portfolio and update the files periodically. You can have it ready for those tight deadlines when you happen across job postings. It can be at an employer's computer in minutes, if need be.

Almost every job in the United States involves a hiring interview in the selection process. In a perfect world, the most qualified person would be hired for an open position, but the truth is, it's the best interviewees who are getting the callbacks. Knowing the answers to interview questions is significant, but the person who learns and masters all the additional factors has the edge over other candidates. Practice! Practice! Practice! As in many areas in life, there are a good, a better, and a best. Do your best!

DISCUSSION QUESTIONS

1. Are there any suggestions about your appearance for an interview that you strongly agree or disagree with? Explain.
2. Do you agree with the level of importance placed on smiling? Why or why not?
3. Do you agree that it is better to let the interviewer offer a hand for a handshake instead of being the first to do so? Why or why not?
4. The author suggests that when answering questions, you should make eye contact with all the interviewers, not just the person who asked the question. What is the reasoning behind this strategy? Do you agree or disagree with this reasoning? Why or why not?
5. What are some things you can do to prepare for the hiring interview questions?
6. Do you agree with the author's assertion that there will always be some prejudice and bias in the workplace? Why or why not?

REFERENCES

Common Job Interview Questions and Answers. (2013). *Paid and unpaid internships at law firms.* Retrieved from http://commoninterview.com/Interview_Advice/paid-and-unpaid-internships-at-law-firms-2/

National Conference of Bar Examiners. (2017). *Study aids.* Retrieved from http://www.ncbex.org/study-aids/

INDEX